INNER STRENGTH

INNER STRENGTH
The Mental Dynamics of Athletic Performance

Ralph A. Vernacchia, Ph.D.

Western Washington University

WARDE PUBLISHERS, INC.
Palo Alto, California

Warde Publishers, Inc.
530 University Avenue, Suite 102-7
Palo Alto, CA 94301
(800) 699-2733

ISBN 1–886346–08–9

Printed in the United States of America
10 9 8 7 6 5 4 3 2 1   06   05   04   03

Design: Detta Penna; Copyeditor: Pat Brewer; Composition and paging: Penna Design and Production.

For Carolyn—my inspiration and the love of my life.

Contents

Preface

I first became interested in the psychological side of athletic performance as a high school track and field athlete. I ran the mile, which in the late 1950s and early 1960s was quite a respected undertaking since only several years earlier Roger Bannister had broken the "psychological barrier of the century" by running a mile in less than four minutes. I was well aware of Bannister's feat since I had read his book *The Four Minute Mile*, in which he eloquently describes his quest to achieve athletic immortality. After reading his book it became quite clear to me that psychology had played an integral role in his ability to achieve his dreams of athletic greatness, especially since he had limited time to train because he was pursuing a medical degree at the time.

As a high school and collegiate athlete I became fascinated by the role thinking and emotion played in athletic performance. Initially I related the psychoemotional aspects of sport to my own performances, but soon I became interested in the relationship of psychology to all sports. My undergraduate education recognized the importance of the psychological aspects of physical activity but never really addressed this issue in depth. It was a sign of the times (1963–67) that the psychological aspects of human performance were addressed primarily as part of the course work in motor learning, exercise physiology, and coaching classes. To learn more about this intriguing area I enrolled in graduate school and began to specialize in the psychological aspects of athletic performance.

While in graduate school I served as an assistant track coach and therefore had a golden opportunity to apply the theoretical concepts I was studying to real life training and performance situations. I soon discovered that the psychosocial and emotional aspects of athletic performance were an integral part of coaching effectiveness. I came to the realization that coaching the whole person was the key to successful coaching—athletes are human beings, not machines that are cued up to perform flawlessly on command. I sought to develop an integrated approach to coaching that would effectively unify the mind and body in pursuit of athletic excellence.

When I pursued a doctoral degree in physical education with an emphasis on the psychosocial aspects of physical activity (1971–73), sport psychology programs were relatively nonexistent. I continued to coach so that I could retain the opportunity to test the validity of sport psychology theories in the "real world" of intercollegiate athletics. I became even more convinced that sport psychology could enhance athletic performance more effectively than the Darwinian (survival of the fittest or "the cream rises to the top") approach most of my colleagues took toward coaching.

In my first collegiate teaching and coaching position, I taught motor learning, psychology and sociology of sport, and a coaching track class in addition to serving as the men's head cross country and track coach. During this period (1973–87) I came to realize that cultivating the mind-body-spirit relationship was the key to effective athletic performance and coaching. The athletes I had coached had consistently performed at high levels, winning individual and team district championships and All-American honors. Two of my former athletes went on to make two U.S. Olympic teams. The credit for these accomplishments goes to the dedicated efforts of the athletes I had the privilege and honor of coaching and to, I believe, the principles of sport psychology that I implemented and refined throughout my coaching career.

In 1987, after 22 years of teaching and coaching I decided to leave coaching and focus on the teaching and practice of applied sport psychology. I did not sever my ties with coaching but remained active in coaching education and worked directly with coaches and athletes as a sport psychology consultant. During this time (1987–present) I met colleagues (sport psychology professionals and coaches) and athletes who provided a deeper understanding not only of the discipline of applied sport psychology but of the culture, politics, and mentality of the achievement-oriented athletic world. These persons include my graduate advisor Keith Henschen and the following professionals with whom I share a passion for the field of applied sport psychology: Rick McGuire, David Cook, Jim Reardon, Gloria Balague, Rich Gordin, Tommie Lee White, Tracy Shaw, Jodi Yambor, Jeff Simons, Mark Thompson, Lew Curry, Bruce Ogilvie, Deidre Connelly, John Heil, Bob Nideffer, Bill Moore, Glen Albaugh, Dave Yukelson, Ken Ravizza, Wes Sime, Burt Giges, John Kootnekoff, Lori deKubber, and Dave Templin. Special appreciation is also given to Bob Rotella and Linda Bunker, with whom I spent a sabbatical leave in 1990 at the University of Virginia. In addition to these sport psychology professionals, many coaches over the years have provided me with valuable lessons and insights regarding the psychology of athletic performance, including Ed Wall, George Horn, Stan Huntsman, Carl Crowell, Pete Carlson, Gary Schwartz, Tony Bartlett, Rick McGuire, Hal Werner, and Joe Vigil. In addition to these great coaches, I have had the opportunity to learn about the psychology of athletic performance from my former athletes and assistant coaches as well as the Western Washington University athletic coaches and the many USA Track and Field (USATF), National Collegiate Athletic Association (NCAA), and National Association of Intercollegiate Athletics (NAIA) coaches whom I have come in contact with over the course of my career.

This book could be characterized as a "back to the future" perspective regarding applied sport psychology since it is an attempt to help sport psychology professionals, coaches, and athletes refocus on the psychology of athletic performance. In the mid to late 1960s the psychology of coaching and the psychology of athletic performance were the focus of the emerging field of sport psychology. It has always been my contention that sport psychology is primarily about sport and athletic performance. Coaches and athletes are the main players in sport and they have a passionate desire to pursue and achieve athletic excellence, and I firmly believe that mental skills education and training can help them achieve this goal.

This book is directed toward defining a peak performance model for achieving athletic excellence through mental skills training. I hope this model can be used by prospective sport psychology professionals who aspire to work with coaches and athletes in a variety of sports and performance environments. While many of the concepts presented in this book are easily understood, they are not easy to master. I hope this book will also provide insight into the challenges and obstacles that can so often derail an athlete's desire to pursue athletic excellence. I have written the book in such a way that it can be used by sport psychology professionals, coaches, and athletes who desire to enhance athletic performance through the understanding and mastery of mental skills training.

RAV

Acknowledgment

The author would like to thank Western Washington University for the sabbatical award that initiated and supported this writing project.

PART ONE

An Overview of Peak Performance

1

From Inner Strength to Peak Performance

Athletes are focused on doing their best in any given athletic performance situation, and most realize that physical and mental preparation go hand and hand in uniting the mind, body, and spirit in the pursuit of athletic excellence. Mental skills that develop such attributes as concentration, confidence, composure, and commitment can strengthen, compliment, and maximize the effectiveness of an athlete's physical skills. Therefore sport psychology has become both an acceptable and practiced avenue of performance enhancement for athletes of all ages, at every competitive level. Sport psychology is the instrument an athlete can use to develop a personal reservoir of *inner strength* that is so crucial to performing effectively in sport.

Applying psychology to sport to produce effective athletic performances involves logical thinking prior to performing, hence, the term *psychology* or *psycho-logic*. We all have great insights about our performances once they are history—we know exactly what our performance responses should have been in pressure situations. The key to performing well in pressure situations is the ability to think clearly and make good decisions just *prior* to performing and *during* performance.

Athletes utilize sport psychology and mental skills training, not because there is something wrong with them, but because they want to get better at their sport and enhance their performances. Performance enhancement and self-improvement are the underlying themes of this book, and they will be presented in a model that is directed toward developing peak performance through mental skills training.

The Roots of Athletic Performance and Sport Psychology

Athletic participation as a vehicle for competitive excellence has its roots in the educational practices of the ancient Greeks who instructed their youth, "to be the best, and excel over others" (Andronicos, 1979). This perspective was fueled by the obvious influence of militarism in the education of Greek youths, who were ultimately expected to sacrifice their lives to defend their city-states. Athletes of today refer to this perspective or approach to sport as a "warrior" mentality.

Since so much was at stake in warfare, Greek athletes were taught to bring all their intellectual, physical, and spiritual resources to bear in athletic competition as well as in war. This mind-body-spirit emphasis on athletic participation enabled Greek citizens to protect and perpetuate a great civilization.

Despite this ancient concept of mind-body-spirit unity for enhancing athletic performance, the fact of the matter is that in contemporary sport the mind and body are viewed as two separate entities that effect and affect athletic performance. The 1984 Olympic Games perpetuated the mind-body dualism by constructing two enormous and headless sculptures of athletes at the entrance to the Los Angeles Coliseum.

Athletics in large part are viewed as physical endeavors whose outcome is predicated on speed, strength, power, endurance, and coordination. The notion of physical perfection and athletic excellence are closely linked, while the intellectual and spiritual sides of athletic performance are often ignored. Contemporary movements in sport psychology stress the mastery and application of mental as well as physical skills as prime prerequisites for effective athletic performances.

Sport Psychology and Athletic Performance

Sport psychology can contribute to performance effectiveness by helping athletes understand the culture, politics, and mentality of their sport, as well as the achievement-oriented world of athletics. Sport psychology can shed light on the challenges of athletic participation by helping athletes to understand, master, and cope with the adversity and disappointment that accompanies athletic performance.

Athletes who are effective performers understand that it is of paramount importance that they are "in the moment" or present when they engage in athletic competition. Great athletes play each play as though it was their last; they give their best at the time because they know they aren't guaranteed another opportunity or a next time. They also realize the reality of athletic performance; that is, that you may prepare to do your best and then give your best in competition, but you won't always do your best. Therefore they strive to execute their skills effectively in each performance situation, in effect to "win ugly" if need be, and to persevere and improve their skills if they are ineffective.

 Mental Key to Success

Performance effectiveness is an enduring attribute of successful athletic performers.

Ultimately the athlete who performs effectively realizes that there is no right way or wrong way to perform, only different ways, and they have complete confidence in their style or way of doing things and getting things done. The recognition and understanding that peak performance and effective performance are one and the same is a common realization among high achievers in the athletic world.

Seasoned athletes focus on self-improvement while everything around them focuses on the opponent, the "big game," and the scoreboard. They realize that their only control is over their own performance and the execution of their skills especially in light of the many distractions that surround them.

Pursuing Peak Performance

Contemporary research and teachings in sport psychology are geared toward facilitating the attainment of peak experience, ideal performance state, peak performance, flow, and "the zone." Sport psychology professionals have attempted to create programs that develop a mental template or prerequisite characteristics for attaining effective athletic performances.

The qualities of peak experience in sport (Ravizza, 1984) include focused awareness (centered present focus, narrow focus of attention, and complete absorption); complete control of self and the environment (perfection and loss of fear); transcendence of self (harmony and oneness, noncritical and effortless). In a somewhat similar vein the ideal performance state is described as one in which the performer experiences the following changes: thinking (less paralysis by analysis); memory (amnesia); perception (slow motion, enlargement of objects); dissociation (pain detachment); and information processing (parallel processing) (Unestahl, 1986).

We also know that certain psychological characteristics separate elite from non-elite athletic performers. Elite athletes tend to be able to moderate worry and performance anxieties; are more efficient in their concentration abilities; maintain stronger and more stable self-confidence; use kinesthetic or body imaging for mental preparation; and attach more personal meaning to doing well in their sport (Mahoney, Gabriel & Perkins, 1987). The general psychological profile of peak performance includes: self-regulation of arousal (energized yet relaxed, no fear); higher self-confidence; better concentration (being appropriately focused); in control, but not forcing it; positive preoccupation with sport (imagery and thoughts); determination and commitment (Williams & Krane, 2001, pp. 174–175).

Achieving a flow state while participating in sport is thought to be helpful in creating higher levels of enjoyment and achievement (Jackson, 1996). Flow (Csikszentmihalyi, 1990; Jackson, 1992, 1995, 1996; Jackson & Csikszentmihalyi, 1999) is characterized by the following characteristics:

1. *Challenge–skill balance* (the match between perceived skills and challenges in a particular situation

2. *Merging of action and awareness* (deep involvement leads to automaticity and spontaneity)

3. *Clear goals* (a sense of purpose)

4. *Unambiguous feedback* (clear and immediate feedback that one is succeeding in his or her goal)

5. *Concentration* (on the task at hand)

6. *Paradox of control* (trying less)

7. *Loss of self-consciousness* (immersion in the activity)

8. *Transformation of time* (loss of time awareness)

9. *Autotelic experience* (intrinsic satisfaction and enjoyment).

Finally many athletes have described being "in the zone" while performing at their best. Being in the zone creates a feeling of transcending one's body, and sometimes even sport itself, taking on a spiritual dimension (Cooper, 1998). Other dimensions of "the zone" include (1) *mystical sensations* (acute well-being, peace, calm, stillness; detachment; freedom; floating, flying, weightlessness; ecstasy; power, control; being in the present; instinctive action and surrender; mystery and awe; feelings of immortality; unity); (2) *altered perceptions* (size and field; time; extrasensory perception; out-of-body experiences; awareness of the "other"); and (3) *extraordinary feats* (exceptional energy; extraordinary strength, speed, endurance, balance, and ease; psychokinesis or affecting objects by mental means alone; elusiveness; uncanny suspension; invisible barriers; and mind over matter) (Murphy & White, 1995).

The opposite of "being in the zone" is known as *choking* and is characterized by various physical (tight, tense, shaky, unsteady, weak, heavy, tired, hard, choppy, awkward) and psychological feelings (beaten, scared, weak, dominated, upset, panicked, worried, rushed, confused, overloaded) (Nideffer, 1992). In contrast, an athlete who is "in the zone" is empowered by his or her physical (loose, relaxed, solid, balanced, strong, light, energetic, effortless, fluid) and psychological feelings (controlled, confident, powerful, commanding, calm, tranquil, peaceful, easy, clear, focused) (Nideffer, 1992).

A Peak Performance Revisited

In 1954, Roger Bannister broke what many considered to be the "psychological barrier of the century" by running a sub four-minute mile (3:59.4). His eloquent description of this performance highlights many of the characteristics attributed to peak performance and experience, ideal performance state, flow, and the zone:

> At one and a half laps I was still worrying about the pace. A voice shouting "relax" penetrated to me above the noise of the crowd. . . . Unconsciously I obeyed. If the speed was wrong it was too late to do anything about it, so why worry? I was relaxing so much that my mind seemed almost detached from my body. There was no strain. . . . I had a moment of mixed joy and anguish, when my mind took over. It raced well ahead of my body and drew my body compellingly forward. I felt that the moment of a lifetime had come. There was no pain, only a great unity of movement and aim. The world seemed to

stand still, or did not exist. The only reality was the next two hundred yards of track under my feet. The tape meant finality—extinction perhaps. . . . I felt at that moment that it was my chance to do one thing supremely well. I drove on, impelled by a combination of fear and pride. The air I breathed filled me with the spirit of the track where I had run my first race . . . . My body had long since exhausted all its energy, but it went on running just the same. The physical overdraft came only from greater willpower. . . . With five yards to go the tape seemed to recede. Would I ever reach it? Those last seconds seemed never-ending. . . . I leapt at the tape like a man taking his last spring to save himself from the chasm that threatens to engulf

". . . I had a moment of mixed joy and anguish, when my mind took over. It raced well ahead of my body and drew my body compellingly forward. I felt that the moment of a lifetime had come. There was no pain, only a great unity of movement and aim."

him. My effort was over and I collapsed almost unconscious. . . . It was only then that the real pain overtook me. . . . I just went on existing in the most passive physical state. . . . I knew I had done it before I even heard the time. (Bannister, 1955, pp. 213–215)

Athletes experience different physical and psychological dimensions of their best ever performance. An insightful exercise for athletes is to take some time to reflect on their best athletic performance (see the "Peak Performance Assessment" exercise on the next page). Athletes can create a personal peak performance profile to use as a target and template for future athletic performances. Physical and mental training can help athletes replicate past effective performances so that they can perform with consistency in competitive settings. Occasionally recalling their peak performance profile will help them focus on their target for effective athletic performances.

The Pyramid of Peak Performance

As athletes strive to perform consistently at their best, they refine their physical and mental approaches to competition into routines that will ensure their performance effectiveness. These routines provide a model or roadmap for the physical and mental strategies and techniques that can be used in competitive settings.

The mental training concepts and skills presented in the remainder of this book are organized into a peak performance model that represents a systematic approach to developing the "inner strength" necessary to achieve performance excellence. This model is derived from hierarchical models suggested by prominent sport psychologists (Gordin & Reardon, 1995; Moore & Stevenson, 1991, 1994) and blends the physical, mental, and philosophical principles of athletic performance, including attitude, motivation, emotion, motor learning and performance, and mental skills (concentration, confidence, composure, and commitment). This model (see Figure 1.1) will be explained in more depth in Chapter 2.

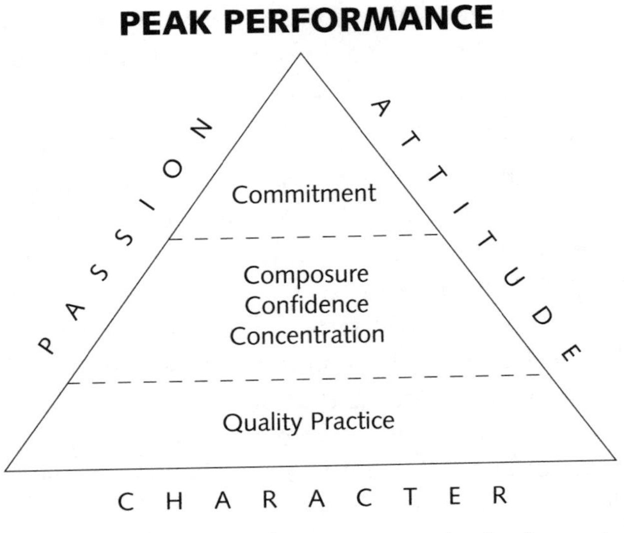

PEAK PERFORMANCE

Figure 1.1   A peak performance model leading to the development of "inner strength" and athletic excellence.

Peak Performance Exercise 1.1

Peak Performance Assessment

Reflect on your best athletic performance ever, and check the characteristics listed below that best describe your physical and psychological feelings at the time of this performance:

Focused	Committed	Absorbed
Effortless	Relaxed	In the present
Calm	Challenged	Effective
Confident	Absorbed	Energized
Composed	Enjoyment	Automatic
In control	Fun	Spontaneous
Heightened awareness	Fluid	Fearless
Powerful	Detached	Painless
Strong	Peaceful	Loose
Positive	Free	Balanced
Determined	Awesome	Smooth
Controlled	Commanding	Tranquil
Slow-motion	Non-critical	Centered
Physical	Trusting	Worry-free
In the moment	Spiritual	Fast

List other feelings here:

Effective athletes focus on the consistency of their performances, that is, their ability to deliver their best possible performance even though they may be having an "off" day. In sport this is referred to as "winning ugly." In essence, an athlete is only as good as his or her worst day. While athletes continually pursue peak performances and experience them on occasion, they pride themselves on how effectively they can meet the unpredictable challenges that are woven into athletic training and competition.

"Winning ugly" is a distinguishing attribute of highly effective and successful performers—most athletes can perform well when everything is going their way and when they are "on" or feeling good, but the *best* athletes can continue to give their best and perform effectively even when they are at their worst. In reality the most effective athletes learn to take the good with the bad as they respond and adapt to the ebb and flow of athletic competition.

In the final analysis, peak and effective performance are one and the same. Peak performances are just that, spikes in the course of effective performances. By focusing first and always on consistently delivering effective performances, that is, by striving to be at the top of their game, athletes can give themselves the best chance for being successful.

2

The Values and Beliefs of Athletic Excellence

Because all athletes have dreams of summoning up their best performance possible at the most important time of their athletic
career and all athletes aspire to be consistently at their best each
time they perform, coaches and athletes are constantly searching
for a method to consistently set themselves up for successful athletic performances. Various aspects and models of peak performance have   intrigued the athletic and sport psychology
community. This chapter will explain the philosophical and
foundational components of the peak performance model shown
in the following figure.

PEAK PERFORMANCE

Toward a Philosophy of Peak Performance

A basic question often asked regarding peak performance is: "How do you separate the contenders, from the pretenders, from the rear-enders in sport?" Peak performers have three personal attributes that enable them to become successful athletes: passion, attitude, and character. As the peak performance model on the previous page suggests, the triangulation of these attributes establishes the "mental" atmosphere for successful and effective athletic performance.

Passion

Love of sport, that is, an amateur perspective toward athletic participation, provides the internal spark that lights the flame of passion, which fuels an athlete's desire to be the best.

 Mental Key to Success

Passion is the enduring love of sport.

Athletes at all levels who have achieved fame and glory often refer to their love of sport as one of the prime reasons for their involvement in athletics. An example of this concept is found in the words of one of the greatest athletes of the twentieth century, Jesse Owens, who humbly stated:

> I always loved running. I wasn't very good at it, but I loved it because it was something you could do all by yourself, and under your own power. You could go in any direction, fast or slow as you wanted, fighting the wind if you felt like it, seeking out new sights just on the strength of your feet and the courage of your lungs. (Baker, 1986, p. 11)

This is a very striking statement from an athlete who achieved Olympic glory and immortality by his Olympic performances (four gold medals at the 1936 Berlin Games). He also accomplished one of the greatest athletic feats of the twentieth century by breaking five world records and tying one in the span of 45 minutes at the 1935 Big 10 track and field championships.

Pursuing the amateur ideal, that is, participating in sport for the love of sport, provides athletes with the motivation and reason for their involvement in sport. To train and perform at effective levels requires dedication and sacrifice, and love of sport provides the inner drive to view the hard work and sacrifice as a requirement of the athletic participation and achievement that generates feelings of self-fulfillment and joy.

Passion is actually the *enduring* love of sport. *When it comes to attaining athletic success, many athletes have the dream but not the drive.*

While love of sport is a prime prerequisite for successful athletic participation, passion is what keeps athletes going in the face of challenge and adversity throughout the ebb and flow of their careers. Passion enables athletes to persevere and realize their talents over time as they invest themselves in the traditional athletic values of hard work, continual striving, and deferred gratification (Eitzen & Sage, 1993).

Athletic participation focused on achievement requires tremendous investments of passion and emotion. Passionate persons, particularly coaches and athletes, often deplete the emotional fuel they direct toward effective athletic performances as they experience the paradox of passion, that is, "the endeavor that excites you the most, exhausts you the most."

This paradox of passion often leads coaches and athletes to become overly passionate or obsessive regarding their athletic endeavors. Overly passionate coaches and athletes sabotage their performances by overtraining and burning out. There is a fine line between the passion and the poison of athletic participation, training, and performance.

Character

While many athletes rise to the pinnacle of athletic success, fame, and glory, those without character soon fade from the athletic spotlight. Some athletes may lack the strength of character to endure the many visible and invisible tests of personal integrity and honesty that the athletic world and athletic competition presents.

 Mental Key to Success

Hunger will get you to the top, but character will keep you there.

For this reason, young athletes in particular must serve their apprenticeship in sport under the guidance of coaches who live, promote, demonstrate, and oversee the value and values of athletic participation. In reality, sports don't build character, coaches do—coaches are the teachers of sport (McGuire, 1998). We must always remember that the athlete meets sport at the coach and that ". . . the coach is the definer, creator, provider, and delivers the sport experience to the athlete. . . . The quality of an athlete's experience can never exceed the quality of the leadership providing it" (McGuire, 1996b, pp. 15–16).

Sportspersonship is the manifestation of an athlete's character, and true champions are remembered not only for what they have accomplished but for how they accomplished it. There are many winners in today's athletic world but only a few true champions, especially in the world of professional athletics. One of the foundational beliefs expressed later in this chapter will address this issue: "Winning is important, but it is not the only thing—character counts."

 Mental Key to Success

Adversity reveals character.

Attitude

In response to the question "what separates the contenders, from the pretenders, from the rear-enders?"—one attribute of highly effective athletic performers arises—attitude. Attitude is the mind-set that an athlete adopts and implements in each and every practice and performance situation. Attitude is everything, and highly effective athletic performers bring their attitude to practice or to the athletic arena—they don't just "show up" and then try to figure out what their attitude is going to be as situations arise during practice or competition.

In the following quote Jesse Owens emphasizes the importance of attitude in the quest to realize athletic dreams:

Everyone must have a goal or a dream to strive for.
Here are the four things you have to do to achieve your goal.
First is your determination to be able to reach your dream.
Second, you have to have dedication.
Then comes self-discipline and sacrifice.
And lastly, is the *attitude* with which you assume your quest.

As mentioned in the previous chapter, sport psychology suggests the application of logical ways of thinking to sport, hence *psychology* or *psycho-logic*. Therefore if we believe that thought precedes action, then prior to and during performance, athletes and coaches must engage in ways of thinking and feeling that will facilitate their performance.

Peak Performance Exercise 2.1

Attitude Check

Think about the last year of your life. During this year, have you had a great attitude concerning your sport? If your answer is yes, describe what it means to have a great attitude and how your attitude has benefited you. How have you been able to maintain your attitude when the going gets tough? If your answer is no, describe what is lacking in your attitude and what it needs to be in order to be "great." How have your ways of thinking and feeling held you back from being the best you can be? (adapted from Rotella, 1990a)

As simple as this sounds, this concept is difficult to realize, since the stress of athletic competition can often distract both athletes and coaches from executing their skills with confidence. Doubt, fear, and worry can creep into preperformance thoughts, creating feelings and actions that are counterproductive to effective performances. Applied sport psychology is directed toward creating a practice and performance mind-set or attitude that will set athletes up for success by helping them focus on what they would like to have happen versus focusing on what they would not like to have happen.

Highly effective athletic performers anticipate and physically and mentally prepare for various performance scenarios by focusing on what they can control in performance settings. One of the basic performance factors that an athlete can control is his or her attitude. Athletes can take the "Attitude Check" exercise to assess theirs.

Obtaining a "great" attitude about athletic performance requires a childlike attitude, that is, a return mentally to the time when an athlete participated in sport for fun, enjoyment, and pleasure. As children we all possessed the inherent abilities to succeed at sport—we had great imaginations, could focus seemingly forever on sport, and thought we could take our chosen sport to the highest levels.

Peak Performance Exercise 2.2

Revisiting the Child Athlete Within

Compare the attitude you had as a child participating in youth sports or dreaming about your future sport performances and your attitude now. What experiences and/or people in your life seem to have caused your attitude toward your sport to grow crusty and make you prone to self-limiting habits such as doubting yourself in crucial moments; losing the joy of competing; and becoming overly serious, overly analytical and overly self-conscious? How have these ways of thinking and feeling held you back from being the best you can be? How have your family's, your friends', and your own concerns about being admired, respected, and winning the approval of others (family, friends, etc.) affected your attitude toward your sport? (adapted from Rotella, 1990a)

As a result of socialization, children are soon taught to limit their imagination and creativity—to quit "daydreaming" and focus on reality. When once an athlete could shoot baskets for hours on end while imagining him or herself scoring the winning basket in the "big" game, now he or she is introduced to the regimentation of organized sport and soon spontaneity diminishes as conformity supersedes creativity. Social comparison and validation also become important as children grow and become more self-conscious of their every move when they once were confident with their own style and way of doing things. After completing the Attitude Check exercise, athletes should take time to revisit their childhood attitude toward sport and athletic performances.

In many ways attitude can make or break an athlete, and in some cases, predetermine the level of athletic success or failure. Athletes should reflect back on the Peak Performance Profile exercise from the previous chapter and think about their attitude at that time. Did it reflect confidence and did this attitude set the athlete up for success? Attitude is the precursor of success—bringing a "great attitude" to practice and competitive situations sets the tone for quality effort in the athletic arena.

Foundational Beliefs and the World of Athletic Performance

Individuals who choose to pursue athletic excellence soon realize that they need to establish guiding principles to help them survive and thrive in the achievement-oriented world of athletics. These principles regarding athletic performance help coaches and athletes keep sport in perspective and soon become precepts for those who have the character to pursue and attain athletic excellence. Developing a sound personal philosophy toward athletic participation or formulating personal performance precepts and standards helps guide an athlete's actions as he or she pursues athletic excellence.

Today's athletic world is full of individuals who have climbed the athletic ladder of success only to find out it is leaning against the wrong wall—they are disillusioned and unfulfilled with and by the reality of their success. In the athletic world this is known as a hollow victory because it lacks substance and meaning. The philosophical statements that follow are presented with the intent of generating thoughts, ideas, and ideals that will provide meaning and relevancy to an athlete's training and performance efforts.

The Art and Science of Athletic Performance

Effective athletic performance is both an art and a science, and while many coaches and athletes understand and implement the scientific principles of athletic training and performance, only a few actually master the artistic side of these same principles.

 Mental Key to Success

When it comes to performance methodology there is no right way or wrong way, there are different ways and athletes must find the way that works best for them.

The artistic side of athletic performance is composed of the athlete's ability to trust his or her individual approach to or style of athletic performance. Some people consider this intuitive and creative side of athletic performance to be instinctive (an athlete's aptitude for athletic performance) and to a large degree is only refined by experience in a variety of athletic performance situations. In essence, this is the head and heart battle that rages within each athlete just prior to performing or in the midst of a performance. The ability to blend instinct and reason in "the heat of battle" and make good performance decisions and choices free from doubt and without hesitation is often referred to as "winning the battle within" and can often make or break the success and effectiveness of an athlete's performance.

Athletes are artists who display their talents on a very visible stage, and athletes can learn a great deal from other performing artists. A director gave the following comments to his cast members (actors and actresses) just prior to an opening night's performance:

> It's time to share what we've found. Actors are sent out on a journey to find the fire. When we find it, we bring it back to share with others. Enjoy it. It is a great obligation and privilege to be on stage in the light while others watch from safety. It takes courage, discipline, and constant vigilance to keep the extraordinary people in this play as fresh, vibrant, and alive for our audience as they are for us. Never stop working, and never let them see you sweat.

The Reality and Truth of Athletic Performance

Athletes must be realists and understand that even though they prepare to do their best and give their best in each and every performance setting, they will not always do their best. A variety of factors an athlete has no control over (e. g., environmental conditions, illness and/or injury, the talent level of an individual opponent or team, scheduling) can influence the outcome of a performance. Understanding the reality of sport is the first step toward developing the mental attributes that ultimately affect athletic performance, namely, perseverance and persistence.

Developing the mental attributes of perseverance and persistence must be complimented with developing the physical attributes of one's talent or ability to perform. For this reason athletes seek out the "truth" about their performances. This "truth" or feedback about how they performed their skills in performance situations and settings leads to self-improvement and greater performance effectiveness. Mature athletes seek out feedback about their performances, as well as information, techniques, and strategies that will make them more effective in the future. Most importantly, they seek constructive criticism through performance evaluations because they realize that the feedback they receive is about their performance and not about themselves personally.

Another major reality of sport that is often unacceptable to athletes and coaches is that athletes are human and make mistakes. In essence, sports *are* games of mistakes—what really counts in sport is not making mistakes but how one performs *after* making a mistake (Rotella, 1990c). Striving for perfection in sport can often be a real performance obstacle or block for many athletes unless they shift their performance focus toward effective performances rather than perfect performances. "Winning ugly" is an acceptable reality of sport—being effective is preferable to being correct or perfect. In the final analysis, "getting the job done" is highly respected in the athletic community.

Sport Isn't Always Fair

If sport was conducted in a perfect world, everyone would be treated fairly. Unfortunately, sport is a human endeavor and subject to the imperfections that we experience in all aspects of our lives. Politics, officiating, and the luck of the draw can often determine the outcome of an athletic contest. These factors, beyond the control of coaches and athletes, can be very upsetting and disrupting to athletes who are giving their all. The challenge for athletes is then to continue to "play their game" or "play on" in the face of a referee's "bad" call or unfair playing conditions. Focusing on the aspects of their performances that they can control—execution of their physical and mental skills (motor skills, mental preparation, attitude, composure, etc.)—becomes essential.

 **Mental Key to Success**

Execution is the solution to performance effectiveness.

Once an athlete accepts the fact that sport isn't always fair, he or she must still continue to play fair since fair play is the moral cornerstone of sport. Character, or striving to pursue athletic excellence with integrity in an imperfect and unfair world, is one of the greatest challenges faced by today's athletic community of administrators, parents, coaches, and athletes.

Avoiding the Achievement "Trap"

A great number of coaches and athletes desire to board and ride the achievement train on their way to glory and fame. Unfortunately very few understand the stops along the way and see their dreams of athletic success derailed. The athletic world is one of accelerated and forced achievement that stresses a timely execution of physical and mental skills in an atmosphere of urgency. For this reason athletes must learn to perform under pressure and to understand the mental pressures that can influence the outcome of their performance.

Picture the word *pressure* in your mind and then mentally erase the last three letters—you are left with the word *press*. The fact of the matter is that experienced and effective athletic performers respond to performance pressures by "trying less" while inexperienced and ineffective performers "try harder."

 Mental Key to Success

A confident, clear, and quiet mind focused on the present is a prime prerequisite for effective athletic performance.

Unfortunately our minds can become cluttered with scoreboard mentality and thoughts of "what's at stake." Doubt, fear, and worry creep in where confidence used to be, physical and mental tension prevents us from trusting our talents and preparation. Before we know it, we have sabotaged, undermined, or derailed our confidence and ability to achieve when it counts.

Once an athlete achieves success he or she needs to stop and "smell the roses" and take the time to evaluate his or her accomplishments. Without pausing to evaluate and get feedback, an athlete can easily fall into the "achievement" trap. The athlete becomes snared in a world of "can you top this" and soon becomes overwhelmed and dissatisfied with the performance expectations of others rather than achieving at his or her own pace, in his or her own time.

The reality of the achievement trap is that there is no way out—athletes can never make everyone happy with or by their performance. One's performance is never good enough, and before the glow of athletic accomplishment dims, performance expectations will be pushed to the "next level." It becomes very easy for athletes to begin performing for others rather than for themselves and soon the athlete feels as though he or she *has* to perform rather than *wants* to perform. Once the athlete loses his or her spontaneity and joy and feels pressured to perform, athletics are no longer fun but work and drudgery. The once "great" attitude that empowered the athlete soon begins to erode, leading to ineffective performances that pale in light of his or her past athletic accomplishments.

Foundational Beliefs of Peak Athletic Performance

Since athletes choose to commit enormous amounts of time, energy, and emotion to mastering their sport, it is imperative that they be guided by a set of personal beliefs that express the "why" as well as the "how" of their involvement in athletics. Adherence to this personal performance philosophy, or foundational beliefs, is an essential first step in pursuing athletic excellence because it helps athletes focus on the process rather than the outcomes of athletic achievement. Foundational beliefs give meaning to the attainment of athletic excellence. This concept is best illustrated by the Olympic Creed:

The most important thing
in the Olympic Games is not to win
but to take part,
just as the most important thing in life
is not the triumph but the struggle.
The essential thing is not to have conquered
but to have fought well.
—*Pierre de Coubertin*

A sport creed is a statement of beliefs regarding an athlete's actions that can provide meaning, direction, and perspective to both the process and product of athletic performance. Possessing a personal creed or statement of beliefs is critical for an athlete because that creed guides them in their practice and performance efforts. Foundational beliefs provide the inspiration, understanding, and perspective necessary to navigate the road to athletic excellence in a meaningful and personally relevant way.

The foundational beliefs presented here are examples of the type of statements that athletes can create in constructing their own performance creed or personal standards for pursuing athletic excellence. The important point here is that athletes need to establish a set of personal standards that will guide their actions and determine their performance outcomes. The following belief statements reflect a success orientation:

- *Hard work pays off in the long run—there are no short cuts to success.*

- *Focusing on the process of self-improvement provides the best chance to succeed as an athlete.*

- *Being "in the moment" enhances athletic performance.*

- *Having fun and enjoying the challenge of athletic performance leads to athletic success and self-fulfillment.*

- *Participating in athletics will make you a better person.*

- *Winning is important, but it's not the only thing—character counts.*

Hard work pays off in the long run—there are no short cuts to success. Adherence to the traditional values of hard work, continual striving, and deferred gratification (Eitzen & Sage, 1993) is necessary to naturally realize one's athletic talents. In today's impatient athletic world of accelerated and forced achievement and "highlight film" mentality, we often lose sight of the amount and duration of training and setbacks that pave the way for successful performances.

Like most worthwhile endeavors, attaining athletic excellence involves hard work, dedication and sacrifice—if it was easy, then everyone would be a champion. Conscientious and prolonged practice of the physical and mental skills necessary to succeed as an athlete are developed over time and tempered by the ebb and flow of athletic competition. Seasoned athletes learn to "take the good with the bad" and to endure the highs and lows of their training and performances. In the final analysis, no athlete ever attained greatness without "going to work early and leaving late"—there are no shortcuts to success.

Focusing on the process of self-improvement provides the best chance to succeed as an athlete. Experienced coaches and athletes learn that winning is elusive at best and depends on a variety of factors beyond their control including talent, scheduling, and their ability to be at their best in every time in every situation (McGuire, 1996b). Therefore these same coaches and athletes succeed by focusing on the one thing that will ultimately affect the outcome of their performances and the one thing that they can control over time—self-improvement.

The Olympic motto, "Swifter, Higher, Stronger," is perhaps the best example of this concept since it is a comparative phrase that urges athletes to constantly seek to improve their performances. Self-improvement is a constant theme for athletes who strive to be the best.

The process of self-improvement comprises several factors including pride, preparation, work ethic, and "extra effort" (McGuire, 1996b). An athlete cannot control a competitor's training and preparation, but he or she can work hard and make the extra effort to anticipate and prepare for upcoming competitions. By constantly asking themselves, "what can I do today to be a little better than I was yesterday," athletes can take control and responsibility for their ability to perform effectively. Ultimately an athlete must perform with a pride that reflects his or her preparation and willingness to dedicate himself or herself to achieving performance excellence.

Being "in the moment" enhances athletic performance. For an athlete being mentally present at the time of performance is extremely important to the outcome of the performance. Many athletes are mentally absent during their performance—lost in either the past or in the future—replaying their past performances, trying to change history, or worrying about their next or future performances. All this takes away from their ability to concentrate on the effect they can have on what they are actively doing in sport. As the saying goes, "The past is history, the future is a mystery, the present is a gift, that's why they call it the present."

Furthermore many athletes need to be reminded that "sports are important, but they're really not very important at all." When practicing or performing at sport, *that* is the most important thing in the athlete's life, but when practicing or performing is done, then whatever the next activity (classwork, homework, job, watching a movie, etc.) or whomever is there (friends, family, etc.) should be the most important thing in the athlete's life. Being present or "in the moment" provides the opportunity for an athlete to summon, focus, and maximize all of his or her physical, mental, and emotional resources at the time that he or she is performing.

Having fun and enjoying the challenge of athletic performance leads to athletic success and self-fulfillment. Mastery leads to fun and enjoyment in athletics. When an athlete can finally, after hours of practice, match the challenge a particular performance situation presents, then he or she begins to have fun at sport. Self-mastery of attitude and emotions coupled with the acquisition of the motor skills and fitness necessary to succeed at their sport can result in achieving personal and performance excellence. Such an enjoyable feeling of achievement is known to coaches and athletes as the glory of sport. This euphoric feeling stems from the intersection of dedicated and committed preparation with the effective and timely execution of athletic skills.

Participating in athletics will make you a better person. A number of promises are made to athletes regarding the value and benefit of athletic participation, but one promise usually holds true—participating in athletics will make you a better person. The educational spillover effect of athletic participation can teach athletes many valuable life lessons and skills.

In the athletic world the experiences are fleeting, but the lessons are lasting. By engaging in the sport experience athletes can learn valuable leadership skills, personal attitudes, and attributes that will benefit them later in life, including work ethic, perseverance, sacrifice, patience, persistence, focus, confidence, composure, commitment, dedication, and ethics, to name just a few.

Winning is important but it's not the only thing—character counts. Fair play is the moral cornerstone of sport, and pursuing victory with honor is a prime moral dictate for coaches and athletes. Protecting the sanctity of sport and the sport experience while balancing both these aspects of sport participation with the instrumental concerns of sport (winning and materialism) is a shared moral responsibility of coaches and athletes.

Many athletes and coaches do conduct themselves according to a code of ethics, but unfortunately some of these same coaches and athletes practice a code of ethics composed of false ethics. Some of these false ethics include: "the ends justify the means"; "it's OK as long as you don't get caught"; "winning at all costs"; "everyone else is doing it"; "whatever it takes." A strong sense of moral responsibility, fostered by sound leadership, can counter the false ethics that exist in contemporary sport.

Winning is important but it's not the only thing—sportspersonship counts, the great Olympian Jesse Owens stated: *Sportsmanship itself is the ultimate victory.* Champions are remembered for how they achieved athletic excellence, not merely for what they achieved. Even if athletes don't win each time they compete, they can always be champions if they pursue athletic excellence with integrity.

The following exercise is designed to help athletes develop their personal philosophy of performance.

Peak Performance Exercise 2.3

Toward a Personal Philosophy of Athletic Performance

Take time to reflect on your personal philosophy of athletic performance. This philosophy will serve as a foundation for the principles that will guide your performances. These guiding principles or foundational beliefs will provide meaning and perspective for both the process and outcome of your performances. They will help you keep athletic performance in perspective and to deal effectively with the successes and disappointments that result from your performances. Write out several foundational belief statements that will serve to create and maintain a "great attitude" toward your sport by providing personal meaning and understanding to your athletic performances.

3

Dreams Do Come True

At the heart of the peak performance model, framed by passion, character, and a great attitude, are the physical, mental, and emotional characteristics that will enable an athlete to realize his or her dreams of athletic excellence.

The realization of athletic dreams results from an approach to athletic excellence that unifies the mind, body, and spirit in pursuit of athletic excellence. Athletic dreams can come true—that is, they can be facilitated—through the mastery of physical and mental skills. As the peak performance model suggests, the mental skills of concentration, confidence, composure, and commitment are built on the foundations of sound philosophical and ethical principles, as well as a sound work ethic toward achieving athletic excellence.

Sports Are 50% Mental

Sports are 50% physical and 50% mental. Mastering the mental skills necessary to excel in athletic performance settings are virtually useless without equal mastery of the necessary physical conditioning and motor skills—and vice versa. The peak performance model can aid athletes in constructing their dreams of athletic excellence and glory. Through a head (mental skills training), heart (philosophy, ethics and foundational beliefs), and hand (physical preparation and work ethic) approach toward athletic excellence, athletes can realize their dreams. The head, heart, and hand process begins with a dream.

Let's pretend that you have been given unlimited funds to build your dream house. You would probably image, without limitations, the location and type of home you have always longed for. Perhaps you would see the land covered with trees but soon you would be able to imagine the land being cleared in preparation for your dream house. You may be able to see your dream house at the top of a mountain or on a bluff overlooking the ocean, or perhaps the beach and ocean are only a few steps from your property. You would also see the architecture of your dream house, property, and view. The layout of the interior of the house would be designed to meet your every need and desire and would compliment and enhance your lifestyle. Once you have seen all of this in your mind and created a mental blueprint of your dream house, you would start to construct your dream house by clearing the land and laying the foundation for your dream house.

Constructing or building one's athletic dream is no different. It requires planning and enormous expenditures of resources to make it a reality.

 Mental Key to Success

Great things don't happen by chance, they happen by design, and an athlete must decide to be the architect of his or her own destiny.

The Dream Cycle

Once an athlete has a clear and vivid vision or dream of athletic success, he or she can set a course for making that dream a reality by following the dream cycle of athletic excellence (Figure 3.1).

Dreams

One of the simplest and most overlooked strategies regarding athletic excellence is to ask oneself, "What's my athletic dream?" As the dream cycle suggests, this is the first step not only in identifying one's vision and mission but also in retaining or reawakening one's childlike attitude toward his or her sport.

As children we were often asked, "What do you want to be when you grow up?" and both the people asking this question and the child who answered it believed that "dreams do come true" and that "everything is possible." As children a certain person or persons encouraged us to "reach for the stars" and to "follow your

Figure 3.1   Dream cycle and athletic excellence

dreams". As we grow older it becomes more difficult to find support for our dreams in a skeptical, cynical, and critical world that tends to shake our self-confidence and our ability to reach our dreams.

A childlike attitude toward athletic excellence must be protected and nurtured by parents, family, teachers, and coaches who believe in the value and values of athletic participation. By the same token these same individuals can help young persons become student-athletes by nurturing their professional dreams and helping them retain their childlike wonderment and curiosity toward learning. Social support and resources are needed to enable athletes, especially student-athletes, to realize their dreams.

Goals

Sometimes the hardest part of realizing dreams is getting started on the road to success. Goals provide the roadmap (Cook, 1996b). Dreams may seem unrealistic or impossible at first, but they begin to feel attainable once we break them down to manageable tasks or devise a plan that will simplify the challenge of realizing them. This concept is illustrated by the riddle, "How do you eat an elephant?" The answer of course is "one bite at a time." Goals provide the step by step process that at least give us a chance to realize our dreams.

Mental Key to Success

Effective athletic performers take small steps to glory.

Goal setting and attainment strategies, which will be discussed in more depth in Chapter 6, help effective athletic performers keep their eye on the ball, that is, retain their ability to focus on the ways and means for realizing their dreams. Goal setting and attainment strategies help athletes pay attention to details of their preparation and performances because they realize the importance of, "taking care of the little things before the little things take care of you."

Visualize

For a dream to become a reality, the dreamer's "mind's eye" must be able to hold a clear and vivid vision of the dream. Sharpening our dream focus is essential for success, otherwise it is like looking at your favorite television program on a set with an out-of-focus picture. You soon lose interest in your favorite program—it's merely a blur. The skills of visualization help us to see the workings of our dreams with the clarity and vividness necessary to guide our actions to an effective end.

Visualization skills will be covered in more depth in Chapter 5, but the important thing to remember about visualization is that it helps us get the "feeling" for a desired performance. For an athlete this means both the kinesthetic or "body" feeling and the "emotional" feel for a performance. Thought precedes action, but there is an intermediate step in this process, that is, thoughts create images that stimulate feeling and feelings that result in action (Zinsser, Bunker & Williams, 2001).

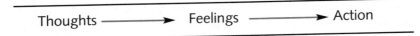

This is why visualization is often referred to as mental imagery. Athletes who perform effectively will often comment that they are "feeling it," and when they comment on their performance they say that it "felt" great, not that it "thought" great.

Action

Once an athlete can see and feel his or her dream, he or she needs to "get busy" working at making that dream a reality. It has been said "motion creates opportunity," which is why athletes must have a positive, can-do, and realistic attitude toward realizing their dreams. Performing at one's best in each and every athletic contest is a challenge, it's hard work—if it was easy then everyone would be the best.

"Getting busy" on the road to success and athletic excellence requires conscientious practice and mastery of the basic motor skills and physical conditioning necessary to excel in athletic performance situations. Chapter 7 will address the importance of quality practice in preparing to perform at one's best.

At its most basic level, the dream cycle, as described to this point, can be condensed into three phrases, "see it (dream goals), feel it (visualize), do it (short-, intermediate-, long-term goals; practice; and perform with trust free from doubt, worry, and fear) (Cook, 1996b, 1996c). Action, free from hesitation, self-doubt, and second thoughts, is the key to successful and effective athletic performances.

Effective athletic performers display their talents with a freedom of expression that gives them the opportunity to artistically perform at their highest level.

Mental Key to Success

Peak performers take pride in autographing their performances with excellence.

Evaluation

Obviously actions have outcomes and consequences. Successful athletic performers who are focused on self-improvement constantly seek out feedback that will help them refine their athletic skills. Constructive evaluation is a necessary prerequisite for athletic success (Orlick, 1992, 1996). Feedback about the effectiveness, appropriateness, and correctness of one's action and attitude in athletic performance situations helps an athlete to design mental and physical training programs that will lead to future athletic performance successes.

The Dream Cycle and Mental Skills Training

To be effective, the dream cycle model must be integrated into a mental skills training program that will progressively aid athletes in mastering the elements of athletic performance. Researchers have identified some of these elements as quality training, setting clear daily goals, imagery training, simulation training, and mental preparation for competition including a precompetition plan, a competition focus plan, a competition evaluation, and a distraction control plan (Orlick & Partington, 1988).

Sport psychologists have promoted and designed a variety of applied training programs that can provide a systematic approach to mental skills training (Nideffer, 1992; Orlick, 1998; Reardon & Gordin, 1992; Weinberg & Gould, 1999; Weinberg & Williams, 2001). The peak performance model presented in this book is designed to help athletes master the physical and mental skills that compliment the dream cycle of athletic excellence. The sequencing of the mental and physical skills training with the dream cycle is depicted in Table 3.1.

The goal of mental skills training is to cycle training so that it coincides with the development and progression of an athlete's physical skills, thus resulting in peak performance. Both mental and physical skills are to be taught and practiced in the preseason educational phase of an athlete's training program. Application

Table 3.1   Dream Cycle and Mental Skills Training

Dream Cycle Component	Mental Attributes	Specific Mental Skills
Dream	Motivation	Foundational Beliefs
		Vision/Mission Statement
Goals	Concentration	Performance Goals
		Mental Routines
	Confidence	Goal Attainment Strategies
	Composure	Baseline Assessment
		Dream Goals
	Commitment	Work Ethic/Attitude
Visualize	Concentration	Distraction Control
	Confidence	Positive Visualization
	Composure	Arousal Control Training
	Commitment	Mental Practice
Action	Concentration	Performance Goals & Cues
		Automatic Processing
		Refocusing
	Confidence	Trust
		Performance Mind Set
	Composure	Emotion Management
	Commitment	Mental Preparation
Evaluation	All Mental & Physical Skills	Constructive evaluation
		Self-Improvement

and refinement of these skills occurs during the competition phase of the season just prior to year-ending championship contests and tournaments that require effective execution of these same skills in critical performance settings [peaking phase (Vernacchia, Austin, VandenHazel & Roe, 1992)]. In athletic training circles this is referred to as the "periodization" of training (Reardon & Gordin, 1992).

With all this in mind, it becomes evident that realizing one's athletic dream is not a process of wishing and hoping but one of learning, developing, refining and mastering the physical and mental skills that lead to peak performance.

A Final Question
What's your athletic dream?

PART TWO

Mastering the Inner Basics of Peak Performance

4

Fueling Your Dream
Understanding Athletic Motivation

Tremendous personal commitments of time, energy, and emotion are required of athletes who pursue dreams of athletic glory. To maintain the enthusiasm and energy necessary to realize effective and glorious athletic performances, athletes need a crystal clear understanding of the reasons why they are striving to achieve athletic excellence. This drive to achieve is known as motivation, and motivation is the mechanism that both ignites and fuels an athlete's quest for success.

This chapter will explore the motives or the "why" of athletic performance.

Knowing the "hot" buttons for achieving athletic success has been a focal point of athletic coaches who seek to encourage and inspire athletes to train and perform effectively. Deep down, athletes know that without the sustained motivation to pursue athletic glory their passion for excellence can soon wane and dissipate. This is why athletes rely on coaches, family, friends, and ultimately themselves to support and re-create the desire to excel at sport.

As stated earlier, love of sport is a key motivator for athletes. Their desire to play at their sport is reminiscent of the childhood enthusiasm and enjoyment that launched them on their journey of athletic participation. Try the exercise "Why Do You Participate in Sports?" on the next page.

The exercise helps examine motivational approach to sport. Does the athlete still have the same motivational approach or inner drive to participate in sport that he or she had as a child? Athletes who play at sport from the heart, just as they did when they were children, seem to retain the basic joy that is essential for sustaining their passion for sport in light of the rigors of training, competition, and adversity that sport brings.

Motivation is at the heart of self-improvement. Self-motivated athletes focus on self-improvement and ask themselves on a daily basis, "What can I do to get a little better than I was yesterday?" In the final analysis athletes fail to improve at their sport not because they lose their skills and talents, but because they lose their desire and drive to improve (Christina & Corcos, 1988).

Determining Your Motivational Baseline

To determine an athlete's motivational baseline, he or she should mark a point on each of the following scales that corresponds to his or her current feelings (McGuire, 1997). Our motives regarding athletic achievement are multidimensional and dynamic (see the exercise "Motivational Rating Scales"). We can best understand these motivations by examining the responses to these scales for what they say about these dimensions of an athlete's motivations: sources, driver, direction, orientation, and ethical reference (McGuire, 1997).

Peak Performance Exercise 4.1

Why Do You Participate in Sports?

Spend some time reminiscing about your childhood experiences with sport. Revisit the pure joy and exhilaration you experienced when you first started to "play" sports. Think of specific play experiences you had as a child experiencing sport through neighborhood games with friends. Why were sports so appealing to you as a child? Write down some of the reasons why you were attracted to play, games, sport, and athletics. Did you just like to be with your friends, to be outdoors, to hit, throw, and catch a ball, or to see how fast you could run? Whatever the reasons, describe them and the feelings they generated inside you. Were these the beginnings of your love affair with sport and physical activity?

Now spend some time thinking about the role sport plays in your current life and lifestyle. Why have you continued your participation in the world of sport? What is your relationship to your sport and those around you who are also involved in your sport? Has your love for your sport and sport in general increased or decreased? Why do you think you have maintained your love of and for sport, or why do you think you have lost that loving feeling toward your sport and the role it plays in your life? Write down a list of the reasons you enjoy participating in sport at this time in your life. What has caused you to continue participating in sport, and why is it one of the most important things in your life? Compare your current motives and reasons for participating in sport with your childhood list. How have your motives changed over the years or are they basically the same? Do you still love sport and the joy it brings you?

Peak Performance Exercise 4.2

Motivational Rating Scales

What is the motivational source of your rewards
for participating in sport?

←————————————————————————————————→

Personal satisfaction   Trophies, awards, media attention,
derived from sport   praise from others

What drives you to participate in sport?

←————————————————————————————————→

Self-motivated   Require motivation from others:
                                                           coaches, parents, etc.

Are you confident or fearful about your future performance(s)?

←————————————————————————————————→

Confident   Fear of failure and/or being
                                                    successful, uptight, worried

Do you enjoy mastering skills or are you bothered
when you do not perform well?

←————————————————————————————————→

Task oriented, focus is   More focused on looking good
on effective performance   and doing things right

Do you do the right thing or will you do "what it takes to win"?

←————————————————————————————————→

Practice good sportspersonship   Willing to bend the rules to win

Understanding Your Motivational Tendencies

The Sources of Our Motivation

Intrinsic   Extrinsic

What is the motivational source of your rewards
for participating in sport?

←————————————————————————————————→

Personal satisfaction
derived from sport

Trophies, awards, media attention,
praise from others

The source of an athlete's motivation toward sport and athletic performance can be either intrinsic or extrinsic. He or she can be motivated to participate and perform in sport from within or by outside forces or by both. As children we participated in sport because of the pure enjoyment it brought us, but as we continued our participation we came to realize that some tangible benefits could be gained from participating in sport. Some of these benefits included getting our name in the paper, pleasing our parents and coaches and receiving their praise, increased popularity with our friends, and obtaining better facilities and equipment.

Thus, initial participation in sport is intrinsic and then moves more toward the extrinsic end of the scale, especially as performance improves. This trend leads young athletes to seek more organized and formal avenues of sport, and they join teams and play for their schools and various community organizations or leagues. Along with this more organized approach to sport comes rewards and increased demands related to training and competition. As the organized challenges of sport increase, so do the pressures to perform. As training and performance demands increase, athletes can get caught up in working at their sport rather than playing at their sport. The challenge for athletes is maintain their love for their sport as the demands increase.

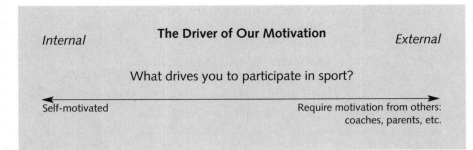

As sport becomes more organized, the drive to attain athletic excellence can come from within or it can be stimulated by others (coaches, parents, friends) and by other external forces such as competition and the media. Once again we find that both internal and external forms of motivation are necessary to drive toward goals. Maintaining control of their own development is a real challenge for athletes as they move through the various developmental stages of their athletic careers.

Athletes who are in control of their development have the presence of mind to realize that they are in the driver's seat and that they will "get behind the wheel" when they are ready. Unfortunately, many developing athletes are pushed or driven to perceived greatness by well-meaning coaches and parents rather than presented with developmentally appropriate sport challenges that keep pace with their physical, psychological, and emotional growth, development, and maturity.

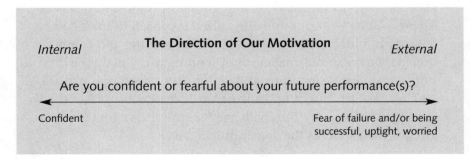

How we view our performance challenges in large part determines the motivational attitude we have prior to and during performances. Confident athletes have no second thoughts about their ability to perform in any given situation—they approach competition with quiet, clear, confident mind, are relaxed, excited, and looking forward to showing off their skills in a performance setting. On the other side of the scale, less confident athletes are filled with doubt, worry, and hesitation, and they tend to avoid or shy away from performance settings because they lack confidence in their skills and abilities. These athletes play to avoid losing rather than playing to win.

Fear of failure results from the way in which an athlete is motivated by him or herself or by others, particularly his or her coach and parents. Athletes who are constantly beating themselves up verbally (i.e., using negative and abusive self-talk such as "you're a loser, give up" or "nice shot, you dummy") because they are not successful, lack patience, and expect themselves to be perfect every time they perform are placing unrealistic performance pressure on themselves. When negative self-talk and the negative reinforcement of coaches and parents are added to the "fear of failure" motivational profile, then athletes are well on their way to avoiding competition. Sometimes these athletes remain in sport but they expect to be punished by others, it is the only way they can seem to gain the motivational fuel to perform. Even though "fear of failure" athletes may be successful, they very seldom enjoy the performance or competitive process because they are outcome oriented and judgmental regarding their performances. They lack the self-acceptance that self-confident athletes possess. Truly confident athletes compare themselves to themselves and focus on self-improvement and trusting their talents and skills, especially in performance settings.

Athletes who fear failure can overcome these feelings by separating their identity from their performance (Cook, 1996a). Chapter 10: Confidence will discuss fear of failure athletes who judge themselves by how they perform—their feelings of self-worth depend on how they perform. Athletes, particularly young athletes, can learn from coaches and parents that regardless of performance outcomes, they are valued and respected individuals who have given their best effort.

In the same vein, athletes who fear failure must learn to

accept that they will make mistakes and to view mistakes as a mechanism to gain feedback on how to improve or make their performances more effective. Effective athletic performers embrace their human imperfections not only in sport, but in all aspects of their lives. Lastly, fear of failure athletes must release themselves from the grasp of scoreboard mentality or outcome goals and focus on the process of achieving success (i.e., relationships with coaches and teammates, attaining physical and mental fitness, motor skill acquisition)

On the other hand, fear of success often results from how athletes learn to be successful. We spend a lot of time in the athletic world teaching people how to be successful but very little time if any teaching them what to do when they do achieve success. Furthermore, athletes are seldom taught how to maintain success, and they tend to worry about losing their spot at the top of the competitive heap.

Athletes who fear success are focused on pleasing others (fans, coaches, parents) rather than on the process of their own performances. This need to please and seek the approval of others creates a tremendous distraction for the fear of success athlete who often avoids placing him or herself in situations of expectation. In essence, this athlete needs to formulate and adhere to a personal plan for effective performance based on his or her skills, abilities, development, and maturation. Fear of success athletes need to play their own game rather than the game they feel others expect of them (Cook, 1996a).

Success is a learned process that is maintained through the relentless pursuit of self-improvement and focus on one's own performance, rather than on the performances of others. To maintain success athletes must focus on their own talents and abilities and what they can do to improve from play to play and day to day—all we can control is our own athletic development and performance. At the top of their game, athletes need to look ahead and not behind. If those people who are behind had it figured out they would be ahead—successful athletes use this mindset to stay one step ahead of their competitors.

Performers who sustain their success are focused on self-improvement and on being at their best consistently in each and every competitive setting. With this type of approach and attitude toward athletic competition, athletes can feel good about themselves and their performance, win or lose.

Task   **The Orientation of Our Motivation**
                                                                  Ego

Do you enjoy mastering skills or are you bothered
when you do not perform well?

← ─── →

Task oriented, focus is   More focused on looking good
on effective performance   and doing things right

This dimension of the motivational scale uncovers whether the athlete is task oriented. Does he or she enjoy mastering the skills of sport and mastering the performance of those learned skills in competitive settings? Task oriented athletes are constantly seeking out feedback regarding their performances—they want information about how to improve existing skills and learn new skills that will make them more effective in similar or new situations. A poor performance doesn't derail the task-oriented athlete; he or she learns from mistakes and uses mistakes as feedback to detect and correct errors that can result in ineffective performances. Task oriented athletes tend to be tough-minded and seek constructive evaluations of their performance, realizing that information about their performance is not about them as people but about their performance. This type of athlete does not take criticism personally.

On the other side of this continuum is the ego-oriented athlete who does take attempts to correct his or her performance skills personally. This athlete has difficulty separating performance feedback from personal criticism and is very tender-minded. He or she is often threatened by performance settings and tends to be avoidance oriented because, instead of improving on his or her skills from performance to performance, he or she is too emotionally overwhelmed by poor performance outcomes to focus on mastery and self-improvement.

Both task- and ego-oriented athletic performers are very

proud individuals. Their pride is one of the prime sources of their commitment to their sport and athletic excellence.

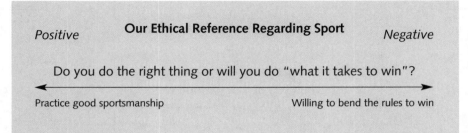

To achieve athletic excellence with integrity by playing fair and practicing good sportspersonship is a goal of a true champion. There are a lot of winners in sport, but not all winners are champions. Champions are remembered not only for what they achieved but for how they achieved it. While everyone cannot be a winner in sport, everyone can be an ethical champion who is motivated to protect the sanctity of sport by practicing good sportspersonship and pursuing athletic excellence with integrity. A winning at all cost motivation toward sport can often result in a hollow victory because it is a result of poor moral reasoning and unethical decision making.

A Motivational Profile of the Success-Oriented Athlete

Reviewing motivational baselines and orientations we see the following motivational profile for athletic success emerge:

- *Love of Sport:* Intrinsic motivation based on one's love of sport.
- *Self-Responsibility:* An internal drive to succeed in sport, one that stresses self starting, does not place blame, and makes no excuses.
- *Self-Confidence:* An approach to sport that focuses on self-

confidence rather than the fears that generate self-doubt and worry.

- *Self-Improvement:* A strong desire to improve, to master the athletic and performance skills that can lead to effective performances.
- *Sportspersonship:* The desire to practice good sportspersonship.

This motivational profile stresses a learned effective (Rotella, 1981) motivational approach to sport, that is, a motivational profile that is mastery oriented. A challenge-seeking motivational profile encourages high persistence in the face of obstacles, the maintenance of effective strategies, or the development of new and sophisticated strategies under adverse situations, and it promotes pride and satisfaction in both successful and unsuccessful situations (Prapavessis & Carron, 1988).

Athletes who display ineffective motivational profiles are considered *learned helpless* because they avoid challenge and have low persistence in the face of obstacles. The learned helpless athlete experiences a deterioration of performance strategies or fails to develop new and sophisticated strategies under difficult or adverse situations, experiences pride and satisfaction only from ability exhibited in successful situations, and equates failure with low ability, little pride, and personal satisfaction (Prapavessis & Carron, 1988).

The ability of an athlete to attribute success or failure to skill, physical ability, and effort has a profound effect on his or her perceived and real feelings of competence or confidence regarding past or future performances. Attributional reasoning is widely recognized as an important aspect of human and athletic performance (Brawley & Roberts, 1984; Earley, 1988; Gill 1980, 1986; Grove & Pargman, 1986; Mark, Muturie, Brooks & Harris, 1984; McCauley & Gross, 1983; Roberts, 1982; Roberts & Pascuzzi, 1979; Spink & Roberts, 1980; Weiner, 1972, 1974, 1979; Weiner, Russell & Lerman, 1979).

In essence, the athlete's *perceptions* regarding these attributions ultimately determine his or her ability to perform effectively in a particular competitive setting. An athlete who is unable to take responsibility for the sources of his or her successes and failures in sport often adopts learned helpless behaviors (Dweck, 1975, 1978, 1980; Prapavessis & Carron, 1988). Learned helpless athletes perceive or feel that they are not in control of determining the outcomes of their performance.

A Five-Step Approach to Effective Athletic Motivation

To assist athletes in overcoming learned helpless behaviors and to help them feel more in control in performance settings the following five-step approach to gaining an intrinsic motivational or "inside-out" approach to athletic performance can be used (Vernacchia, 1998). This approach is focused on learned effective behaviors in athletes (Cook, 1996a) including:

- No excuses
- Acceptance of self-responsibility for performance outcomes
- Viewing weaknesses as challenges
- A primary focus on the athlete's strength
- Strong emotion of pride
- Confidence based on preparation
- The ability to set and attain performance, process, and personal goals
- Determination of success by internal attributes such as persistence, effort, will, and commitment.

The learned effective approach to athletic performance is enhanced by the following five steps, which can be employed by athletes and coaches prior to athletic competition. The precompetitive phase of athletic performance is critical because it identifies and outlines the athlete's mental preparation plan for competition. The precompetitive phase also includes many and varied distractions that can cause athletes to forget or lose track of their intended mental plans for success. The following competitive focus and refocusing plan (Vernacchia, 1998) is especially helpful a day prior to, the day of, and just prior to competitive efforts:

1. *Identify Performance Goals and Cues.* Help athletes focus on how they can do (performance process) what they want to do (outcome process). Task-relevant cues and behaviors are employed in competition to help the athlete focus or refocus (concentrate) on what they would like to do rather than to be distracted by situations and happenings that they have no control over (Anshel, 1990; Magill, 1989; Singer, 1980). Have the athlete write out his or her performance goals along with the cues that are associated with attaining these goals. Use concentration cards as shown in Figure 4.1 to help athletes review their performance goals and cues.

2. *Focus on Strengths and Talent.* Aid athletes in attributing their successes or failures to their own talent, abilities, skills, and effort so that they can increase their feelings of *competency* and *control* (Weiner, Hierenberg & Goldstein, 1976).

   Confidence = Control   Confidence = Competency

   The focus here is on the performance factors within the athlete's circle of control and within his or her skills, abilities, and efforts to effect.

3. *Stress Effort-Conscious Performances.* Encourage athletes to focus on effort rather than doing things perfectly in performance settings. In other words, focus on making the effort to be as effective as possible in performance settings, that is, winning ugly if necessary. This will help athletes let performances "flow" and develops trust and belief in previously mastered skills that can be activated by making a "concentrated" effort to excel in performance situations.

4. *Emphasize Self-Improvement.* Emphasize competition against one's self or focusing on doing one's best in the performance situation and avoiding comparing one's self to others. In effect, play their game as best they can, and let the chips fall where they may. This step should also emphasize the training and performance improvements the athlete has made to reach his or her goals.

5. *Emphasize Enjoyment and Fun.* Emphasis on involvement and enjoyment in the "process" of achieving successful athletic performances is an important and final step for any athlete. This emphasis will free them up to *play* their sport with creativity, style, and vigor rather than grinding away at their sport with mechanical and workmanlike efforts that are oftentimes ineffective.

To help an athlete focus on the fun and enjoyment of athletic performance, have him or her visualize in their mind's eye their best performance ever. Have the athlete describe the feelings of self-fulfillment and satisfaction and pure joy that accompanied this performance. In essence, focus on having a love affair with success and bring these feelings and images to upcoming performances.

The Overs and Unders of Athletic Motivation

To completely understand athletic motivation it is necessary to explore the relationship between motivation, confidence, and achievement (Rotella, 1990b; Vernacchia, 1997). This relationship determines an athlete's motivational style and includes: (1) the undermotivated, overconfident underachiever and (2) the overmotivated, under- confident underachiever. These two styles are common among ineffective athletic performers. A third motivation style is employed by successful athletes, namely: (3) the motivated, confident achiever.

The Undermotivated, Overconfident Underachiever

This motivational pattern is demonstrated by young athletes who are just entering sport. In many cases they may have considerable talent and may, in fact, be precocious and enjoy a great deal of success without training very much or working very hard. The task for the coach working with this athlete is to develop the athlete's work ethic so that he or she understands the relationship

Figure 4.1 **Concentration Card for Defensive Rebounding (Basketball)**

Cue	Concentration Goals and Performance Behaviors
"Shot"	Reach out and locate opponent (tagging)
	Turn toward opponent
	Back to opponent
	Box out
	Go to the ball
	Jump, grasp, and hold the ball
	Land with feet apart and maintain balance
	Secure the ball (hold to chest)
	Look for outlet pass

between conscientious training and effective athletic performance.

The young athlete who does not learn to work hard in practice will soon meet his or her match in the higher levels of competition. Where once the athlete had been the "big fish in the little pond," he or she soon becomes the "little fish in the big pond," and without a solid work ethic, this athlete will feel unprepared and helpless as competitive levels and situations become more challenging.

While coaches are responsible for instilling a proper work ethic in their charges, they also must teach them the importance of training intelligently at appropriate intensities and volumes that allow for rest and recovery from demanding workouts. Hard work alone does not guarantee effective or enhanced athletic performances. Young athletes must realize that as they begin their athletic careers their performances will improve dramatically, especially if they are working hard. However, they reach a point at which performances plateau or take a considerable amount of time to improve. This performance paradox—the better you get, the less you improve—must be clearly understood. At this point patient and intelligent training leads to improved athletic performances. The frustrated athlete who does not understand this will continue to work "harder" rather than "smarter" and soon becomes an overmotivated, underconfident underachiever.

The Overmotivated, Underconfident Underachiever

The overmotivated, underconfident underachiever is the motivational pattern that typifies the overtrained athlete. These athletes have learned their lessons well, adhering to and glorifying the work ethic in their training programs. These athletes love the ritual and routine of sport and training and have lost their focus regarding the purpose of training, that is, to perform well. These athletes will practice and practice and then get in the game and practice some more. This type of athlete must be confronted with the question: "Do you practice to practice or do you practice to perform?"

The realization must be that a "nose to the grindstone" approach to training eventually results in a flat nose. Working hard will get athletes about half-way or two-thirds to their goal—training "smart" will get them the remainder of the way. Essentially there comes a point when athletes must trust their talent, training, and preparation and focus on performing in a confident manner. Athletes who lack confidence go to the performance setting doubting their talent and preparation because a particular training session didn't go as planned or wasn't perfect. In light of this realization they try "harder" in the performance situation, just as they do in training, rather than trusting themselves and being patient—the key here is to try "less" in the performance situation and let talent take over.

The overmotivated, underconfident underachiever is often a perfectionist who cannot accept being human and is constantly afraid of making mistakes (fear of failure). Perfectionistic track athletes, for example, (Connelly, 1992) overwork at their training until they get it right, or they force themselves to hit the times prescribed for a particular workout, thus leaving all their racing energy at practice. When they get to performance day they are "flat" and lack the energy and excitement needed to compete effectively. This leads to frustration and a renewed dedication to work even harder during practice—a vicious cycle.

The following strategies can help the perfectionistic athlete develop a more realistic, human, and effective training and performance style (Burns, 1980; Connelly, 1992; Cook, 1996a):

1. *Develop a Process Orientation to Sport.* Rather than constantly focusing on the outcome of sport and endeavoring to make it "just right" and perfect, focus on the pleasure of the training and performance process. Identify the by-products of training and athletic performance that make it fun and enjoyable (e.g., being with friends and teammates, travel, relationships with coaches, self-improvement, attaining superior physical and mental fitness, playing the game).

2. *Understand the Sport Work Ethic.* Engage in quality practice or training, but more importantly, engage in quality rest to allow recovery and rejuvenation from the training, travel, and performance demands of sport. Provide a balanced time orientation to training or a "work by the job, not by the hour" approach to avoid overtraining. Be as effective in training sessions as one can within the time allotted and the resources available—focus on effectiveness and not perfection, which will sharpen an athlete's focus during training, enabling him or her to get the most out of practice sessions. Many athletes overwork at practice, trying to get everything just right or perfect, but in effect they are getting tired and end up practicing their mistakes, and creating bad habits.

3. *Confront Fear of Failure.* Remember we are human and imperfect at best, and as the saying goes, "That's why they put erasers on pencils." Sports are games of mistakes, it's really all about using mistakes as feedback to improve one's performance. Rather than dwell on mistakes made in practice or performance settings and view them negatively, embrace them and use them to provide the feedback to be more effective in the next practice trial or performance effort.

4. *Confront Feelings of Inadequacy.* Athletes can develop the mental discipline to focus on their strengths following poor practices or performances by eliminating self-defeating thoughts. To do this an athlete must learn to retrain or "flip-

flop" the thoughts that can lead to feelings of inadequacy. For example, an athlete may have the following thoughts related to his or her performance, "I can't believe I messed up like that, that's like me, I always fall apart when it counts." Change this thought to, "That was my best effort, I know I can do better, my practices have been great, I always perform better as the game goes on."

5. *Make a Concentrated Effort to Change Ineffective Behaviors.* An athlete can change perfectionistic behaviors by making the choice to trust his or her coach and training, by focusing on and counting successes, by practicing saying "thank you" for compliments, by learning to practice relaxation techniques, by developing interests outside of sport, and, most importantly, by being patient with him or herself and the process of change.

The Motivated, Confident Achiever

The motivated, confident achiever in sport realizes first of all that there is no such thing as overachieving—you either achieve your goal or you don't. Overmotivated, underconfident underachievers constantly feel they could have or should have done better, or that their performance wasn't good enough to meet their standards, or good enough in comparison to the competition or past performances. If overmotivated, underconfident underachievers do succeed in competition, they believe they are "overachievers" who really don't have as much talent as everyone else, they just outworked their competitors.

Motivated, confident achievers in sport go to the performance setting with the express intent to perform as effectively as they can under the existing circumstances, while at the same time placing complete trust and belief in their training and preparation. These athletes are "in the moment" at the time they are performing and focus all of their energy on the execution of their specific game plan or performance strategies and techniques. Motivated, confident achievers play "their" game once the competition starts.

For this athlete the performance situation is ego-enhancing rather than ego-threatening. He or she is truly looking forward to performing—excited by the opportunities for self-improvement and achievement that competition can bring.

One Final Motivational Assessment

Use the following exercise to examine your motivational style in light of the three types just presented.

Peak Performance Exercise 4.3

Motivational Styles

Some athletes tend to be very goal oriented and constantly think about attaining their goals. These people fill themselves with worry and concern over the consequences of not achieving their goals, thus developing a level of "wanting" that leads to ineffective levels of perfectionism and fear of failure. By doing so, these athletes never become as good as they could be. Other athletes tend to be not so goal oriented and thus have much lower levels of commitment and dedication. Many of these athletes experience constant early success in their athletic careers and just seem to ride on their natural talent, thus limiting their chances of becoming the best they can be.

What's your tendency? Do you think more about how great you'll play or more about how terrible it would be to lose? Do you spend more time looking for ways you can become great or more time looking for the security, comfort, and safety of never losing? Do you have the physical discipline for doing all the hard training and preparation but lack the discipline to free yourself mentally and play all out on game day? Or vice versa, do you lack the discipline to prepare thoroughly but have the ability to let go at game time and totally play all out?

If you tend to be the first type (overmotivated type who is able to work out hard and fears failing and thus can't let go and play freely), reflect on how your perfectionistic attitudes and tendencies have hindered your performance. What are the advantages and disadvantages of your perfectionism? How do self-critical tendencies hinder your self-confidence? Monitor your thoughts for three days while practicing and playing, and compare the frequency of positive and negative statements you make to yourself. How have these perfectionistic tendencies made you develop a fear of failure and made you a candidate for overtraining and burnout?

If you tend to be the other type (the undermotivated type who plays freely but doesn't put in enough training to really develop all his/her potential), reflect on how your lack of self-discipline and dedication has bred some work habits that leave you short of full preparation. Take a careful look at your past, and explain how the rewards given by our culture for winning at previous levels of competition have bred these less than effective work habits. Evaluate any forms of self-sabotage that may prevent you from making the commitment necessary to become the best you can be.

If you don't tend toward either of these types but have a more balanced motivational style, reflect on how you keep your balance, especially in difficult and boring situations. How will you keep this balance throughout your life and career as it brings you greater success? How will you keep your balance when you get to the point of always taking on more than anyone can possibly handle? (Adapted from Rotella, 1990a.)

5

Dreaming Your Dream
The Power of Visualization

Visualization is a powerful mental training technique for athletes of all abilities. Often referred to as mental training, mental practice, mental imagery, and/or mental rehearsal, visualization can enhance the acquisition of sport skills as well as athletic performance. Visualization involves use of all the senses to vividly and clearly re-create, simulate, or create, in our mind's eye, successful and effective practice and performance outcomes (Vealey & Greenleaf, 2001).

Sport psychology researchers and practitioners wholeheartedly support the use of visualization to improve concentration, build confidence, control emotional responses, acquire and practice motor skills, acquire and practice strategy, and cope with pain and injury (Feltz & Landers, 1983; Moran, 1996; Murphy & Jowdy, 1992; Weinberg & Gould, 1999).

. . . I've tried to always visualize myself being the best, giving a hundred percent in a situation and going out and actually achieving a world rank or Olympic medal. Over and over in my mind, every day, maybe a thousand times a day, I see myself being the best. After a while the body just responds to that. You step into a situation and the body feels like it's already done that, it's already been the best, so it's just going out there and doing it again. I can't tell you how much you have to let your mind dwell upon what you really want in life. . . .
—*USA Track and Field Athlete, Olympic Bronze Medalist* (Vernacchia, McGuire, Reardon, & Templin, 2000, p. 15)

> "*Over and over in my mind, every day, maybe a thousand times a day, I see myself being the best. After a while, the body just responds to that.*"

Visualization: Why It Works

Visualization works because it connects our imagination with reality. Our minds think in images and images create feelings, and our thoughts and feelings can influence the effectiveness of our actions. Our dreams in effect are visions of who we are and what we would like to be or do. Our imagination provides the creative energy that encourages us to act out our dreams.

A young boy or girl who dreams of becoming a champion athlete is influenced toward acting on his or her dream by media images and tales of athletic glory conveyed by parents, coaches, teachers, and friends. As young children we are suggestible, but sometimes children lose their *suggest-ability* as they experience the reality and harshness of life and sport. As children mature and develop, they can be socialized out of their ability to visualize by constant reminders to "stop daydreaming" about unrealistic goals. In many cases we must become children again in order to realize our dreams of athletic glory, by allowing ourselves to access our imagination through visualization techniques and strategies.

Advertisers, for example, know how suggestible we really are and successfully use our imaginations to promote and sell their products. Popular magazine and television ads associate products with the images of people and scenes that project such socially desirable attributes as wealth, power, fun, physical prowess and athletic skill, and sexuality. The suggestion is that if you use their product you'll experience happiness and success.

A vivid imagination can result in a physical response—try the visualization exercise "The Lemon Exercise."

Peak Performance Exercise 5.1

The Lemon Exercise

Sit or lie down in a comfortable position, close your eyes and relax by taking several deep breaths. Now imagine yourself at home in the morning waking up from a good night's sleep. You feel rested and completely relaxed. It is a day off for you, and you are looking forward to participating in your favorite recreational activity. It is a warm summer day and the sun is streaming into your room-you get out of bed and dress comfortably in shorts and a tee shirt and head to your kitchen for breakfast. After arriving at your kitchen, you sit down at the kitchen table-you are relaxed, energized, happy and looking forward to the day. On the table in front of you is a cutting board, a knife, and a lemon. You pick up the lemon in one hand and the knife in the other and slice the lemon in half. As you slice the lemon, juice squirts onto your fingers and hand. The juice is cool and glistens as it filters the sunlight that is streaming into your kitchen. You take a half of the lemon and cut it in half and once again the cool juice of the lemon lands on your fingers and hand. Now you take a quarter of the lemon and place it in your mouth and suck on it. . . . Now you take the lemon from your mouth and place it back on the cutting board. . . . Open your eyes.

What was your physical response to the lemon exercise? Did you feel your lips pucker? Did your mouth start to actually water? Did you actually have a physical response to the images you were creating and experiencing in your mind even though you didn't really suck on a lemon? Repeat the exercise and create more vivid and clear images in your mind—did you experience a stronger response?

In learning sport skills, visualization allows an athlete to mentally practice movements so that he or she can get the "idea" and "feel" of the movement or sequence of movements for a sport skill. This is important because the first stage of learning a sport skill involves *imaging* how a sport skill or movement pattern is to be performed (Oxendine, 1986). Athletes who are being taught a new skill often say to their coaches, "I don't see what you mean." Coaches then demonstrate skills again, or provide other examples, verbal descriptions, or methods (films, video-tape) that help an athlete form the mental picture of how a skill is to be performed.

In terms of athletic performance, visualization allows an athlete to pre-image success by mentally rehearsing and reviewing the effective performance in an environment of "virtual reality." The key here is the mental discipline and composure to image what the athlete would *like* to have happen in a performance situation. As the saying goes:

 Mental Key to Success

Successful people see what they want to have happen, and unsuccessful people see what they don't want to have happen.

To help themselves maintain their focus on success, athletes practice and master visualization strategies that will enable them to anticipate and mentally prepare for distractions and obstacles they may face in competition. Visualization, properly utilized, helps athletes maintain their focus on success in a nondistractible way. An Olympic track and field athlete who was a finalist in his event explains this process as follows (Vernacchia, McGuire, Reardon & Templin, 2000, pp. 15–16):

> You have to prepare up here (pointing to his head)
> and get your mind going and prepare for what the race is
> going to be and that means running pictures through
> your mind about what you're to expect, and you have to

do that prior to getting on the race line. You can't wait until the day of the race or the hour before. You have to do it Monday, Wednesday, Thursday, and keep thinking about it in your mind how you're to prepare for that race on Saturday, and then try to put into image how the stadium looks and how the track is going to feel and what the crowd is going to be, put all those things in your mind and make it very bright and analyze it, and then try to apply that the day of the race.

Another Olympic track and field athlete who was a silver medalist in her event made the following observations about visualization (Vernacchia, McGuire, Reardon & Templin, 2000, p. 16):

> I think the visualization technique is best for me. . . . I do it usually the night before, and it helps if you know your lane assignments or you at least know your competition or whatever and can expect what they're doing . . . right before I go to bed I think about the race and I run it, and I run it, and I run it, and then it just falls together . . . I rerun it a hundred times, it's like a video camera.

The Mind Is Like a Parachute

To utilize visualization techniques most effectively, athletes need to first master relaxation training. It has been said that "the mind is like a parachute, it works best when it's open." Achieving a state of physical relaxation, that is, relaxing the body, is the first step to calming and relaxing the mind. In a calm or relaxed state the mind is more receptive or open to suggestions and affirmations related to personal and performance goals. In a relaxed state the athlete's mind can clearly and vividly see the mental images of successful performance, free from stress and tension.

While we often recognize the effect that stress and tension can have upon athletic performance, few athletes develop the mental and physical skills necessary to relax or loosen up prior to, during, and after competitive efforts. Many coaches encourage or instruct their athletes "to relax," but athletes are rarely given, let alone develop and master the mental and physical tools of relaxation training.

Successfully employing relaxation strategies and skills prior to, during, and after athletic competitions has five phases:

1. *The Recognition Phase.* This initial phase alerts the athlete to the fact that he or she is experiencing mental and physical tension that can be potentially counterproductive to effective performances if not mediated.

2. *The Exercise Phase.* Athletes can use mild forms of exercise, for example, go for a walk once they feel tension mounting as they ready themselves for a performance. Basketball players, for example, have a morning team "shoot around" prior to an afternoon or evening game. Physical exercise creates relaxation.

3. *The Calming Phase.* In addition to mild forms of exercising, athletes can make a conscious and concentrated effort to choose visual and auditory stimulation (e.g., music) that will calm their mind and body. The mental skill of visualization can be utilized to re-create calming scenes and sounds that will provide a relaxing mental and physical climate for relaxation. This process may also allow an athlete to nap prior to a performance—sleep can be a welcome form of relaxation for an "uptight" athlete.

4. *The Clearing Phase.* Sometimes athletes can relieve mental and physical tension by engaging in progressive relaxation exercises that, in effect, act as a "body scan" to bring about relaxation. Conducted in a quiet place (many athletes prefer to lie down while engaging in this technique) and beginning with deep breathing exercises, an athlete can release tension within various muscles and muscle groups starting with the scalp and top of the head and ending with the tip of their toes. This is a great way of clearing or freeing up the mind and body from stress and tension.

5. *The Performance Phase.* Most importantly and most often overlooked is a way for an athlete to use relaxation skills and technique during competition. Calmness or relaxation under

fire is essential for effective athletic performances. Maintaining the state of relaxed readiness that was developed prior to competition is a performance challenge even the most seasoned athletes face.

Key Relaxation Exercises and Skills to Be Mastered

The ability to relax is a learned physical and mental skill. Coaches and athletes should recognize this fact to master and properly implement relaxation training techniques. The exercises presented here should be practiced daily, preferably in a quiet place while the athlete is in a relaxed and comfortable position (e.g., lying on a bed in a quiet room).

The author is reminded here of a conversation he had with Lee Evans, the great American Olympian who set world records in the 400 meter dash and the 4 × 400 meter relay. His 400 meter world record set in the 1968 Olympic Games stood for twenty years. Lee Evans would always win his races, many times by the slightest margins, but he always won. When asked how he did it, he responded, "I just wanted to win." When probed further regarding his specific techniques for winning, he stated: "I would find a quiet place to relax and then I would see everything about the upcoming race, the stadium, the track, the weather conditions, my opponents and I would run the race in my mind. If I did that for 5 or 6 hours, I could break the world record." This is a very revealing statement, not only because it validates the use of relaxation and visualization techniques, but because it demonstrates the tremendous mental discipline champion athletes have.

For 5 hours Lee Evans was able to think about how he would successfully run his race. Unsuccessful or less successful athletes, especially newcomers to sport, think about what they want to do and how they want to do it for 15 minutes and then about what they don't want to do or what they don't want to happen to them for the other 4 hours and 45 minutes.

Training sessions for mastering relaxation skills and techniques require a 20-minute practice session, usually at the end of the day prior to going to bed, for a 21-day period (preferably 21 consecutive sessions). The athlete can practice one or more of the exercises described below each evening.

Compare and Contrast

This phase one (recognition phase) compatible exercise is known as differential relaxation and teaches athletes to know the difference between relaxation and tension within their bodies. A very basic exercise that illustrates this recognition or awareness skill is to have the athlete flex his or her arm at a 90 degree angle. The hand should be held in a fist. Now ask the athlete to make a fist and to completely (100%) tighten up all the muscles in the upper and lower arm as well as the chest, shoulder, neck, and back areas of the body. Hold that state of tension for 5 seconds and then relax the fist and all the tightened muscles completely (0%). Now compare and contrast the tension levels that were just experienced. Continue with the exercise by asking the athlete to exert a 75% level of tension and then relax to 0%. Progress through the various levels of tension and relaxation from 100% to 75% to 50% to 25%. Once the athlete reaches the 25% level, decrease the levels of tension by 5% (i.e., 20%, 15%, 10%). Once the athlete reaches the 10% level, decrease the levels of tension by 1 or 2% (i.e., 10%, 9%, 8%, etc. to 0%).

The key is to have the athlete recognize and identify his or her own tension threshold for various skills and movement patterns. The tension threshold is the point at which too much physical tension begins to interfere with performance or effective execution of skills and movement patterns. The tension threshold is the point at which an athlete begins to lose his or her "flow" in sport and starts to become mechanical and ineffective. Athletes can learn to identify this threshold and use various relaxation techniques to return to or remain in a "flow" state.

Ravizza and Hanson (1995) refer to the tension threshold as the "yellow light" phase of performance by comparing the various awareness stages of tension that an athlete faces to a stop-light. When the athlete is flowing, loose, and relaxed, he or she is in a "green light" situation. When tension begins to interfere with performance, the athlete is in a "yellow light" situation and needs to respond appropriately by using various mental and physical skills to reduce tension before it reaches the "red light" stage and is too late to reverse.

Deep Breathing or "Internal Massage"

Simple breathing techniques, that is, "internal massage," can help to relieve muscle tension and ready overexcited or anxious athletes for competitive challenges. A simple breathing exercise to utilize when athletes need to regulate their tension and excitement levels just prior to competition is to close their eyes and take several slow deep breaths. On the inhale, see the letters RE and breathe deeply, taking in refreshing, relaxing, and rejuvenating fresh air of self-regulation and self-confidence. On the exhale see the letters LAX while releasing stress, tension, fears, doubts, overexcitement, and worry about the approaching competition. *Inhale RE, exhale LAX.*

Clearing the Body to Achieve Mental Calmness

Using progressive relaxation exercises to clear the body is the first step to achieving mental calmness. Progressive relaxation training can ready the mind for accurate decision making that leads to successful performance outcomes and to increasing the mind's receptivity to the visual images of success that so often precede great performances. Visual images of success can only take root in the mind once the body is relaxed—a relaxed physical state results in an open mind that favors creativity and trust in one's abilities to deliver the best performance possible.

Progressive relaxation or "body scanning" occurs during the "clearing phase" of relaxation training. Start at the top of head and progressively relax various muscle groups by focusing on each muscle group, feeling loose, warm, and free of tension. Relax muscle groups in the following order—top of the head, scalp, facial muscles, neck muscles, shoulder and upper back (especially the area from between the shoulder blades to the back of the neck, chest, arms (upper and lower), hands and fingers, stomach area, lower back, hips (front and back), thighs (front and back), lower legs (front and back), and finally the ankles, feet, and toes.

Once the body has been totally relaxed then the athlete can continue the exercise by creating images of a scene or place that represents a quiet, calm, serene mental state. This scene or place can be created in the athlete's mind and can then be replicated and revisited each time he or she wishes to practice visualization, mental imagery, or mental rehearsal of performance skills. For example, the scene the athlete creates can reflect the solitude and serenity of nature (e.g., ocean, forest, or mountain scene) in order to reach a deeper state of relaxation and then to build inner strength through mental imagery and affirmations. An example of mentally constructing such a scene would be:

> . . . stepping through a doorway into a beautiful, pleasing scene that is unusually appealing to you. Plants, fresh air. You can see the sky, blue and clear with a few clouds rolling by. And you can hear water running nearby, a stream or a river. And as you relax in this scene for a few moments, what you can do is to take some time to communicate to your inner self the images and affirmations that can provide your inner mind with a clear understanding of your desired goals, your desired realities, and desired athletic achievements.
>
> So spend a few moments mentally rehearsing and communicating with your inner self, building inner strength. See yourself enjoying each day, all aspects of your life, more free each day from the self-limiting, distressing reactions that can interfere with and can inhibit your quest for excellence in sport and life. Use these mental skills that you are learning now and practicing during the day for momentary rest and refreshment. And whether it's for five seconds or five minutes, at strategic times during the day, to quiet and clear your mind, to reduce the building tensions and stress and then to be able to relax at the end of your daily activities—to clear your mind and enjoy your own free time.

Communicate to your inner self, your goals, ideas, and successes, and then see yourself executing and performing successfully and effectively in a variety of settings. Build your inner strength by using these images and affirmations while you are deeply relaxed. (Adapted from Vernacchia, McGuire, & Cook, 1996, p. 183)

The Five Finger Exercise

The five finger exercise is a quick relaxation technique that athletes can utilize during competition. Athletes must master progressive relaxation exercises prior to utilizing the five finger exercise because this technique essentially creates a relaxation response by associating particular muscle groups with a specific physical cue.

In this exercise the athlete learns to specifically target certain muscle groups by associating the muscle group with one of four fingers. The athlete then trains him or herself to relax or release tension within the muscle group or a specific muscle within the group. For example, when the athlete touches his or her index finger and thumb, it serves as a cue to relax the muscles of the head, face, and neck. When the athlete touches his or her middle finger and thumb, it serves as a cue to relax the shoulders, chest and arms. When the athlete touches his or her ring finger and thumb, it serves as a cue to relax the upper and lower back and hips, and finally touching the little finger and thumb serves as a cue to relax the upper and lower legs, including the ankle and feet.

Most athletes first feel tension and stress in the back of the neck (hence the expression, "pain in the neck"). By simply squeezing the thumb and index finger and taking a deep breath, the athlete may be able to reduce tension quickly in this area of the body. Similarly, a golfer who experiences tension in the arms as he or she is standing over a shot can relieve this tension by gently pressing the middle finger of one hand against the grip/shaft of his or her golf club. Some athletes, such as swimmers, use this technique in the middle of strokes to remain relaxed. A backstroker can touch his or her thumb and index finger during the recovery phase of his or her stroke to relax the shoulders.

Visualization: How It Works

Once athletes have mastered progressive relaxation, they can be trained in visualization techniques. Athletes engage in systematic visualization exercises to produce automatic and effective practice and performance outcomes. Visualization or mental practice can allow minute muscular contractions that simulate the real movement (Schmidt, 1991). Visualization exercises are usually practiced in a four-phase sequence (Vernacchia, 1996b):

1. *Relaxation Phase*—In this phase the athlete utilizes a particular relaxation technique that induces physical and mental calmness (e.g., progressive relaxation or deep breathing). The athlete's goal during this phase is to be free of muscular tensions. Once the athlete is free of muscular tension and as relaxed as possible (i.e., in a state that is experienced just prior to falling asleep), he or she will be mentally and physically receptive to suggestions regarding the learning and execution or sport skills and strategies.

2. *Programming Phase*—Once relaxed, the athlete is ready to receive practice and performance enhancement suggestions with a clear and quiet mind. These suggestions can take the form of mental pictures and images of successful outcomes of training and performance experiences. This visualization can be composed of mental images that recall the athlete's most enjoyable and successful performances or to image desired future performances.

    The athlete's initial goal in the programming phase is to see him or herself performing skills effectively in practice and performance settings while at the same time experiencing and enjoying athletic success.

    The next goal of the programming phase is to itemize the steps that must be taken to achieve this success. The athlete is encouraged to focus on specific strategies and skills that will promote a successful performance. The athlete mentally rehearses his or her skills and actually pictures him or herself performing these skills successfully in training and/or competition. A mental plan is established that specifically and vividly describes what steps an athlete needs to take to achieve success.

3. *Associative Phase*—To help an athlete recall the previously programmed suggestions, cues should be established (colors, words, numbers, etc.) that will trigger an appropriate performance response. In competition, for example, an athlete might have a number cue that triggers an appropriate arousal level. Or an athlete may relax and be reminded of skills by focusing on a uniform color, or by repeating a word or phrase, such as *relax*, or by using an affirmation, such as "I am performing well." These cues will help the athlete to perform effectively under pressure.

4. *Mind to Muscle Phase*—To be effective, visualization training must be practiced daily. This mental skill must be practiced and refined, just as physical skills are practiced and refined. It is helpful to engage in visualization training each day, sometimes just prior to practice or at the end of the day prior to going to sleep, in a quiet environment that is free of distractions and conducive to relaxation and concentration.

How to Use Visualization Techniques

Visualization techniques or strategies that can be used to enhance motor skill learning and athletic performance are mentioned throughout this book, particularly regarding goal attainment, quality practice, injury rehabilitation, and the 4C's of concentration, confidence, composure, and commitment. The following section of this chapter will focus on a variety of ways to apply visualization techniques including imitation, highlight music videotapes, reminiscence, repetitious visualization, and creative concentration tapes or CDs.

Imitation

Imitation is really the "monkey see, monkey do" principle of visualization and can be the most influential form of mental training or practice. The athlete is presented with an image or demonstration of how a skill is to be performed in practice or competition and then attempts to perform the skill. This technique is particularly effective with visual learners of high motor intelligence.

Oftentimes coaching techniques are centered on auditory or verbal explanations of skills, which may be difficult for athletes to translate into particular movement patterns or performance skills. For this reason the adage, "one picture equals a thousand words" is very applicable, since many athletes have the physical ability or motor intelligence to immediately understand and produce complicated movement patterns.

The key is to always present the athlete with a picture or visual image of the skill being performed correctly and effectively. This is why a less skilled athlete will improve his or her skills if matched with an athlete of greater ability and skill. A beginning tennis player who practices with a more advanced player has the image of how to execute the various strokes correctly and effectively whereas a beginning player who practices with another beginning player has the image of an incorrect, ineffective, and inefficient performer in constant view. Athletes in the initial stages of learning a sport skill should be presented with demonstrations, and videos of someone performing the skill correctly and effectively.

An interesting way of employing imitation to enhance sport drills is to use the "ready, aim, fire" approach to skill mastery. In volleyball, for example, players might be practicing a drill to improve their defensive skills for diving and "digging" a spiked ball. While waiting in line to return the spiked shot, athletes can "ready" themselves by closing their eyes and mentally imaging the proper technique as well as anticipation strategy they will employ. Athletes can then take "aim" as they move up in line by opening their eyes and watching the flight, velocity, and direction of the ball. Athletes can take "dead aim" by actually moving toward the ball and pretending to return the ball. Finally, athletes can automatically "fire" off the motor program (actually "dig" the ball) they have created and mentally practiced while standing in line.

Highlight Music Videotapes/CDs

The most effective way to use imitation as a performance enhancement technique is to provide the athlete with images of him or herself performing effectively. Today's advances in video technology can provide athletes with models of successful performance. Highlight video footage or images from an athlete's best performances have the potential to be one of the most influential models available to coaches and athletes (Halliwell, 1990; Malroy, 2000; Perry, 2001; Templin & Vernacchia, 1995).

As mentioned in the previous section, imitation visualization strategies create a mental image of what a successful skill performance is supposed to look like. Athletes may also be able to enhance an image through the regular use of mental training techniques that develop control to further enhance existing images of successful and effective performances (Orlick, 1986; Suinn, 1976).

Highlight music videotapes/CDs can be created to provide successful visual images of an athlete's outstanding and creative performances, and the tapes are further enhanced by the athlete's selection of stimulating or inspirational music (Chighisola, 1989; Franks & Maile, 1991; Halliwell, 1990; Leavitt, Young & Connelly, 1989). The tapes are focused on presenting the athlete's best or most effective and creative performances as opposed to those performances that may be biomechanically or technically correct but ineffective. Best performances are those in which the athlete adapts and adjusts his or her performance style and physical skills to the flow and demands of the competitive environment. Focusing on technically correct movements while performing can make athletes mechanical whereas focusing on "best" performances can help athletes become more adaptive, flexible, and creative in the application of their performance skills.

Highlight music videotapes are created this way (Templin & Vernacchia, 1995):

1. Identify an athlete's "highlight-type" plays throughout the course of a season.

2. Primarily include times when players felt as if they were performing at a high level or in an ideal performance state.

3. Edit these plays together, and incorporate special effects such as slow motion, repetition of big plays, freeze frame, and positive self-talk statements/graphics.

4. Ask the athletes to select music they feel will be both motivating and enjoyable.

5. Finally, record the music over the original audio of the tape/CD to produce a 3–5 minute highlight peak performance music video.

Implementation of the highlight music videotape/CD (Templin & Vernacchia, 1995) is accomplished by:

1. Explaining to athletes that the tape is a visual aid that will help them construct and reinforce images of high-level physical and mental performance

2. Asking athletes to replay this image of their performance and to imagine themselves actually performing in the video/CD

3. Instructing athletes to remember the "feel" of the particular performance, especially if they are highly concentrated or in an ideal performance state

4. Creating a three-step, 5–10 minute daily viewing routine (before or after practice and/or games):

    a. *Relaxation exercise*—Take 5 deep breaths while visualizing the letters RE when inhaling and LAX when exhaling.

    b. *Review cues*—"Imagine" yourself actually performing in the video/CD and "feel" as if you were inside the person on the tape/CD who is playing the game.

    c. View the tape/CD.

Interviews with basketball players who used highlight music videotapes revealed increased levels of confidence, an emotional boost, increased motivation, a feeling of being "pumped up" for games, and more enjoyment of playing roles (Templin & Vernacchia, 1995). The production of highlight music videotapes and CDs is time-consuming and requires access to video and audio technology, but it can be a worthwhile and extremely effective mental training tool.

Reminiscence

One of the most effective ways of helping athletes keep their minds on how they'd like to perform is to ask them to recall their "best" performance ever. This technique is particularly helpful for the anxious athlete who has a tendency to entertain images, thoughts, and feelings that can be potentially counterproductive and detrimental to an upcoming performance. As competition draws nearer, many athletes are distracted by images that create a preperformance mind-set of worry, doubt, and fear rather than one of a calmness and confidence.

Having athletes recall and verbally describe their "best" performance(s) can help them refocus on images of "what can go right" with a performance rather than "what can go wrong" with a performance. Furthermore the athlete can experience a greater sense of control over his or her performance because he or she can describe the details of a previous "best" performance that has actually been implemented in the competitive setting. By mentally "walking through" a previous "best" performance athletes can also create a sense of excitement for an upcoming performance by recalling the uplifting and positive emotional feelings that accompanied their most successful and effective performances.

Repetitious Visualization

To ingrain a mental image of correct and effective sport skill performance, an athlete must repetitiously engage in mental practice. The first step in this process is to make sure that he or she is imaging correct movement patterns with positive or effective results. The second step is to mentally and physically repeat the movement pattern or sport skill until it can be stored in motor memory as a consistent motor program. The third step is to be able to "cue up" the motor program at the appropriate time so that the athlete can automatically respond to the performance demands of any competitive situation.

Here is a method for helping athletes apply repetition training:

1. First image the skill to be performed at the speed and with the accuracy of movement and outcome you'd like. Include the sounds and sights of the desired movement pattern. In essence, image the skill just as you'd like to perform it. Now perform 10 mental repetitions of the skill.

2. Now see yourself performing the skill in slow motion. Feel the movements, feel muscle groups contract and relax. Perform 10 slow-motion mental repetitions of the skill.

3. Now focus on the personal performance characteristics of your movements, including center of gravity, focal point for the eyes, rhythm, flow, and breathing. Baseball players may focus on watching the ball come off the bat, golfers may focus on the rhythm and feel of their swing, football players may focus on the explosiveness of their movements, a pistol shooter may focus on the refined movements of the hand. Now perform 10 repetitions of the skill, focusing on a personal performance characteristic that will have a major impact on your overall performance.

4. Now reverse this process by performing 10 slow-motion mental repetitions of the skill.

5. Now perform 10 full-motion mental repetitions of the skill, just as you would like to perform it in practice or competition.

Repetitious visualization helps athletes because it allows them to practice and refine their physical skills without actually making physical mistakes. The beauty of mental practice is that it can be performed correctly and effectively all the time. This is particularly helpful for athletes who are in the midst of learning new skills or making corrections to existing skills that are no longer effective. Repetitious visualization can also help injured athletes who would like to retain existing skill levels even though they are not able to physically practice. While repetitious visualization will not accelerate skill learning and performance, it will facilitate the effectiveness of physical practice.

Creative Concentration Audiotapes or CDs

Creative concentration techniques for enhancing athletic performance (Cook, 1989; Cook 1996c; Neubauer, Miller & Vernacchia, 1994; Vernacchia & Cook, 1993) involve the use of mental mastery and rehearsal strategies that are directed toward simulating the athletic event prior to the actual competitive experience. These techniques combine visualization and concentration strategies (Nideffer, 1985) in order to provide the athlete with a structured or self-generated method to enhance their performance.

Athletes are asked to write out a script of how they would like to perform, and in some cases they are asked to write a script (see example presented in Appendix A) that incorporates any anticipated occurrences that may distract them from performing effectively. The mastery script is then recorded on an audiocassette tape or CD with background music, which the athlete listens to daily prior to the actual athletic event. The specific mastery rehearsal techniques include preparation, creating the tape, and using the tape (Cook, 1996c):

- *Preparation*

1. Rehearse mastering the event using imagery.

2. Utilize realistic and believable images.

3. Develop from positive personal experiences, perceptions, and descriptions bringing your personality into play.

- *Creating the Tape/CD*

1. Imagine the perfect experience—mastery.

2. Write a script describing the total experience—pre-event, event, post-event.

3. Use first-person affirmation statements (e.g., I feel relaxed and ready to perform; I am confident and prepared to play the game of my life).

4. Include:

   a.   Environmental considerations (weather, etc.)

   b.   A mental description of the event and actions

   c.   Each of the senses—sights, sounds, smells, etc.

   d.   Movements and feelings associated with the entire event.

5. Read the script with expression onto a audiocassette tape or CD.

6. Use music or sound effects in the background.

7. Limit the tape to three to five minutes so that it is usable in many settings.

- *Implementation*

1. Begin listening to the tape/CD one to two weeks in advance of the event—up until the actual event.

2. Regularly—three to four times a day.

3. Whenever it fits—or at other convenient times.

4. Receptivity is the key—listen and believe.

5. Rehabilitation setting—mastery rehearsal can be used while healing from injury.

The following response of the captain of the University of Kansas men's basketball team is typical of the value attributed to the use of creative concentration tapes by athletes:

The practice of mastery rehearsal helped me to perform by setting myself up for success. It also helped me fight off negative thoughts that were making me nervous and causing tension. Before I started listening to the tapes which I made, negative thoughts in my head were preventing me from doing my best. Sometimes when I was playing and there was nothing in my head, negative thoughts would come into my mind. After experiencing and using the tapes, I gradually started performing better and that was because mentally I started thinking positive. I saw I could battle negative thoughts with positive thoughts. Through rehearsing and listening to the tapes, I prepared my mind positively for each game. At times when my mind was blank I would think something positive before something negative would appear. After making the tapes and going over it, my confidence came back and my performance got better. . . . The positive mastery rehearsal method helped me because it set my mind up for success. I think it helped me to deal with problems mentally before they occurred. It also helped me to rebound faster from adversities. (Vernacchia & Cook, 1993, p. 195)

Remember

Seeing is Believing and
Believing is the First Step to Achieving

A picture is worth 1,000 words

If we can see it we can achieve it!

6

Living Your Dream
Goal Attainment

Goal setting is one of the most researched and frequently discussed sport psychology topics, yet athletes who set goals often have difficulty attaining them. Goal setting enables an athlete to take aim at a target or purpose for their training and competitive efforts, and goal attainment strategies provide the ways and means to hit the target. Goal attainment strategies are action oriented, and if followed in a progressive manner they can aid athletes in realizing their dream, intermediate, and short-term goals. The goal attainment strategies presented in this chapter will enable athletes to set themselves up for success by establishing a plan of action.

In Chapter 3, athletes were asked to reflect on and describe their athletic dream. The important point was to dream without limits or restrictions. Athletes don't need to be realistic when setting dream or long-term goals. Realistic thinking creates doubt, worry, and fear both of success and failure that can interfere with establishing a true motivational target for an athlete's training and performance efforts.

It may seem unrealistic for a young person to aspire to be a professional athlete, but the realistic thing to do is to begin working toward that goal. In effect set a dream goal, and see how close an athlete can come to attaining it. This stair-step approach to goal attainment results from taking progressive actions in the direction of our goals. For example, an athlete may never become a professional, even though this was his or her dream, but by participating in athletics, he or she will become more fit and healthy, more skillful, and more competent at sport than when he or she started. While striving to attain their dream goal, athletes may benefit from travel opportunities, making new friends for life, attaining an athletic scholarship, becoming more healthy and fit, mastering sport skills, becoming a better student-athlete, selecting a sports related career, etc. In effect, engaging in an athletic process of self-improvement will not only draw them closer to their dream goal but also bring them long-term satisfaction and happiness.

In reality, athletes are encouraged to dream about accomplishing great things in their sport despite the adversity they may face. Accomplishing the impossible in light of the seemingly insurmountable is what distinguishes high achievers in sport from the also-rans. Athletic achievement is a process of self-improvement, so if dream goals are not completely realized, athletes can look back on their athletic journey and feel proud of the accomplishments they did achieve. The journey of athletic participation will have made them not only better athletes but better people.

A Goal Attainment Plan for Peak Athletic Performance

The goal attainment plan above incorporates goal setting techniques and strategies into a step-by-step approach to achieving athletic success. Each step in the plan provides an integrated progression toward success based on the effective application of an

A Goal Attainment Plan for Peak Athletic Performance

Establish a vision or mission statement.

Balance your goals.

Clarify, negotiate, and accept your role and responsibilities within the team.

Be specific-write out your goals.

Focus on performance and process goals.

Affirm your goals.

Rest, relax, and visualize your goals.

Use time management skills to realize your goals.

Stay healthy and physically fit.

Practice slipstreaming.

Avoid end-watching.

Go for it!

Stop and "smell the roses."

Evaluate the results and outcomes of your efforts.

Reset your goals.

athlete's physical, mental, and life skills. Here's the plan—we'll discuss each step in detail.

Establish a Vision or Mission Statement

The athlete's first step is to review his or her personal foundational beliefs regarding athletic achievement. Essentially this is the process of establishing a personal creed, or "belief theme," or mission statement that will guide his or her actions in the achievement-oriented athletic world.

The word *creed* is derived from the Latin word *credo*, which means "to believe." A belief theme in line with an athlete's personal athletic philosophy might be, "Work hard and always give your best." This belief theme or statement expresses a commitment to a way of acting in all athletic performance settings. Other belief themes would be "Play hard, play fair, and be the best you can be," "Victory with honor," or "Athletic excellence with integrity." Coaches can condense their philosophy into a belief theme to guide their leadership actions, such as, "Be honest, be fair, and be yourself."

Each athlete's definition of success is different, but each athlete should have a clear and purposeful vision of his or her success target. For some athletes their mission may be to be an effective team player; for others it may be to be the best athlete on their team, or in their league or state or in the nation. Other athletes may simply strive to give their best in each and every practice and competitive setting. The bottom line to establishing a mission statement is that it should reflect the athlete's purpose for participation in athletics within the framework of the values of sport.

Balance Your Goals

Athletes will have a number of goals, both inside and outside of sport. Balancing goals, that is, giving equal time, energy and effort to the goals we establish can go a long way in preventing us from becoming one-dimensional. Athletes who focus solely on their athletic goals to the exclusion of other academic, social, or family goals soon lose their self-identity in sport. By clarifying their personal values and prioritizing their goals (see the Values Clarification exercise on the next page), athletes can lead a balanced and multidimensional lifestyle that enables them to "step out of sport" once practice, performance, or their athletic careers are over. Figure 6.1 illustrates the various goals athletes may have in their lives.

If an athlete's goal wheel is to spin true, then he or she must spend an equal amount of time in each area of life. Balanced

Figure 6.1   Goal Wheel

goals lead to a balanced lifestyle and a holistic or total person approach to sport and life. Spending too much time in one goal area at the expense of other personal responsibilities will cause the goal wheel to wobble and spin out of control.

"There's a time for everything and everything in its own time" is a good motto for athletes if they want to avoid the "spillover" effect of unattended responsibilities in their lives. Not attending to studies and schoolwork will cause an athlete to worry about his or her academic eligibility for athletic participation—this worry can become a distraction that spills over to his or her game, adversely effecting attitude and performance. By the same token an athlete who is unwilling to regulate his or her social life and partying may be unable to recover sufficiently from the travel, practice, and performance demands of his or her sport.

Peak Performance Exercise 6.1

Values Clarification for Athletes

Make a list of the various roles that you assume in your everyday life. Examples of roles are sister or brother, athlete, musician, student, employee, family member, friend. After making the list, prioritize it, placing the most important thing or role in your life at the top and the least important at the bottom. Now consider the following scenario-you have just come from a doctor's appointment in which you are told that you have a terminal illness and have only 6 months to live. In light of this news, review and reprioritize your list. The final list should reflect your *real* values and priorities in life, whereas the initial list you made reflects your *apparent* values in life.

*Clarify, Negotiate, and Accept Your
Role and Responsibilities within the Team*

Successful athletes pride themselves on being team players. In the athletic world, conformity is a prerequisite for acceptance and in many cases is directly related to the amount of playing time an athlete will receive. For these reasons, it is important that an athlete understands and accepts his or her assigned role and responsibilities on the team. Even "individual" sport athletes have certain performance roles and responsibilities that will contribute to the overall effectiveness of his or her team.

Team roles are usually related to the position a player fills on a team—he or she may be a starter or a substitute or perhaps a practice player. In most sports, especially those of a highly interactive nature (football, basketball, volleyball, soccer, etc.) the coach assigns roles to athletes based on the athlete's ability to perform the skills necessary for the role as well as the athlete's ability to blend his or her talents and abilities with teammates. Other intangibles may also enter the mix including, seniority, politics, and leadership ability.

Team responsibilities can be coach and/or team driven and involve adherence to team standards, training rules, and the team's mission and goals. Even though an athlete may be frustrated by his or her lack of playing time, the coach and other team members should always be viewed as those who can provide the support necessary to realize athletic dreams.

Open and honest coach-to-athlete communication is essential in helping an athlete understand his or her team role and responsibilities. Discussing, clarifying, and negotiating one's team role and responsibility are healthy and effective first steps to role acceptance and performance.

Be Specific—Write Out Your Goals

Actually writing out goals will help athletes focus on and commit to their goals. Placing written goals in visible and prominent places (e.g., an athlete's locker or training diary) will help athletes to retain their goal focus and keep their goals in mind. Frequently viewing goals will aid athletes in making the performance of goal-enhancing behaviors routine. A popular goal saying advises athletes as follows:

 Mental Key to Success

GOALS: "Ink 'em and think 'em, view 'em and do 'em, believe 'em and achieve 'em."

When writing out specific goals, consider the following guidelines (Cook, 1996b; Gould, 2001; Vernacchia, 1996a):

- *Set goals that are measurable.* If an athlete's overall goal is self-improvement, then three things need to be done to monitor the progression of an athlete toward that goal: (1) Get a baseline performance to determine the actual ability of the athlete before determining the desired or ideal goal level for that same athlete (this will help athletes set a reasonable progression toward the goal); (2) devise a means to record and measure an athlete's improvement (statistics, videotaping and task analysis of skills, performance evaluations, etc.); and (3) review the measured outcomes of athletic performance-seek performance feedback (informational, corrective, and prescriptive).

- *Focus on short-term goals in order to attain dream goals.* Dream or long-term goals may provide inspiration and motivation for practice and performance efforts, but short-term goals can provide specific strategies and techniques that will lead to goal attainment. Before an athlete is selected as a starter, he or she needs to come to practice on a consistent basis. While at practice the athlete would strive to master specific skills through daily drills that promote automatic and effective skill execution. While most athletes set game goals, the most *effective* athletes set clear daily goals for practice as well as for game performance (Orlick & Partington, 1988).

- *Keep goals flexible.* The road to athletic success and self-improvement has many roadblocks, obstacles, and distractions. Athletes encounter such setbacks as lack of resources, poor equipment and facilities, or illness and injury, or they can simply be outclassed by an opponent. Adjusting goals in the dynamic world of athletic training and performance enables athletes to ward off frustration and discouragement by allowing them "to take one step backward before taking two steps forward."

- *Time is on your side.* Be careful not to limit goal progression by adhering to unrealistic timelines for goal attainment. In many ways the athletic world is one of "forced achievement," one that often creates an unrealistic sense of urgency that leads to perceived and real failures. An athlete's goal for the season may be to shoot a round of golf at par, and he or she may get only to 2 over par—does that imply failure because the athlete didn't reach the goal? Carry the goal over to the next season, continue improving skills in the off-season, and strive once again to shoot par.

- *Keep in mind the performance paradox of sport.* The performance paradox of sport demonstrates that the better an athlete gets, the more he or she may fail. As an athlete approaches his or her performance ceiling for a season or even a career, the smaller the increments of improvement and the longer it takes to see even the smallest improvements. A golfer may shoot a dream round of 59, well under the par of 72. This is a phenomenal score. If the same golfer shoots a 65 (7 under par), is he or she a failure—65 is still an excellent score that will win most tournaments. Or the golfer may have won the tournament and been very effective in doing so but still has not improved on his or her best score and may never for the remainder of his or her career. Remember the performance ceiling reached during one season may be the performance floor or entry level for next year's season.

- *Leave goals open-ended.* Many times athletes will place a limit on their outcome goals by stating them in absolute terms (I will average 7 rebounds a game; I will jump 7 feet in the high jump; I will be a starter on the basketball team). Add two words to that outcome goal—"or better." These two words allow or give athletes permission to go beyond the self-limiting barriers they sometimes place on themselves.

- *Set goals outside of sport.* In line with the importance of maintaining a goal balance in life, an athlete should set goals in a variety of areas. It is important to have several passions in life and to focus on each passion in its own time, but when a passion becomes "the" passion, it soon becomes an obsession. Once sport becomes the only thing in an athlete's life, it becomes very difficult to "step out of sport," especially when he or she needs a break from training and performance demands that can lead to staleness, overtraining, injury, and burnout.

Focus on Performance and Process Goals

The key to reaching and surpassing the outcome or product goal (e.g., time, distance, number of rebounds or points per game, attaining an athletic scholarship, making an all-star team, becoming a starter) is to focus on *performance goals*—mastering the performance components that will lead to the accomplishment of the outcome or product goal.

For example, a basketball player's goal may be to be a good rebounder. To get a rebound, several skills must be performed sequentially (performance goals) to assure that the player has a chance to get a rebound (outcome goal). If the player is on defense, he or she must always be between his or her opponent and the basket; once a shot is taken, the player must "block out" the opponent while at the same time judging if he or she will be positioning him or herself for a long or short rebound. The player must then use certain techniques to actually "grab" and retain the rebound, including making an outlet pass to a teammate as his or her team transitions to offense. If all these rebounding actions and skills are performed correctly, the athlete has a reasonable chance to rebound effectively.

It is also important for athletes to focus on *process goals* that will enhance his or her performance. Process goals focus on the educational and social aspects of athletic participation. Educational process goals include development of carry-over attitudes and values that contribute to lifetime health and fitness habits (i.e., nutrition, relaxation techniques, strength and aerobic development); academic achievement; development of attitudes that will assist athletes in goal attainment (i.e., commitment, achievement, motivation); development of self-esteem and self-confidence. Social process goals include establishing friendships, relating to individuals of diverse backgrounds to achieve a common goal, and developing respect for authority.

Affirm Your Goals

Affirmations are positive belief statements about one's self or one's talent and abilities. If a basketball player aspires to be an effective rebounder, the player would affirm his or her ability to realize such a goal by using the following affirmations: "I am a great rebounder"; "I love to rebound"; "I'm a great leaper"; "I'm a tough defensive player"; "I enjoy triggering our offense by making great outlet passes."

Rest, Relax and Visualize Your Goals

Since the pursuit of athletic excellence requires tremendous investments of time, energy, and emotion (McGuire, 1996c), it is imperative that athletes balance the training and performance demands of their daily schedules with rest and relaxation. The next chapter will address the issue of quality practice or training and will emphasize the point that athletes who engage in quality training sessions also need quality rest sessions. Rest or restoration, primarily in the form of sleep, provides athletes with the opportunity to re-energize and rejuvenate themselves after demanding practice and performance efforts.

It is wise for athletes to provide structured "down" time for themselves during the day—a 20-minute nap after lunch, for example, does wonders to restore an athlete's energy and focus for practice and performance. Other forms of relaxation training were described in Chapter 5. Rest and recovery are important factors for athletes to attend to while in hot pursuit of their goals.

As mentioned in Chapter 5, relaxation skills are a prerequisite for athletes who seek to use visualization techniques for performance enhancement.

 Mental Key to Success

We cannot achieve what we cannot imagine or see in our mind's eye.

Stimulating the imagination or creative subconscious is often overlooked in the goal setting and attainment process. Creating the images and feelings of a desired goal, whether it is related to sport or life, can serve to fuel our motivation, emotional energy, and the physical efforts required.

Employ the visualization techniques described in Chapter 5 to stimulate the imagination to "find a way" to achieve and realize goals. For example, a golfer can post sequenced photographs obtained from a golf magazine that model his or her desired golf swing. The golfer can then frequently view these photographs to provide a model to help image his or her desired swing.

Use Time Management Skills to Realize Your Goals

One of the most overlooked life skills associated with goal attainment is time management. Athletes can easily get caught in a time crunch and are not able to devote the necessary time and energy to their athletic development or, in some cases, spend too much time in athletics and neglect other areas of their lives. Athletes must learn to compartmentalize their roles and responsibilities into a time frame that will allow them to take everything in its own time and to have the time to do everything. Time management is closely linked to an athlete's ability to balance and prioritize goals.

 Mental Key to Success

> Most athletes fail to realize their goals not because they lack ability or talent but because they simply run out of time.

Many time management strategies can be utilized by athletes, and for the most part these strategies involve mapping out daily tasks in relation to their priorities and demands. Time management helps athletes to perform their daily tasks effectively and efficiently, not perfectly. The key is to accomplish tasks within a given time frame and not to underwork or overwork these tasks, that is, to work smarter not harder.

8 Steps to Efficient and Effective Time Management

1. *The night before, make a list of the tasks you want to accomplish the following day.* Include all your required and/or desired tasks and responsibilities, school related, team practice, game, work, family, social, etc.

```
********************************
        WESTERN AS BOOKSTORE
          360-650-3655
        WWW.BOOKSTORE.WWU.EDU
********************************
SALE
11-18-05 15:11
 REG#3  TRAN#8865  CSHR#500


T INNER STRENGTH:THE MEN
978188634608                    23.95
SUBTOTAL                       $23.95
TAX 8.300%                       1.99
TOTAL                          $25.94
Visa                            25.94
ACCOUNT # XXXXXXXXXXXX6445
EXPIRATION DATE: 01/07
APPROVAL CODE: 018733
CHANGE DUE                      $0.00
        THANKS FOR SHOPPING YOUR
          WESTERN AS BOOKSTORE
        RECEIPT REQUIRED FOR REFUND
```

2. *Prioritize the list.* Review your list and prioritize the list according to the importance of the task in your life and according to the amount of time it will take to effectively perform or accomplish the task.

3. *Block in your prioritized task list/activities on a time sheet.* See Figure 6.2. First assign blocks of time to your required tasks/activities (e.g., class schedule, practice or game time, employment time). Then fill in your time sheet with the remaining tasks or activities you would like to accomplish or take part in. Allow for transition time to move from one task to the next.

4. *Picture yourself accomplishing these tasks successfully.* Visualize yourself going about your daily activities, see yourself at the site of each activity, and image yourself performing tasks/activities effectively.

5. *Relax, Rest, and Sleep.* Now that you have planned your next day's activities, get some rest and allow yourself to gather the energy necessary to complete the next day's tasks/activities effectively.

6. *Review your time management sheet in the morning and throughout the day.* Your time management sheet is a flexible plan or script for excellence in your everyday life. Refer to your script frequently throughout the day, especially if you have a large number of tasks to complete.

7. *Check off tasks/activities once they are effectively performed.* Remember your time management script is flexible—you may be unable to do certain aspects of each task or did not anticipate another aspect. Do the best you can in the time allotted to effectively accomplish each task. If you run out of time, move on to the next task—work by the job not by the hour.

8. *Begin the process over again in the evening.* Give the task/activities you were not able to perform, or did not "get to" that day a high priority for the next day. Remember first things first—take care of your highest priority first and in time all your priorities will be met.

Time	Activity(ies)	Location	Transition	Time	Evaluation
8 AM					
9					
10					
11					
12					
1 PM					
2					
3					
4					
5					
6					
7					
8					
9					

Figure 6.2   Time Management Script

Stay Healthy and Physically Fit

This may seem like strange advice to give to athletes, but the fact of the matter is that many athletes are very fit and not healthy. They are so focused on training and competing that they can overtrain, overcompete, and are susceptible to injury, illness, and mental and physical fatigue. The key to being both healthy and fit is to factor rest and recovery time into the goal attainment plan. Recovery time enables them to recover not only from training, travel, and competitive efforts but also from the additional educational, social, and economic demands of everyday life.

As simple as it sounds, it is important to get at least 8 hours of rest each night and to include rest, sleep, and relaxation in a goal attainment plan. Athletes can benefit from a 20–30 minute nap prior to practice or in the middle of the day. Making and taking the time and finding the place to get the rest and rejuvenation benefits of a nap or a good night's sleep require planning.

Practice Slipstreaming

One of the best ways to attain goals is to emulate someone who has already attained the athletic achievements that the athlete is striving to achieve. This hero or shero is a "success mentor" who has already navigated the journey, so his or her advice can be invaluable in helping attain goals. Athletes and coaches can read the biographies of successful athletes—goal attainment and wisdom go hand and hand. Seek the advice of successful athletes. "Rubbing shoulders" with the best can only serve to enhance goal attainment strategies.

Avoid End-Watching

Sometimes the goals that athletes set for themselves, especially dream goals and long-term goals, appear to be overwhelming and unattainable. For this reason it is important for an athlete to focus his or her energies on short-term and performance goals. Short-term and performance goals help us focus on the task at hand in a very nondistractible way-they are the stepping stones to success. Avoid doing too much too soon, and focus on one step at a time.

Go For It!

"Motion creates opportunity." A goal attainment plan looks great on paper, but it's useless unless it is acted upon. Athletes must get busy and consistently work toward making their dream a reality through conscientious training, focused performances, and a managed lifestyle that is conducive toward attaining their goals. They should focus on short-term goals and take small steps to glory.

Stop and Smell the Roses

Once athletes have reached a hard-earned goal, be it short, intermediate, or long term, they should take the time to celebrate their achievement. A self-administered pat on the back delivered in a personal and quiet way can go a long way toward maintaining momentum along the goal attainment trail. Athletes should reward themselves for a job well done before moving on the next goal challenge.

Evaluate the Results and Outcomes of Your Efforts

Once athletes have attained a significant goal, they should take time to assess the effects that their goal attainment efforts have had on their life and lifestyle as a whole. How has their success or lack of it affected the people around them, especially family members and friends. Were the accomplishments and sacrifices worth the effort? Are they really happy now that they have achieved their goal or goals? Should they continue to participate at a competitive level, or would it be best to participate at a recreational level? Are there adjustments that need to be made? Some athletes may decide at this point to get out of sport all together or for a period of time. Some will also decide to continue in their sport by rededicating themselves to a higher level of achievement.

Reset Your Goals

Once athletes have decided to continue in their sport, they must reset their goals to achieve a new level of accomplishment. Sometimes this needs to be done in the middle of the sport season if they have exceeded their initial seasonal goals and perhaps even one of their dream goals.

Mental Key to Success

Most people fail to reach their goals not because they aim high and miss, but because they aim low and hit.

A Final Question

What short-, intermediate-, and long-range goals will help you realize your athletic dream?

7

Cultivating Your Dream
Quality Practice

A sound work ethic in sport is a prime prerequisite for athletic success. To succeed in sport an athlete must be willing to not only work hard but to learn to work smart at sport.

Successful and more experienced athletes soon come to realize that a nose to the grindstone approach to their sport is only going to give them a flat nose. Hardworking athletes are often victims of overtraining and burnout, while smart-working athletes are able to maintain their motivation and enthusiasm for athletic training and performance. Rather than simply going through the motions during practice, coaches and athletes design and engage in *quality* practice sessions that are both efficient and effective in facilitating motor skill acquisition, development, and refinement.

Furthermore, engaging in quality practice increases the chances of an athlete experiencing more "fun" in sport. Performing in a challenging situation or environment that they are unprepared to face is not much fun for athletes. Mastery of the physical and mental skills associated with particular sports is really the first step in achieving athletic success and enjoyment in sport. Athletic participation and performance become fun when athletes are able to match their ability with the physical and emotional demands of their sport. Quality practices provide the opportunities for athletes to master the conditioning, motor skills, and performance demands of their sport.

Three Principles of Quality Practice

The three principles of quality practice are (1) practice makes permanent, (2) make a concentrated effort, and (3) practice with a purpose.

Practice Makes Permanent

Contrary to popular belief, practice does not make perfect, but "practice makes permanent." Quality practice makes performers effective because it protects athletes from perfecting their mistakes. Many athletes practice for long hours at their sport and become mentally and physically tired. The fatigue of overpracticing can lead to increased errors or mistakes, and practicing mistakes can create bad habits.

Knowing how long to practice is just as important as what and how to practice—knowing when to stop practice, even though it's not perfect, can go a long way in creating an effective athletic performer. Practices are for making mistakes, mistakes merely provide the feedback necessary for improved and effective performances. Performances are for displaying effective skills, not being perfect—performing effectively and sometimes "winning ugly" is a reality of successful athletic performances.

Make a Concentrated Effort During Practice Sessions

Many athletes lose sight of the true purpose of practice and need to ask themselves the following question, "Do you practice to practice or do you practice to perform?" Unfortunately the athletic world is filled with frustrated athletes who practice and practice and then get in the game and practice some more. The purpose of practice is to prepare to perform.

Knowing the how and why of each daily practice session and how each day's practice fits into a seasonal plan for peak performance gives purpose and meaning to often demanding practice sessions. Practicing with a purpose makes practice relevant to high-performance sport settings. For this reason athletes periodize their training and change the focus of their training/practice programs as they progress from preseason to the competitive, peaking, and restoration phases of their sport season.

Designing practice to facilitate the learning of sport skills, or maximizing the effectiveness of skill drills, can enhance the transfer of skills learned in practice to game or performance skills. For example, rather than have a baseball player take unlimited batting practice, it would be best to regulate his or her practice according to the number of swings. Instead of going into the batting cage for 10 or 15 minutes, it would be best to limit the total number of swings the batter takes during the entire practice to 30.

Furthermore the batter would be limited to only 5 swings each time and then would leave the batting cage and rotate with other players on the team until a total of 30 swings are taken. This type of practice more closely simulates the actual number of swings a player is likely to take in each at-bat in a game. This strategy also allows the player to rest between visits to the batting cage, keeping him or her fresh rather than exhausted from taking 30 swings, allowing time to process feedback gained from practice attempts and to utilize mental rehearsal to prepare for their next at-bat. These strategies produce a quality practice session by allowing for rest between sets of swings so the player isn't practicing or repeating mistakes and by closely simulating game conditions.

Practice With A Purpose

Effective athletes know exactly what they want to achieve during daily practice sessions and how each aspect of practice contributes to future performance outcomes. Experienced athletes focus on self-improvement—"What can I do today in practice to make myself a better athlete, a better performer?"

 Mental Key to Success

Elite athletes develop a practice as well as a game focus by setting clear daily goals for practice sessions (Orlick & Partington, 1988).

To reach self-improvement goals, athletes can review the conditioning, skill, and simulation drills that will be conduced at practice before practice, preferably the night before practice. Rather than just showing up for practice an athlete can mentally prepare him or herself to maintain focus throughout practice by anticipating the demands and requirements of each drill that will be conducted in the practice session.

Athletes can also maintain a simple focus by concentrating on improving one skill at a time during a practice. Focusing on mastering too many skills at once can often lead to frustration. After each game or performance an athlete can select one skill that he or she would like to improve to be more effective in upcoming athletic contests. The coaching staff can then help an athlete identify existing drills or design new drills and activities to improve his or her performance effectiveness.

A sharpened focus during practice helps athletes concentrate on the real purpose of a particular practice session and promotes a *quality* as opposed to a *quantity* mentality toward practice. For example most golfers head out to the practice range with a large bucket of golf balls (a quantity approach). A quality approach to practice would encourage a golfer to head out to the practice range with only 10 golf balls, with the intent of striking the 10 best shots of his or her life.

Lastly, setting clear daily goals for practice and reviewing them just prior to or during practice can ensure that athletes are paying attention at the time practice drills and activities are conducted. The physical and mental demands of practice can often

distract an athlete from his or her practice goals, and an occa-
sional review of "practice cues" can prevent an athlete's mind
from wandering during practice. "Being in the moment" during
practice and during performances is a learned attribute of highly
effective athletic performers.

The Unders and Overs of Quality Practice

Underlearning vs. Overloading

Trying to do too much, too soon and expecting too much, too
soon is a common mistake made by many young athletes in the
early stages of learning and performing sport skills. Patience and
understanding the cumulative effect of quality practice, that is,
focusing on self-improvement from day to day, week to week,
month to month, and year to year, can go a long way in relieving
practice and performance frustration.

Unfortunately many coaches and athletes have a sense of
urgency approach to practice once the season begins and as they
draw closer to the competitive portion of their sport season. For
this reason many practice sessions are packed full of conditioning
and skill drills, as well as simulation training directed toward
preparing athletes for upcoming competitive challenges. Practices
are often long, and concentration can waver in the light of
increased learning and performance demands.

Underlearning during practice, that is, establishing a learning and retention threshold for athletes, can be an important
element of quality practice. Monitoring practice sessions so athletes terminate practice when they feel as if they can do more or
practice longer takes a mental discipline on the part of both
coach and athlete that will pay off in the long run. Athletes who
underlearn know when they are at the point of diminishing
returns, and they regulate their practice by the number of trials
they take in a practice session. For example, a discus thrower will
take between 15 and 20 quality throws during practice because
he or she realizes that performance effectiveness (accuracy and
speed of throwing movements) decreases with fatigue brought
about by overthrowing.

Furthermore, athletes who end practice when they feel as if they can do a little more go back to the locker room excited about the next day's practice rather than mentally and physically exhausted and dreading the next day's practice session. This strategy goes a long way in preventing athlete staleness and burnout, especially over the course of a long season.

Overlearning vs. Overpractice

Athletes engaging in quality training should practice to the point of fatigue—but not while they are mentally and physically exhausted. While athletes often practice in a fatigued state, they should never practice while they are exhausted. Knowing the line between fatigue and exhaustion delineates working smart from overpracticing. Practicing while exhausted, or overpracticing, can result in athletes practicing their mistakes and creating bad habits.

 **Mental Key to Success**

Quality practice involves overlearning not overpracticing skills.

Athletes who are just being introduced to a skill will need to establish a performance criterion that will demonstrate that the particular skill has been mastered. Performance criteria can be subjective, such as artistic style, or objective, such as being able to perform skills or movement patterns effectively and repetitively with speed and accuracy.

Skill mastery indicates that an athlete can perform skills instinctually or automatically. For this reason athletes engage in skill and simulation drills to master their skills prior to being placed in emotionally charged performance settings. While repetition may be the parent of knowledge, mindless repetition driven by the routine and ritual of overworking at practice can only lead to exhaustion, frustration, and ineffective skill execution.

Athletes who have already mastered a particular skill may have to relearn skills by reviewing and drilling movement pat-

terns and sport skills to the point of reaching a level of performance effectiveness. This process is really one of refreshing the
motor memory as it relates to the application and performance of
previously mastered sport skills.

Overcoming Learning and Performance Plateaus

One of the natural by-products of athletic training is coping
with the learning effect of skill mastery. Depending on an athlete's abilities, the practice and performance of athletic skills
can often lead to a leveling off of enthusiasm for self-improvement. This "leveling off" phenomenon is referred to as a learning plateau.

Training and performance plateaus usually result from three
things: fatigue, boredom, and frustration. The fatigue of overtraining or overpracticing can lead to mental and physical staleness, whereas the inability to learn and perform skills in a timely
manner can lead to frustration. In some cases, athletes who are
extremely talented when it comes to learning sport skills and performing in their sport can become bored with the lack of challenges they face.

Regulating practice sessions to prevent overpracticing and
overloading by providing adequate amounts of rest and recovery between both demanding practice sessions and competitive efforts are key elements in helping athletes maintain a
refreshed and rejuvenated outlook toward their sport. Individ-
ualizing practice sessions to challenge athletes of various skill
and developmental levels is a first step to alleviating practice
boredom. Boredom created by the sheer repetition of the same
practice sessions and drills throughout the sport season can
also be countered by modifying or providing a variety of practice techniques and drills that will "spice up" training sessions.

Frustration experienced by athletes can be relieved by providing insight or technical knowledge to athletes that will enable
them to master the "little things" of skill and performance mastery that make a big difference in getting over the hump of a
stalled learning or performance goal.

Elements of Quality Practice

Planning or designing practice sessions with performance effectiveness in mind involves consideration of these key elements of quality practice:

- Knowledge of Learning Styles
- Feedback—Internal and External
- Feedforward—Mental Practice and Simulation Training
- "Going to the Next Level"
- Quality Rest

Knowledge of Learning Styles

Each athlete has a preferred learning and performance style for learning. Athletes can learn sport skills and their applications through three modes—visual, auditory, or kinesthetic (body awareness).

A visual learner depends on skill demonstrations and pictures or images of proper skill execution and application to get the idea or mental picture of how a skill is to be performed. The visual athlete learns by imitating proficient or popular athletic performers who are very effective at performing their skills. Videotapes and taping of athletic performance and skill execution can benefit the visual learner. For this type of learner, a picture is worth a thousand words. Coaches can appeal to this type of learner by using verbal descriptions of skills that include vivid and clear mental images.

Auditory learners can benefit from in-depth verbal or written descriptions of skill execution, as well as athlete-coach discussions. Kinesthetic learners are very focused on the "feel" of particular athletic skills and movements. This type of athlete likes to try several repetitions of a particular movement so he or she can get the feel of the skill and how it is performed.

While athletes should learn a skill using all three of these modes, they should identify their primary or preferred learning mode because it will enhance their ability to learn and perform skills. A coach can determine the primary learning mode of an athlete by watching the athlete's eye movements as skills are being introduced and explained to them. Once explanations have been made and while the athlete is absorbing the newly acquired information, he or she may look up (visual learner), to the side (auditory learner), or downward (feeling or kinesthetic learner) (Vernacchia, 1996a).

Feedback—Internal and External

The most critical factor in determining the effectiveness of quality practice is feedback, or information an athlete can receive about his or her performance. Information sources sought by athletes regarding the process and product of their performances can come from both internal (self-regulation) as well as external sources (coaches, sport scientists, technology, etc.).

"Listening to one's body" and developing a "feel" for one's movement patterns and skills are two forms of internal feedback that are often overlooked and underdeveloped by athletes. Athletes can become easily distracted by the external factors in the performance environment (crowds, scoreboard mentality, weather, opponents, mistakes) and lose focus on performing their skills from the inside out, that is, under the control of self-regulation. Listening to one's body can prevent athletes from trying too hard in competitive settings by being aware of the optimal level of activation for their own best performance.

In the Peak Performance Assessment in Chapter 1, athletes were asked to reflect on their peak athletic performance. To help develop internal feedback, they should revisit those feelings and recall how their body felt before, during, and after that performance. Focusing on the emotional and physical or kinesthetic awareness of his or her peak performance is important so that the athlete can replicate the "feel" of that moment for future performances. When athletes are performing well, they often say that they are "feeling it" when they report being in the zone or in the midst of a peak performance.

Being sensitive to one's body before and during performances can help athletes identify the appropriate levels of muscle tension or relaxation and emotional arousal that are necessary for effective performances. For example, simple breathing techniques, that is, internal massage can help to relieve muscle tension and ready overexcited or anxious athletes for competitive challenges. A simple breathing exercise for athletes who need to regulate their tension and excitement levels just prior to competition is to close their eyes and take several slow deep breaths. On the inhale see the letters RE and breathe deep, taking in refreshing, relaxing, and rejuvenating fresh air of self-regulation and self-confidence. On the exhale see the letters LAX while releasing stress, tension, fears, doubts, overexcitement, and worry about the approaching competition. *Inhale RE, exhale LAX.*

Other forms of internal feedback for creating body awareness involve athletes focusing on the "feel" of the movements of their bodies during practice. For example, while performing warm-up stretches and flexibility exercises athletes can close their eyes and image and feel the particular muscle or muscle group that is being stretched. By moving slowly and purposefully through such exercises, athletes can become more in tune to their bodies as they prepare for the demands, focus, and stress of practice and performance settings. Additionally, athletes can incorporate "feel" into their training programs by employing such practice strategies as using weighted implements while practicing or rehearsing movement patterns (weighted bats and golf clubs); performing movements in slow motion; eliminating the visual field by practicing movements or skill blindfolded; and by eliminating outcomes of skills (hitting a baseball into a net, or shooting a basketball against a wall) so that the athlete can focus on "feeling" the mechanics and movements of their swing and shot).

Technology can provide excellent sources of external feedback for athletes, especially videotaping. For example, athletes can use the following video feedback and evaluation process to enhance motor skill acquisition or the refinement of learned motor skills (Vernacchia, 1996a):

1. Prior to practice, the athlete can view videotapes that demonstrate the correct execution (form/style) of their sport skills. The videos give the athlete a mental picture of how these skills should be performed. Athletes should allow

20–30 minutes to review these videotapes and images of their desired performance. To increase the effectiveness of this method include video "highlight" tapes (Templin & Vernacchia, 1995) of the athlete performing his or her skills effectively in game and practice settings;

2. Utilizing specific practice drills, the athlete should then perform their sport skills during practice while they are being videotaped;

3. The athlete can view the videotape of his or her learning and performance attempts either during or after practice in order to evaluate feedback regarding their effectiveness.

4. Upon the completion of practice, the coach and athlete analyze the practice session. Athletes can then compare the videotape of their actual practice with tapes of their desired skill execution that were viewed prior to practice. The videotapes of the actual performance can be shown in slow motion or frame by frame to compare and contrast the actual with the desired skill response.

Other forms of external feedback regarding the effectiveness of skill performance can be obtained from verbal comments by coaches and teammates, and task analysis evaluation procedures that provide written feedback regarding practice and game performances. Strength training and conditioning machines and devices can also provide other forms of feedback that are helpful for athletes. Less sophisticated methods such as performing movement patterns in front of mirrors (i.e., strength training exercises) will provide helpful visual feedback to improve an athlete's form and accuracy.

Feedforward—Mental Rehearsal and Simulation Training

While providing athletes with feedback that will help them evaluate and refine their sport skills is important, *feedforward* can mentally prepare athletes to maximize their practice and performance efforts. Through the use of mental practice and simulation training, athletes can mentally and emotionally create a virtual practice and performance atmosphere that will facilitate skill learning and performance, especially in competitive settings.

Mental rehearsal can serve to help athletes master their athletic skills in both practice and performance settings since it provides a means to develop an athlete's creativity and decision-making abilities; it allows athletes to rehearse possible actions and strategies, including the possible outcomes of such strategies; and it builds confidence for future performances because it allows for effective stress and anxiety management (Schmidt, 1991). Athletes utilize mental rehearsal to help them reach their training goals, to overcome injury, to retain their skills during injury rehabilitation, to improve their focus during practice and performances, and to simulate performance conditions (Hemery, 1986; Mahoney, Gabriel, & Perkins, 1987; Orlick & Partington, 1988; Vernacchia, McGuire, Reardon, & Templin, 2000).

Visualization and mental imagery were covered in depth in Chapter 5, but one way to facilitate quality practice among athletes is to couple daily goal setting for practice with mental rehearsal.

Athletes who set clear daily goals for practice do so the night before each practice session and then spend 20 minutes a night mentally rehearsing their skills prior to going to bed. The mental rehearsal process helps athletes to see and "feel" themselves accomplishing their goals while at the same time creating a "clear and present" purpose for the upcoming practice session. This combination gives an athlete time to anticipate and mentally prepare an effective physical response to the challenges each practice session presents (handling fatigue and frustration, etc.).

Simulation training or model training (Orlick & Partington, 1988; Vanek & Cratty, 1970) is a useful offshoot of mental practice that allows an athlete "to picture" the exact conditions that he or she may ultimately face in performance settings. Once again this allows an athlete to call up both the emotional and physical "feel" that the competitive environment generates, as well as a variety of emotional and physical responses to obstacles and distractions that may arise unexpectedly during competition. In the final analysis, anticipation and preparation are the keys to mental toughness, and for this reason, simulation training is a key ingredient of quality practice.

Going to the Next Level

Today's athlete is often concerned with taking his or her game or skills "to the next level." While we have noted the importance of self-improvement, athletes need to know where their true level of effectiveness is, especially given the time and energy they have available to dedicate and commit to their sport. When considering whether to invest more of his or her personal resources into sport an athlete must carefully weigh the cost and benefits of attempting to go to the next level.

First of all the athlete must assess whether he or she is capable of moving to advanced skill levels. Does the athlete have the motivation, ability, and aptitude for his or her sport?

Moving to advanced skill levels may sound like a positive step to take for any athlete, but it can have a negative effect on performance. Some athletes never regain their past form and effectiveness once they have reworked or overhauled their style and skill techniques. Sometimes relearning skills or adjusting movement patterns that are deeply ingrained through years of practice and performance may not be an advisable undertaking.

The athlete who is considering making skill, style, or movement pattern changes should ask three questions: (1) Am I capable of making the change? (2) Is there enough time to make the change? and (3) Am I motivated to make the change? (Christina & Corcos, 1988). In light of these questions, the athlete may decide to focus on refining existing performance skills and style rather than adopting a new one that will take him or her to the "next level."

Any change in skill or performance style has an accompanying *learning effect*, that is, the athlete's performance effectiveness may decline at first, until the new style or skill is learned, mastered, and integrated into the game setting (Christina & Corcos, 1988). Recreational golfers, for example, who take lessons and change their grip find that their scores decline for a while until they become comfortable with the new grip. The key question is whether the athlete can be patient enough to continue believing in his or her new style or skill in light of frustration, discouragement, and poor performances.

Athletes must also assess where they are in their athletic careers (beginning, middle, or end) as to the value of making any significant changes in their performance style or skills (Christina & Corcos, 1988). An athlete may decide to stay with his or her current style since there may not enough time left in his or her career to realistically and effectively make the change or correction.

Lastly, while the athlete has both the capability and time to make style changes and skill corrections, he or she may lack the motivation to practice appropriately (Christina & Corcos, 1988). The relearning process requires forming new motor programs, which tend to break down or become ineffective in performance settings, and for this reason the athlete will need to draw on personal and external sources (coaching) of motivation to reach his or her new goals.

Sometimes "heaven is where you're at" in terms of skill mechanics and performance effectiveness, and athletes may need to focus on the enthusiasm and commitment with which they perform their existing skills rather than constantly changing their style. Athletes may be well served to keep their style and skills the same and change their attitude.

Quality Rest

If athletes are going to engage in quality practice, the demands of which are many, then they must also engage in quality rest. Rest or restoration provides an athlete with the opportunity to re-energize and rejuvenate themselves after demanding practice and performance efforts.

Providing down time in any competitive training schedule can work wonders to restore an athlete's zest and motivation to practice and perform. Sleep, for example, is often overlooked as an integral part of a quality training program but is essential to the well-being and performance effectiveness of athletes. Changes in sleep patterns due to jet lag, emotional stress, or injury can have a negative impact on athletic performance (Savis, 1994). Periodized training programs provide a postseason recovery phase for athletes, as well as rest and recovery periods within seasonal training phases to meet these physical and emotional demands of training.

Lack of sleep is often a problem among student-athletes, particularly at the collegiate level. These athletes put in long training hours, sometimes working out twice a day. Couple training demands with travel, competition, academic and social demands, and those who are not vigilant about protecting and satisfying their sleep requirements soon find themselves in a state of sleep deprivation. Being tired at practice or prior to a performance can cause an athlete's mind to wander, causing him or her to perform poorly and merely go through the motions.

Taking a 20–minute nap is one of the best ways to provide athletes with the rest they need just prior to practice or performance efforts. As children we did this regularly but as adults we tend to be socialized out of this practice. Wise athletes provide structured down time for themselves during the day—a 20–minute nap after lunch does wonders to restore an athlete's energy and focus for practice sessions or performances.

Overcoming Overtraining, Burnout, and Injury

As training programs for athletes become more sophisticated and demanding, coaches and athletes must be constantly vigilant of three factors that can undermine physical and mental preparation for achieving athletic excellence—overtraining, injury, and burnout.

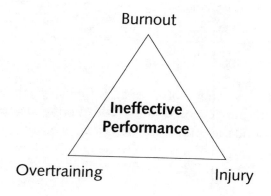

119

Overtraining Is the Downside of Passion

While it is important that an athlete be passionate about his or her pursuit of excellence, he or she must learn to recognize when passion has turned to obsession. Athletes must constantly reflect on one of the truisms of passion, "The endeavor that excites you the most exhausts you the most." For this reason athletes are encouraged to participate in training and competitive programs that emphasize quality training and rest.

A formula for athletic genius can be defined as one-half talent and one-half harness. Young and uninitiated athletes bring unbridled passion to their sport but soon learn that success depends on the ability to blend passion with effort.

Athletes who are susceptible to overtraining often go over the edge in training by becoming obsessed with the ritual and routine of sport and overwork at achieving their athletic dreams. Overworking at success is counterproductive to effective athletic performances—the ability to work smart and rest helps athletes maintain their edge for athletic excellence.

Overtraining Defined

Overtraining can be a part of a negative training cycle that includes the following components: training stress, overtraining, staleness, burnout, and withdrawal (Silva, 1990). Accompanying this training cycle, of course, is the ever present possibility of athletic injury.

The first component of this cycle, *training stress,* can be defined as, "the application of the overload principle designed to extend the boundaries of the athlete's capacity in such a manner that an increase in the capacity is gained via positive adaptation to the imposed demand" (Silva, 1990, p. 7).

Silva (1990) defines the remaining components of a negative training cycle as follows: staleness is "the initial failure of the body's adaptive mechanisms to cope with the psychophysiological stress created by training stimuli" (p. 10); overtraining "occurs when there is repeated failure of the body's adaptive mechanisms to cope with chronic training stress" (p.10); burnout is "an exhaustive psychophysiological response exhibited as a result of frequent, sometimes extreme, but generally ineffective efforts to meet excessive training and competitive demands" (p. 11). The final recourse for the exhausted or burned out athlete is to leave the training setting or to be removed from it so he or she can rest, regenerate, and rejuvenate themselves both physically and mentally (Dale & Weinberg, 1990).

We need to differentiate *overtraining* from *staleness* and *burnout*. The term *overtraining* implies an ongoing process, while the terms *staleness* and *burnout* represent the outcomes of overtraining (Morgan, 1992). The key is to prevent conditions such as staleness and burnout by attacking them at the root of overtraining. Recognizing that an athlete is exhibiting signs of being overtrained is an important step in the remediation or adjustment of training loads by coaches who design and supervise training programs.

The key to training effectively is to stress the athlete to the point of exhaustion but not to exhaustion and not while the athlete is in an exhausted state. Training stress/workloads should be gradually presented to athletes through periodized training programs that allow for proper rest and recovery from intense and demanding workouts. Knowing the point of exhaustion or each athlete's training threshold and tolerance involves the art of training/conditioning as much as it does the science of training/conditioning. Athletes who overtrain become mentally and physically exhausted and worn out from their training rather than strengthened by it.

Each athlete must develop an awareness for his or her own training threshold or exhaustion point, which if exceeded on a regular and continual basis will result in overtraining. Athletes must listen to their body rather than ignore their body when the warning signs and symptoms of overtraining are experienced.

Joan (Benoit) Samuelson, the 1984 Olympic marathon champion, speaks to this point when she states:

> . . . I have always believed the best way to learn your limits is by experience. For myself, I can run hard for a couple of consecutive sessions, but then I need to take it easy for at least two days—rather than follow the one-day-hard/one-day-easy rule. I have learned by experience how to gauge overtraining. . . . Watch for the signs that you've overdone it: feeling flat in training, lack of appetite, insomnia, general apathy or crankiness. Also, when you suspect overtraining, study your running diary and review your lifestyle over the past few weeks. (Samuelson & Averbuch, 1995, p. 65)

Symptoms of Staleness, Overtraining, and Burnout

Coaches and athletes need to be aware of the various warning signs or symptoms of staleness, overtraining, and burnout if they are to prevent or reverse the effects of ineffective and potentially debilitating training programs. The following tables provide a variety of warning signs and symptoms that should be helpful to coaches and athletes who monitor their training programs.

Understanding the Motivations of the Overtrained Athlete

Why do athletes self-destruct by overtraining? Why do they ignore common sense when they know they are overdoing it? What are the motives of athletes who seem to overtrain on a regular basis in light of the negative side effects (i.e., injury, performance decrements) they experience? To answer these questions we need to revisit (see Chapter 4) the primary motivational pattern that typifies the overtrained athlete—the overmotivated, underconfident underachiever.

The overmotivated, underconfident underachiever adheres to and glorifies the work ethic, is in love with the ritual and routine

Psychological Characteristics of Staleness
(Henschen, 2001, p. 447)

- sleep disturbances
- loss of self-confidence
- drowsiness and apathy
- quarrelsomeness
- irritability
- fatigue
- confusion

- emotional and motivational imbalance
- excessive weariness that is prolonged
- lack of appetite (anorexia)
- depression
- anxiety
- anger/hostility

Signs and Symptoms of Overtraining and Burnout
(Weinberg & Gould, 1999, p. 443)

Overtraining
- apathy
- lethargy
- sleep disturbances
- weight loss
- elevated resting heart rate
- muscle pain or soreness
- mood changes
- elevated resting blood pressure
- gastrointestinal disturbances
- retarded recovery from exertion
- appetite loss

Burnout
- low motivation or energy
- concentration problems
- loss of desire to play
- lack of caring
- sleep disturbances
- physical and mental exhaustion
- lowered self-esteem
- negative affect
- mood changes
- substance abuse
- change in values and beliefs
- emotional isolation
- increased anxiety
- highs and lows

of sport and training, and has lost focus regarding the purpose of training, that is, to perform well. This athlete must realize that working hard will only get a person about half-way or two-thirds to a goal—training smart gets a person the remainder of the way. These athletes must learn to trust their talent, training, and preparation and focus on performing in a confident manner.

The overmotivated, underconfident underachiever is often a perfectionist who cannot accept being human and is constantly afraid of making mistakes (fear of failure). The perfectionistic athlete (Connelly, 1992) overworks at training until he or she gets it right or forces him or herself to attain the practice goals prescribed for a particular workout. Then lack of energy and excitement leads to less than effective performance, which leads to frustration and a renewed dedication to work even harder during practice—a vicious cycle.

Recommendations for Preventing Overtraining

Beyond recognizing the signs and symptoms of staleness and overtraining, the following recommendations for the prevention of overtraining can be helpful for coaches and athletes:

1. *Set realistic and flexible goals for training and racing.* The first step in this process is to identify the outcome goals or purpose of a training and performance program. These goals should be expressed in terms of product/outcome—time and place—as well as in terms of process—how these outcomes are to be accomplished.

    Use care in establishing a performance schedule that allows adequate time for recovery between each competitive effort. A poorly designed competitive schedule can create a sense of urgency that can drive athletes into overtraining since it does not allow enough breathing room for recovery from demanding training sessions and competitive performances. Overperforming or overcompeting can be as harmful to the athlete as overtraining.

    Research shows that successful elite athlete set goals for practice as well as for competition (Orlick & Partington, 1988). Setting goals for each training session allows athletes to practice with a purpose and to self-monitor their workouts. Rather than training for the sake of training, they can train to learn and polish their performance skills as well as their conditioning.

Goals should be realistic but challenging if a committed effort is to be elicited from athletes. Goals that are too easily attainable do not seem worthy of a committed effort, and unrealistic goals lead to frustration no matter what the performance outcome may be (Gould, 2001).

Keep goals flexible to allow for the individual differences and development of each athlete. This is particularly important for the perfectionistic athlete who tends to overwork if he or she fails to achieve unrealized goals, even if they have been set at an unrealistic level. Setting unrealistic goals and/or time frames for reaching goals are a trademark of the perfectionistic athlete. Since the athlete's expectations are not in line with reality, he or she usually ends up feeling frustrated rather than pleased or satisfied with effort and performance (Connelly, 1992).

2. *Engage in quality training sessions.* While setting practice goals can help athletes focus on the purpose of their training sessions, it is important to approach and participate in each session with the focus and intensity necessary to maximize the training effect gained through practice.

    Athletes who are in the process of overtraining, simply go through the motions during training sessions; they are, in essence, bored with their training. These athletes begin to demonstrate repetitive stress syndrome, a very common training ailment. Athletes in this frame of mind no longer possess the mental energy to engage efficiently in their training programs and would benefit from workouts/workloads that require less volume and more intensity, from cross-training (e.g., swimming, riding the stationary bike), or from complete rest.

3. *Keep training programs flexible.* Training sessions should allow athletes to make adjustments in their workouts. During their workouts athletes should be encouraged to listen to their bodies to determine if they are crossing into the staleness zone. Regarding this overtraining trap Joan (Benoit) Samuelson states:

Beware of overtraining and reaching your peak too soon before the race. This can happen when I get too wrapped up in seeing continuous improvement and challenging myself. That's because training like this can be enticing and addictive. When I feel this happening, I really have to listen to my training partners, who warn me to cut out of a workout before I go over the edge. Once, I didn't listen and a bad track workout set the stage for a spoiled marathon. I kept trying to make up ground from this one effort, despite the fact that I had been ill and clearly had not recovered. . . . Don't make this common mistake. Marathon training is very tiring. When you don't feel right, back off. It's all too easy to fall victim to the idea that you must run a certain number of 20–milers. When you're tired, it's better to run less. (Samuelson & Averbuch, 1995, pp. 106, 107)

4. *Provide adequate rest and relaxation opportunities for athletes.* The traditional North American work ethic does not encourage rest and relaxation. Athletes are often aware of their need for rest but feel guilty if they miss a training session or workout, or even cut a workout short. For this reason they continue to press on, regardless of their tiredness—they are socialized into "pushing through it" or "sucking it up" rather than being branded a slacker or quitter. At this point the coach must intervene since the athlete will not act on his or her own to leave the training session.

    The strategy of the 20–30 minute daily nap may be helpful for athletes who engage in extensive and demanding training programs. And monitoring the amount and quality of the athlete's sleep is important.

5. *Relieve postcompetitive stress.* Emotion generated by competition can remain with the athlete long after the game is over. If not managed properly, postcompetitive emotions such as depression, anger, elation, anxiety, tension, and other intense psychological feelings can spill over into the athlete's personal

life and/or next training session or competition. Emotions often intensify and take the form of quarrels, fights, drinking behaviors, and other destructive behaviors (Henschen, 2001; Weinberg & Gould, 1999). Unresolved or residual feelings and emotions must be resolved as soon after the competition as possible through the guidance of the coach, parents, and/or a sport psychologist (Henschen, 2001).

Henschen (2001, p. 451) suggests the following ways coaches can reduce postcompetition stress in athletes:

- Provide a supportive atmosphere immediately following a contest.
- Concentrate on your players' emotion, not on your own.
- Try to be with your team after a contest (not on the radio or TV).
- Provide an unemotional yet realistic assessment of each athlete's performance.
- Talk to all team members, even those who did not play.
- Once athletes have dressed, have a team or group activity (e.g., postgame meal).
- Keep athletes away from well-meaning peers and parents.
- Do not allow team members to gloat over success or be depressed over a loss.
- Begin preparation for the next opponent at the very next practice.

6. *Focus on performing—practice with a purpose.* Make it clear that the goal of training is to perform effectively in competitive situations. As mentioned earlier, many athletes and coaches lose sight of this fact and fall in love with the ritual and routine of practice. Athletes overextend themselves in practice rather than in their competitive efforts and can't understand why they are "flat" when it is time to perform.

Some athletes compete in practice in order to determine the best athlete on the team or to establish a team pecking order. This sort of intrateam competition during the training sessions is very counterproductive since it activates the athlete's competitive zest at the wrong time. In essence, the competitive attitude that is needed for performing has been released too soon and is dissipated prior to competition.

7. *Build mental as well as physical confidence.* Teach athletes the mental as well as physical skills necessary to help them gain a feeling of self-control during training and competition.

    Self-regulation skills such as biofeedback are very helpful to an athlete. Biofeedback training includes relaxation training and helps athletes to "listen to their bodies" and to react to the negative aspects of training and racing stress in a positive manner. Additional mental skills related to confidence-building are discussed in Chapter 10.

    Keep in mind that the essence of mental confidence is trust in one's talent and training. Trust will free the athlete up to let his or her talent flow during races. The performance mindset is one of trust, whereas the practice mindset is one of analysis, introspection, and critical evaluation of mechanics, techniques, and racing strategies. During practice athletes should be analytical, thoughtful, and mechanical, whereas in performance situations athletes must trust their pre-race plan and competitive instincts and make a firm commitment to play "their" game.

8. *Have fun.* This may sound like trite advice but great athletes look forward to both practice and performance opportunities. They enjoy practice and training because they know that they are preparing themselves to enjoy their future races. They enjoy the process of training, of being with their teammates and coach, of being outdoors, of being healthy and fit, and of exerting a personal power over nature that few people experience. All of these feelings add up to a sense of physical and mental mastery that they have earned and now feel very proud of attaining. They enjoy the benefits of training, the fruits of their labor.

    Down deep the great athlete knows that there is a purpose to their training, that is, self-mastery through self-improvement.

They know that the competitive environment provides the vehicle for personal excellence, but most of all they return to the athletic arena to experience the glory of sport. This most spiritually uplifting feeling in sport—an intense feeling of accomplishment, pride, and enjoyment—can only be attained through sacrifice, hard work, commitment, and dedication.

Overworking at Sport and Burnout

Athlete, and coaching burnout for that matter, is a result of overworking the processes of sport, that is, overpracticing and falling in love with the ritual and routine of sport. Oftentimes coaches and athletes lose track of the purpose of practicing, that is, to perform. In Chapter 7 on quality practice we saw that effective athletes learn how to train "smart" as opposed to "hard" and retain the physical and emotional energy needed to meet the needs and demands of athletic competition (Vernacchia, 1992, 1995, 1996).

The fact of the matter is that ritual and routine result only in boredom, and this boredom, brought about by the mindless repetition of training (overtraining), can lead to staleness and eventually to burnout. Add a demanding competitive schedule, and an athlete is well on his or her way to achieving a mental and physical state of exhaustion rather than effective performance. Athletes who experience burnout "go through the motions" and soon become too tired to care about their performance outcomes. Furthermore, athletes tend to fit the personality profile for burnout susceptibility—they tend to be achievement-oriented perfectionists who often overwork at tasks, are idealistic, highly driven, and highly responsible (Henschen, 2001; Odom & Perrin, 1985; Vernacchia 1996d).

The Symptoms of Burnout

The symptoms of burnout occur in stages; some of the following symptoms appear in the initial stage: fatigue, sleeplessness, irritability, tension or anxiety, headaches and gastrointestinal disturbances, lower tolerance for frustration, inability to concentrate, and changeable moods (Austin, 1981; Girdano, Everly & Dusek, 1990; Henschen, 2001: Odom & Perrin, 1985; Vernacchia 1996d).

The intermediate stage of burnout (Girdano, Everly & Dusek, 1990) is one of self-protection from increasing amounts of stress as a result of training and performance responsibilities and pressures and is characterized by some of the following symptoms: procrastination, lateness for practice, subpar performances in practice or athletic contests, persistent tiredness in the mornings, cynical attitudes, resentfulness, increased alcohol or cola consumption, or an "I don't care" attitude.

Unable to resist or protect themselves from the training and performance stresses, athletes may progress into the exhaustion stage, which includes some of the following symptoms: loss of caring for others including teammates, family and coaches, suspicion of others, feelings of helplessness and lack of control, depression, stomach or bowel problems, mental and physical fatigue, and a desire to "drop out" of sport (Girdano, Everly & Dusek, 1990; Odom & Perrin, 1985).

Add to all of this the athlete's ability or inability to cope with the demands of his or her lifestyle, and seeds of stress that result from overtraining can easily progress from staleness to a full blown case of burnout. Athletes are "stress seekers" (Cratty, 1989) who maintain a very demanding lifestyle that includes educational, travel, training, social, family, and a variety of other demands on their time and energy (physical and emotional) (Vernacchia, 1995).

Recommendations for Beating Burnout

In addition to recognizing the signs, symptoms, and causes of staleness and overtraining, sport psychologists provide the following suggestions for preventing athletic burnout:

- Engage in realistic goal setting
- Focus on success
- Exercise patience in the expectation of results

- Focus on the process approach to athletics (i.e., socialization, skill development, physical fitness) as well as the product approach (winning)
- Avoid interpreting results self-referentially
- Define success realistically after evaluating talents, abilities, resources, and situations (Odom & Perrin, 1985, pp. 220–221)

In line with these suggestions and those suggested for preventing overtraining, the following strategies can also be effective in preventing and reversing burnout:

- *Learn to "step out of sport" when necessary.* Maintaining a balanced lifestyle plays a key role in helping athletes reach their goals. Athletes who overfocus their time and energies on sport are essentially overinvested in their dreams. Such athletes are always thinking of and doing sport rather than pursuing other dimensions (friends, hobbies, studies) of their lives. Taking time to step out of sport can provide a healthy balance within an athlete's lifestyle and can be a refreshing diversion from sport as well.

- *Adopt a "less is more" mentality toward sport.* Learning to manage time and compartmentalize the day is essential in preventing burnout (Malone & Rotella, 1981). The key is to walk away from a task or tasks. Even though they may not be completed "perfectly," they may have already been effectively accomplished. By realistically evaluating their time and energy resources, athletes can select and prioritize only the most relevant daily tasks to be undertaken.

- *Create an advocacy to reach athletic goals.* Athletes can take advantage of the various support systems available to them as they strive toward their goals. Coaches, parents, teachers, athletic administrators, athletic trainers, sport psychology consultants, and others can all be helpful in providing insights and tangible support and resources for athletes. Being a team player and accepting the support services and resources of those who surround them can be a helpful approach as they pursue athletic excellence.

- *Use mental skills training to cope with the stresses that may lead to burnout.* Relaxation training and visualization are two key mental skills or internal resources that can help athletes overcome and prevent burnout. Knowing when to take a timeout when one is in the middle of experiencing the demands of athletic training and competition is an important skill for an athlete to possess. The use of breathing exercises, progressive relaxation exercises, and visual imagery to quiet and clear the mind before, during, and after training and competitive efforts are essential prerequisites for achievers in high-performance sport.

Stress and Injury

Athletic injuries are a natural part of an athlete's career. Overtraining can result in a variety of overuse injuries and can make athletes susceptible to injury as fatigue disrupts an athlete's concentration or diminishes his or her practice and performance intensity (Brewer, 2001; Heil, 1993; Williams, Rotella, & Scherzer, 2001). The emotional distraction of injury will be addressed in Chapter 11 with the description of a stage model (denial, disbelief, and isolation; frustration and anger; bargaining; depression; and resignation) that will help athletes understand how to respond in a positive way when injured (Kübler-Ross, 1969; Williams, Rotella, & Scherzer, 2001).

In addition to addressing the emotional stages of athletic injury, an athlete must then face the process of injury rehabilitation. This process would also include the review and adjustment of training programs so that potential future injuries can be prevented. To understand the injury rehabilitation and psychoemotional healing process an athlete will experience, the following guidelines are suggested (Vernacchia & Henschen, 2001):

- Obtain and understand injury diagnosis and prognosis.
- Establish a treatment and rehabilitation plan.
- Seek and accept medical, social, and emotional support.

- Use mental skills to enhance healing and the retention of physical skills.
- Regain physical confidence.
- Make technical adjustments to avoid reinjury and ineffective future performances.
- Keep a healthy perspective regarding rehabilitation and future performances and role on the team.
- Plan for an effective emotional reentry to the team and performance setting.
- Establish a follow-up plan.

Obtain and understand injury diagnosis and prognosis

One of the most ignored and overlooked aspects of injury rehabilitation is the obvious first step to healing—attaining an accurate diagnosis. Oftentimes athletes are unable to take this all important first step because of the financial cost of obtaining a complete medical diagnosis of their injury. In some cases, athletes are reluctant to seek a medical diagnosis because of the possible future consequences of an injury, particularly with potentially season- or career-ending injuries.

As a result of the socialization attitudes or mentality that can exist in sport, many athletes disregard or ignore the seriousness of their injuries. Athletic attitudes that fall into this category include: "No pain, no gain," "Act tough and always give 110%," "Play hurt—play through your injury," "Injured athletes are worthless" (Williams, Rotella & Scherzer, 2001). Athletes may also be reluctant to report their injuries, therefore masking them, in order to retain or protect their position on the team (Williams, Rotella & Scherzer, 2001).

The uncertainty of injury diagnosis creates a climate of emotional and physical tension and confusion that is counterproductive to optimal injury rehabilitation and healing. An accurate medial diagnosis of an existing injury can help an athlete gain an emotional and mental understanding regarding that injury and the prognosis for effective return to the training and performance setting.

Establish a treatment and rehabilitation plan

Successful athletes are very good at following training and performance plans and strategies, therefore, establishing a treatment and rehabilitation plan will provide the guidance necessary to recover from injuries that may interrupt training and participation in athletic contests.

Athletes often amaze physicians, medical professionals, and the general public because they seem to recover from their injuries at a more rapid rate than nonathletes. This happens because athletes are motivated and know how to train and how to follow a training plan, or in this case a treatment and rehabilitation plan. For example, Joan Benoit Samuelson, the 1984 Olympic marathon champion quoted earlier in this chapter, underwent arthroscopic surgery on her knee 17 days before the U.S. Olympic marathon trials. She went on to participate in the trials, make the U.S. Olympic team, and win the gold medal.

Accepting rehabilitation as a temporary replacement for normal training programs and methods is helpful in creating a healing mind-set for the injured athlete. Since an athlete may not be able to participate in normal training programs and activities, he or she may need to engage in substitute activities to maintain general fitness (e.g., cross-training such as riding a stationary bike or swimming). This activity enables the athlete to stay physically active while undergoing rehabilitation.

Seek and accept social and emotional support

Many athletes isolate themselves from their support systems once they become injured, but seeking the support of friends, family, and sports medicine personnel (i.e., athletic trainers, team physician, academic support personnel, sport psychology consultants) to replace the normal supportive relationships they have with coaches and teammates is important.

Those people who are part of an athlete's social support system can help an athlete keep rehabilitation in perspective by pro-

viding the following types of support: listening, emotional support, emotional challenge, task appreciation, task challenge, tangible assistance, and personal assistance. Without social support
some athletes can wander aimlessly through the rehabilitation
process and, in some cases, engage in activities that are counterproductive (e.g., poor academic performance, use of alcohol) to
healing in a timely and effective manner. Some athletes feel they
can overcome injuries on their own and are soon frustrated by
the demands and challenges of their recovery and rehabilitation.
It is important for athletes to realize that injury rehabilitation is
not a self-help process; it requires, as does other forms of athletic
excellence, a team effort.

Use mental skills to enhance healing and the retention of physical skills

Mental skills are an integral component of the injury rehabilitation process. The key mental skills to employ in the healing
process are addressed in other chapters and include self-talk strategies (thought stoppage and replacement); goal setting; relaxation
training; visualization; mental toughness training (anticipation
and preparation); and composure or emotion management strategies. Working with a sport psychology consultant to design a mental plan for injury rehabilitation, including reentry into the team
and performance setting, is an important strategy for an injured
athlete.

Regain physical confidence

Probably the most critical aspect of athletic injury rehabilitation
is the athlete's ability to regain his or her physical confidence
prior to reentering the practice and competitive settings. For this
reason, athletes can participate in practice sessions that present
progressive physical challenges appropriately designed by the
coach, sports medicine staff, and the athlete to build physical
confidence.

Make technical adjustments to avoid reinjury and ineffective future performances

One of the common mistakes in the injury rehabilitation process is the failure to consider technical adjustments in an athlete's playing style that need to be made once they have recovered from an injury and reenter the training and competitive environments. Such adjustments can help the athlete avoid reinjury or possibly injury to another part of the body.

For example, a basketball player who has incurred a knee injury may have been a very assertive defensive player prior to the injury. He or she played tight defense and the player's physical abilities (speed and quickness) allowed him or her to get away with incorrect defensive techniques (using a cross-over step rather than a slide step) and still perform effectively when guarding his or her opponent. After the knee injury this same athlete may have to adjust his or her defensive style of play by "playing off" the opponent rather than employing a tight defensive posture. This change would allow the athlete more time to adjust to his or her opponent's moves while at the same time preventing reinjury to the knee.

The athlete may also need to learn new defensive strategies to be more effective. For example, the athlete may spend more time watching game films of opponents to determine their offensive tendencies, strengths, and weaknesses. He or she can then overplay the opponent to one side or the other, depending on which direction the opponent likes to drive to the basket. Similarly, in an effort to create a "steal," the athlete can overplay an opponent to the strong side dribble, therefore forcing the opponent to dribble with his or her weak hand.

Keep a healthy perspective regarding rehabilitation and future performances and role on the team.

Another factor often overlooked in the injury rehabilitation process is the failure of athletes to recognize and accept the cumulative benefits of their previous training. Many athletes feel that "all is lost" when they are injured and consequently lose confidence, both physical and mental, in their ability to remain fit enough to perform if their training is interrupted by the effects of an injury. Athletes must recognize the cumulative effect of their training and that if they can engage in alternate forms of physical fitness and mental training, they will reenter the practice and performance setting with a reasonable chance to perform effectively.

Mental training techniques such as mental rehearsal of physical skills can help athletes retain their skill levels. Mental training and practice can be enhanced by having an athlete attend practice sessions and watch the drills and plays of teammates. In some cases, athletes can engage in forms of physical fitness activities while watching practice (e.g., riding an exercise bike on the sidelines). In any case, a mental picture of what is taking place at practice helps an athlete mentally and physically prepare for the time when he or she will rejoin the team. Furthermore, drills and skills (offensive plays and defensive formats) can be mentally rehearsed with more clarity and vividness since the athlete has had an opportunity to observe the implementation of various practice factors in actual performance situations.

In addition to recognizing the importance of the cumulative effects of training, an injured athlete needs to understand how his or her role on the team may be influenced by the injury. An injured athlete who was initially a starter may need to accept that, depending on the severity of the injury, he or she may now receive limited or reduced playing time. The injured athlete may need to take on a role of support player for teammates, providing encouragement for others even though he or she would rather be playing and be the one receiving encouragement from others. Anger and frustration generated by an unwillingness to accept new or altered roles on the team can only stifle the healing process for an injured athlete.

Plan for an effective emotional reentry to the team and performance setting

The feelings and emotions they experience when they finally return to the practice or performance setting overwhelm many rehabilitated athletes. Distracting feelings regarding reinjury, poor performance, acceptance by teammates (especially if an athlete is replacing another athlete who has been receiving extensive playing time while injury rehabilitation was taking place), and lowered self-confidence are some of the emotional factors that can contribute to an athlete's worries. Worry can prevent an effective transition to the practice or performance environment.

Emotional anticipation and preparation, that is, emotional rehearsal, is an important factor in returning to practice or performance settings in an effective way. Determining beforehand how an athlete will feel, both emotionally (emotional rehearsal) and physically (body rehearsal), can help an athlete prepare an appropriate emotional as well as physical response.

Emotional rehearsal, a form of mental imagery training, can be used to experience the various emotions that a particular practice or performance setting may create. Pre-imaging the feelings associated with both pleasant and unpleasant feelings related to future challenges can aid the athlete in preparing an effective coping response (Williams, Rotella & Scherzer, 2001). Emotional rehearsal enables athletes to feel confident and secure that their rehabilitation has been successful and that they will perform effectively upon returning to competitive situations (Williams, Rotella & Scherzer, 2001). The goal here is to have the athlete produce feelings of competency and self-pride as he or she emotionally "walks through" the various perceptions and potential fears, worries, and doubts (real or imagined) regarding performance effectiveness (Williams, Rotella & Scherzer, 2001).

Establish a follow-up plan

Once an athlete has rehabilitated a particular injury, constant vigilance is needed to prevent reinjury or further injury, perhaps to another part of the body. Injuries can serve to help an athlete gain increased awareness of the body and to adapt training and performance strategies that will help prevent further injuries (e.g., flexibility training, adjustments in the periodization of their training schedules, adjustments in skill techniques used in performance settings).

The upside of being injured is that it enables an athlete to identify and establish a support system that can be accessed again if an injury should occur in the future. Although sport is physical, learning to listen to one's body, thoughts and feelings during training and in performance settings is the real first step in the prevention of athletic injury. Learning how to cope with and recover from injury is an important learned attribute of highly effective and realistic athletic performers.

PART III

Mastering the 4 C's of Peak Performance

9

Concentration
Focus and Refocus For Success

How many times have coaches implored athletes to concentrate? How many times have athletes been at a loss to really know what their coaches mean by *concentrate*? Both coaches and athletes understand the important relationship that concentration has to athletic performance but oftentimes, coaches are at a loss as to how to teach the mental skills of concentration. Athletes are rendered ineffective in competitive situations because they have not learned, practiced, and mastered their ability to concentrate or pay attention in the "heat of battle."

Concentration is simply the maintenance of attention (Magill, 1989). The performer's ability to attend to the details of their performance and performance environment take a great deal of mental strength and discipline (Moran, 1996; Simons, 1998). The most effective athletes have learned to pay attention to the details of their performance and take care of the little things before the little things take care of them. At the highest levels of athletic performance little things make a big difference. Championships are won by inches, or hundredths of a second, or by a last second as a result of an athlete's ability to give a concentrated effort in a crucial situation.

 Mental Key to Success

Concentration is the ability to perform with a clear and present focus.

Concentration is the first step in developing a sequence of mental skills that will cascade into an effective or peak performance. An athlete's ability to concentrate is the first step in gaining control of his or her ability to perform the physical skills that have been mastered through conscientious practice, training, and previous competitive efforts. The ability to concentrate includes the athlete's ability not only to focus on the things that will make them successful during a competitive situation but also to maintain focus and, if necessary, refocus. Furthermore, athletes must develop their ability to deal with the various distractions that are inherently present in performance settings (Orlick & Partington, 1988).

The Mind-Set of Concentrated Performers

The Absence and Presence of the Concentrated Mind

The ability to have both the absence and the presence of mind while performing is another characteristic of highly effective athletic performers. Thinking while performing can disrupt an athlete's ability to let his or her skills flow in competitive settings (paralysis by analysis), and therefore the absence of conscious thought while performing is essential to the fluid execution of well-learned motor programs. At the same time an athlete must have a conscious awareness of the performance environment so he or she can be flexible and adjust motor programs without even thinking about it. In performance settings, effective athletic performers react to cues that trigger well-learned and automatically performed motor programs (Moore & Stevenson, 1991).

Performing "In the Moment"

Being "in the moment" is a prime prerequisite for successful and effective performances, a mind-set that high performance athletes possess (Williams & Krane, 2001). To attain such a mind-set, athletes need to overcome the socialization of a process mentality that emphasizes that there will always be another chance, another tomorrow, or other opportunities to attain one's best performance. Effective athletes perform in the present because they realize that the time is now and they may never have another chance or opportunity to achieve the greatness and glory of their best performance.

In some sports this mind-set or attitude can simply be a matter of survival. For example, the best football players learn to make each play as if it were their last play because the very intense physical nature of their sport brings the realization that, in fact, it could be the last play of their career. Being "in the moment" requires total concentration that is focused on the task at hand if effective performance efforts are to be realized.

The Three Stages of Concentration

To understand and implement focusing strategies in athletic performance situations, it is best to review the stages of concentration from both a theoretical and an operational perspective. The theoretical perspective gives us an understanding of the "why" of concentration, and an operational model explains the "how" of concentration. Knowing and mastering the "how" and "why" of concentration will help athletes perform in the "now" of high-performance sport.

Table 9.1: Concentration Model for Effective Athletic Performance

Stages	Characteristics	Concentration Abilities/ Skills Required
1. Decision- Making Stage (Pre-performance)	Assessing Strategizing Deciding Mental preparation	Selective attention Divided attention Shifting attention Mental rehearsal Identification of concentration goals and cues Mental routines Mental toughness training
Transition from Decision Making to the Performance Stage		Attuning
2. Performance Stage (Performance)	Automatic action Body awareness Emotional control Internal/external cue recognition Use of feedback (FB) Refocusing	Alertness and trust Mental/physical routines Attend to performance goals and cues Selecting the appropriate modes of FB Distraction control
3. Evaluation Stage (Post-performance)	Constructive evaluation	Improvement strategies based on performance Feedback

A variety of concentration theories related to athletic performance are a blend of sport psychology and motor learning principles (Cook, 1996c; Nideffer, 1976, 1985; Nideffer & Sagal, 2001; Nougier, Stein, & Bonnel, 1991; Schmidt, 1991; Stallings, 1982). Each of these models stresses the importance of sequencing of mental processes as an athlete progresses through cognitive stages of attentional focus that ultimately affect performance. Concentration that results in effective athletic performances involves three stages—decision making, physical performance, and evaluation. Table 9.1 presents each of these stages, as well as the characteristics of each stage and the concentration abilities and skills necessary for the efficient and effective operation of each stage.

Stage 1: The Decision-Making Stage of Concentration

The decision-making stage of concentration requires the athlete to be mentally active and interactive with the upcoming performance environment so that he or she can make appropriate and effective decisions regarding the implementation and execution of motor skills. Good decision making in this stage results in sound performance strategies. During this stage the athlete will be mentally active as he or she assesses the performance environment and physically passive as motor programs are prepared for action. The action potential or performance effectiveness of the athlete in any given situation is determined in this stage.

Stage 1 concentration requires that the athlete mentally assess the performance setting, taking into account all factors that could possibly affect performance. For example, before a golfer selects the appropriate club, he or she needs to assess the distance to the hole, the wind direction and velocity, the location of hazards such as sand traps and water, the location of the pin, etc. Once this information has been taken into consideration and the proper club has been selected, the player must complete his or her strategizing by deciding on the type of shot to be hit (draw, fade, high, low, etc.) and the target at which he or she will aim the shot. Once all these decisions have been made, the performer is ready to move into the next concentration stage.

The initial or decision-making stage of concentration is influenced by how much time the athlete has available to formulate, activate, and implement strategies and decisions. A golfer is engaged in a self-paced skill and essentially has control over the amount of time he or she can expend in selecting strategies and making performance decisions. So does a basketball player who is about to take a foul shot, or long jumper, or baseball pitcher. However, many athletic activities require rapid assessment, strategizing, and decision making because the situation is one that is externally paced or depends on how the athlete responds to a dynamic performance environment. For example, a football quarterback may call a play in the huddle but may adjust the play at the line of scrimmage once he or she observes the defense. If a pass play is called, the quarterback must reassess the defense once the ball is snapped, so he or she can decide what receiver will receive the ball (target), what type of pass will be thrown (touch pass, hard and low, etc.), or whether the pass should be thrown at all. The quarterback may decide it is best to tuck the ball away and run with it.

Stage 1 Concentration Skills

Stage 1 concentration abilities and skills include:
- the ability to pay attention to the task-relevant cues and elements in the performance environment (*selective attention*);
- the ability to pay attention to one or more cues at a time (*divided attention*);
- the ability to use a broad and narrow focus when assessing situations (*shifting attention*);
- the ability to see in one's mind how an effective skill or skill sequence is to be performed (*mental rehearsal*);
- the ability to identify key components of the desired skill performance, as well as cues that will trigger a skill execution (*identification of concentration goals and cues*);
- the ability to use mental rehearsal to call up the "feel" of the desired performance (*mental routines*); and

- the ability to anticipate and prepare for variations in the performance environment that could distract one's attention (*mental toughness*).

Selective Attention

The most important skill required of effective performers is the ability to select the important factors in the performance setting to pay attention to if their strategies and decisions are to be effective. For example, before a basketball point guard makes a pass, he or she must evaluate how the defensive player is guarding offensive players. If the guard's teammate is being overguarded in an attempt to cut off passing lanes, the guard may decide to have his or her teammate cut to the basket so a back door play can be run. The defensive player may be positioning him or herself in front of the guard's teammate (fronting the player), and the guard may decide to throw a high pass over the top of the defensive player so the guard's teammate can catch the pass, turn and shoot uncontested. In each of these cases the guard must pay attention to task-relevant cues (how his teammates are being guarded) before deciding to make a pass—this is known as selective attention.

The ability to attend to task-relevant cues in the performance environment in a nondistractible way is the trademark of effective concentration skills (Singer, Cauraugh, Murphey, Chen & Lidor, 1991). Selective attention also refers to the ability of the athlete to separate the important information in the performance environment without being mentally overwhelmed or overloaded by everything around them (Magill, 1989). To revisit our golfing example, the player may be walking down the fairway approaching his or her next shot. While the player is aware of all the aspects of the performance environment (opponent(s), coaches, fans, media, scoreboard, family, etc.), he or she is able to focus on only the factors that will be helpful in assessing the situation (yardage to the hole, lie, wind velocity and direction, etc.) that will result in effective shot making. In essence, effective performers look at everything that surrounds them in performance settings but only see or select the factors that will help them determine effective strategies and decisions.

Divided Attention and Shifting Attention

A basketball point guard, who had a considerable amount of time to formulate strategies on the foul line prior to shooting, may have little time available once he or she is on offense and has to rapidly survey the defense before deciding on what play to call while at the same time maintaining control of the ball, court vision, and the amount of time remaining on the shot clock. This example illustrates two key Stage 1 concentration skills that can ultimately influence the effectiveness of selected performance strategies and decisions. The first skill is that of performing in situations that require "divided attention"—that is, making decisions (what play to select, who to pass to, etc.) in the midst of attending to the execution of ongoing skills (dribbling). The ability to divide attention in the middle of performances is a key to avoiding distractions that can undermine effective performances. It becomes more difficult for a baseball pitcher to be effective once a opposing player is on base because the pitcher must adapt his or her style to "hold" that player on base while also concentrating on pitch selection and execution.

The second concentration skill demonstrated by the point guard is the ability to shift his or her attention from a wide to a narrow focus. The point guard must be able to take in all the information necessary to run an effective offense by assessing the defense while he or she is bringing the ball downcourt. The point guard will need to recognize (wide focus of attention) whether the opposing team is playing a zone or person to person (i.e., a 3–2 zone for example or whether his teammates are double-teamed in a person to person defense). Based on his or her ability to recognize and analyze the defense the point guard will select and call out what he or she considers to be the appropriate offensive play.

Once the point guard calls the play then he or she must initiate the play by passing to a teammate. In order to make an effective pass the point guard must now shift his or her attention to a narrow focus. The point guard will identify the appropriate player who will receive the pass and then the point guard must select the proper pass to execute, as well as the method he or she will use to make sure the pass is completed.

This process of shifting attention is a dynamic process that is repeated many times throughout a basketball game by a point guard. The guard must constantly shift his or her attention from broad to narrow and vice versa in order to perform effectively.

Mental Rehearsal

The ability to mentally rehearse selected performance strategies or movements is another key concentration skill of highly effective athletic performers. Some athletes even combine mental rehearsal with physical movements to help them get the feel of the desired movement pattern. For example, a basketball player about to shoot a foul shot may go through the shooting motion before he or she takes the shot. This helps the athlete get the feel, that is, create the body awareness necessary to make the foul shot. This is why golfers take practice swings. Most athletes can create "feel" by simply visualizing or mentally rehearsing the desired process and outcomes of their movement patterns. Depending on whether skills and movement patterns are self-paced or externally paced, the speed at which athletes visualize desired outcomes can vary. Self-paced skills, such as foul shooting and golf shot making, allow a considerable time for mental rehearsal. Externally paced skills, such as passing a basketball to a moving player, provide a limited window for mental rehearsal and require a rapid review or recall of successful images.

Identification of Concentration Goals and Cues

Since both selective and divided attention affects the athlete's ability to concentrate effectively, it is imperative that athletes have concentration goals to focus on before and during their performances. Concentration goals are determined by reviewing the athletic performance task at hand and identifying the important components of a performance task or skill that, if performed effectively in a sequential manner, will result in a desired outcome.

A defensive basketball player who desires to be an effective rebounder must perform a sequence of movements that will result in "grabbing the rebound." First the player must be conscious of maintaining a position between his or her opponent and the basket. Once his or her player or another player takes a shot, the defensive player must locate his or her opponent by "tagging" him or her. This is usually accomplished by reaching out with either hand and touching the opposing player. Next it is important for the player to step toward and turn his or her back and backside toward the opponent in an effort to box out the opponent, thus preventing the opponent from getting the rebound. Finally the defensive player must jump to the ball as it rebounds from the rim or backboard, catch and hold it, secure it once he or she has landed on the floor, and protect the ball from opponents by holding it to his or her chest. The defensive player's cue or word that may trigger this sequence is the word *shot*. Hearing this cue will trigger an automatic response of the player's rebounding skills. Table 9.2 presents the concentration goals and performance behaviors and the cue for defensive rebounding in basketball.

Mental Routines

Cook's model of concentration relies heavily on structured mental routines, especially for self-paced motor skills that are controlled by the performer (Cook, 1996c; McGuire, 1992). Figure 9.1 outlines the framework and components of a mental routine. The mental routine aids the athlete in assessing and preparing, as well as rehearsing his or her performance response in any given situation. Cook's model of concentration includes mental rehearsal as a tool to review desired performances and to call up the feel of the desired performance. Lastly the model includes a cue word (*Trust*) that is used to trigger the motor program that will lead to effective performance outcomes. Later in this chapter, under Stage 2 concentration skills, this mental routine will be combined with sport-specific physical routines to create automatic athletic performances.

Table 9.2   Basketball Skill—Defensive Rebounding

Cue	Concentration Goals and Performance Behaviors
"Shot"	Reach out and locate opponent (tagging)
	Turn toward opponent
	Back to opponent
	Box out
	Go to the ball
	Jump, grasp, and hold the ball
	Land with feet apart and maintain balance
	Secure the ball (hold to chest)
	Look for outlet pass

Mental Toughness

As stated previously the ability of an athlete to perform his or her skills in a nondistractible way is a key characteristic of effective athletic performers. Athletes who are successful in this endeavor possess the attribute of mental toughness because they react effectively to unexpected situations that occur in game situations. The athlete who has the mental discipline and flexibility to adapt to the dynamics of athletic performance settings has the best chance to be and do his or her best. To this end highly effective athletes mentally prepare themselves to expect the unexpected or handle the what ifs of athletic performance by anticipating and preparing a response to a variety of unpredictable situations before they actually perform in game situations. Anticipation and preparation are the keys to mental toughness (Cook, 1996c).

Mastering Stage 1 Concentration Skills

Concentration Drills

Several concentration drills can help athletes develop total and divided focusing abilities. Some of these drills help the athlete

OBSERVE
Absorb the surroundings

STRATEGY
What do I have to do to make it happen ?

ALL DECISIONS HAVE BEEN MADE AT THIS POINT

SEE IT
Visualize the sport skill being performed effectively

FEEL IT
Feel the body movements needed to produce
the effective performance

TRUST IT
Use the cue word *Trust* to trigger the performance
Choose to *trust* your skills, talent, and preparation

Figure 9.1 Cook's Concentration Model

shift his or her ability to focus on a variety of focal points in the environment to only one performance factor or cue and vice versa. The following mental drills (Henschen, 1995) can improve and master concentration abilities:

1. *The Concentration Grid Exercise*—This fun exercise can be administered individually or to an entire group. Have the athletes work in partners and make sure the grid is held face down so the athletes don't see the numbers until the exercise begins (the grid appears on page 157). One of the two paired athletes then turns over the page and crosses out as many numbers as possible in consecutive order starting with 00, 01, 02. The athlete continues to cross out numbers for one minute. While one person is crossing out the numbers, his or her partner is doing everything possible to distract the person. Partners can talk, whistle, or shout, but they *cannot*

84	27	51	78	59	52	13	85	61	55
28	60	92	04	97	90	31	57	29	33
32	96	65	39	80	77	49	86	18	70
76	87	71	95	98	81	01	46	88	00
48	82	89	47	35	17	10	42	62	34
44	67	93	11	07	43	72	94	69	56
53	79	05	22	54	74	58	14	91	02
06	68	99	75	26	15	41	66	20	40
50	09	64	08	38	30	36	45	83	24
03	73	21	23	16	37	25	19	12	63

touch the other person. After one minute, reverse the roles. It is interesting to note that first graders frequently reach the number 25, while adults can get only into the high teens (Henschen, 1995, p. 179).

2. *Observation and Multifocusing*—(a) Close your eyes and listen to outside sounds in your environment for three minutes. After three minutes open your eyes and list the various sounds you heard. Try this in different environments (at home, traveling, at athletic contests). (b) Look around your environment for several minutes and identify as many different aspects of it as you can. At the end of this observation period, list the various aspects of the environment that you observed. Try this in different environments and situations, particularly while observing various athletic events (at the

site or on TV). See the configuration of the arena and playing floor, where the teams sit, where the officials place themselves, be aware of the weather conditions, the location of the scoreboard, etc. Observing all factors in the athletic environment that surrounds your performance ultimately will help you make effective decisions and adapt your decisions and play in certain situations.

3. *Body Awareness*—Eliminate external distracts by placing your fingers in your ears and closing your eyes, and then listen to the sounds of your body (heartbeat, breathing, joint movement, etc.) for two minutes. Repeat the same drill but this time without blocking out external sounds (remove your fingers from your ears) and sights (eyes open).

4. *Total Focus*—Study an object for five minutes, such as a pencil or a tennis ball, that you can hold and manipulate in your hand. Focus intently on this object. If your mind becomes bored and starts to wander, refocus on the object. Each time you perform this drill, change the object.

5. *Combination Drills*—Once you have attempted drills 2, 3, and 4 separately, then practice your ability to shift your attention from one type of focus to another by combining each of these drills into one drill. Go from multifocusing, to body awareness focus, to total focus on a specific object. Practice this while watching athletic events in person or on TV. Shifting your attention and focal point will prevent you from being overwhelmed and/or overfocused in performance settings.

6. *Shifting Focus and Distraction Control*—In addition to combining drills 2, 3, and 4 to improve your ability to change or shift your focus, try this more demanding 30-minute drill. This exercise involves reading a book, listening to the radio, and watching TV. Read a book (interesting and with no pictures) in a quiet place for 10 minutes, and then tell someone what you just read. For the next 10 minutes, read the book while listening to the radio and then tell someone what you just read and/or listened to on the radio or

describe both listening tasks. You can make this task more or less challenging by increasing or decreasing the volume of the radio. For the final 10 minutes of this exercise, read a book while listening to the radio and watching a TV program. Now describe what you have just read, listened to on the radio, and/or watched on TV. This exercise will not only develop your ability to shift your attention but also help you learn to deal with distractions.

7. *Strategizing*—Pick a problem that has been bothering you and ask your mind to feed it as many solutions as it can. File the first solution away in the back of your mind and then go on to the next solution. Try this for five minutes, and then identify the various solutions you have created and decide which of these solutions would work best for you in this particular situation. Trying this with various sport situations will help you anticipate and prepare for effective responses to performance challenges.

8. *Letting It Flow*—Develop your creativity by letting thought flow through your mind at your own pace. Entertain these thoughts or ideas without evaluating them. Have fun playing with any and every thought or idea that enters your mind. Doing this for five minutes is a good way to develop the ability to focus on what you want to do rather than what you want to avoid.

9. *Clearing Your Mind*—Try to think of nothing for one minute. Control your mind so that it cannot feed you any thoughts. This exercise is great for relaxing your mind when it becomes cluttered with too many thoughts or ideas as a result of overfocusing.

10. *Concentration Card Game*—Play the card game concentration to improve your memory and concentration skills. Spread all 52 playing cards face down on the floor or a tabletop. Mix the cards up so there is no order to them. Each player turns over two cards in each turn. After the first card is turned over, the player turns over a second card that he or she thinks will match the first card (ignore the suits). If a match

occurs, remove the cards and the player is given another chance to uncover a match. If the cards don't match, the player returns the cards face down to their original position and the next player takes his or her turn. Obviously you must remember the placement of the cards as the game progresses. The player who collects the most pairs of cards wins. This game can be played with one or more players.

Mental Rehearsal

Using a variety of visualization methods can enhance an athlete's concentration ability. These methods were described in depth in Chapter 5 and include imitation, highlight music videotapes/CDs, reminiscence, repetitious visualization, and creative concentration tapes/CDs.

Concentration Goal Cards

To identify concentration goals or the focal point of their concentration efforts, athletes can complete *concentration goal cards* similar to the one presented in Table 9.2. Each goal card should include a cue word that can trigger the specific sequenced movements and behaviors that will result in effective performance. This exercise aids athletes in cue identification and recognition, as well as provides a review of learned skills that can be applied in a specific performance setting.

Rehearsing behaviors ahead of time makes athletes more efficient and effective performers once they are caught up in the flow of the performance. Performance effectiveness requires the athlete to be mentally passive and physically active, that is, not to think about their moves but to react to cues that will trigger automatic moves.

The most effective way to use concentration goal cards is to write each skill to be mastered and performed on one index card (3"×5" or 5"×7"). Print the Concentration Goals and Performance Behaviors on one side of the card and the Cue word on the other side of the card. Athletes can then create a file or stack of these cards, essentially flash cards, that can be learned and reviewed before practice sessions or game performances. These cards help athletes to focus on the now of their performances without getting emotionally overwhelmed or "ahead of themselves" as they think about upcoming performances. Concentration goal cards can also be effective in teaching athletes how to refocus because it gives the athlete a focal cue if and when the athlete's mind wanders or the athlete is distracted.

Athletes can be drilled using the concentration goal cards by simply flashing the cue word to the athlete and asking him or her to respond to it by actually going through the actual movements necessary to execute the particular skill or movement pattern. Athletes can sharpen their concentration and performance skills by practicing on their own or with a training partner and randomly selecting different cue words and running plays against imaginary or actual opponents. The concentration goal cards can be reviewed to see if their movements were accurate and complete.

Mental Toughness Training

Athletes can engage in mental toughness training to aid themselves in responding effectively to unexpected happenings or current and future performance distractions and obstacles (Cook, 1996c).

Have the athletes write out their responses to various performance challenges, obstacles, or distractions they can anticipate facing in future competitive settings. After each situation, the athlete should write out their typical response and determine if it has been effective or ineffective for them. If it has been ineffective, the athlete can prepare a mental toughness response to this challenge, obstacle, or distraction. Write out several responses, if necessary, and select the one that would be most effective (Table 9.3).

Transitioning from Decision Making (Stage 1) to Performance (Stage 2)

As the athlete transitions from Stage 1 (mental preparation stage) to Stage 2 (performance stage), he or she must realize and accept that all decisions regarding the performance have been made.

Table 9.3   Mental Toughness Training

Challenge, Obstacle, Distraction	Typical Response	Mental Toughness Response
Weather Conditions: Windy *Sport/Skill:* Tennis Serve	Failure to adapt and double fault (Ineffective)	*If serving into the wind:* Toss the ball further in front of the body and use a flat serve rather than a slice serve to gain more velocity *If serving with the wind:* Toss the ball the ball directly overhead and use a slice serve to reduce velocity and be more accurate.

Once the competition begins, performance is determined by the athlete's ability to monitor his or her physical and emotional states during performance while simultaneously paying attention to performance goals and cues. The athlete's ability to assess, decide, and act on performance strategies through the application of learned and adapted motor skill and movement patterns are challenged and tested in this stage. In many ways practice time is a time of learning for the athlete-an invisible process that can only be truly evaluated by how an athlete performs. The performance stage demonstrates whether real learning has taken place.

The concentration ability and skill needed in this phase is the ability to attune to the Stage 2 performance environment and demands.

Attuning

Transitioning from the mental to the performance stage is accomplished as the athlete becomes more attuned to the performance environment (Syre & Connolly, 1987). Attuning or focusing in this process requires that the athlete mentally prepare for competition by reviewing and establishing a plan to respond effectively to the uniqueness of the setting surrounding the performance.

Attuning or focusing attention—becoming more aware of all the factors that will influence performance—is the transition step from being mentally active and physically passive to becoming physically active and mentally passive while performing. Attuning increases the athlete's sensitivity to the performance setting and situation, their body, thoughts and feelings, their teammates and coaches, and, most of all, with the purpose and plan of their performance (Syre & Connolly, 1987).

Mastering the Transition Skill of Attuning

The athlete's ability to attune or focus on the important aspects of his or her upcoming performance is essential in setting him or her up for success. The concentration skill of attuning mentally readies the athlete for the actual demands that will be faced in competition. Often referred to as "mentally preparing" for performances, attuning involves concentrating on several performance areas (Syre & Connolly, 1987):

1. *Attuning to the Performance Setting and Situation.* Athletes must take the time and make the effort to visit the area, field or stadium where their performances will take place. Athletes need to know the structure of the performance environment so they can adjust their senses to the unique environment that will surround their performance. As obvious as it sounds, it is important for athletes to walk through the performance setting and all the components that are part of that setting (i.e., the locker room, the playing field or floor, the condition of the playing field, location of the restrooms, location of the sports medicine facilities, the media areas, team seating, location of the band, lighting, equipment). This pre-performance exercise enables athletes to mentally and physically orient themselves once the actual competition takes place because they know what to expect and what it feels like to be in a particular performance environment.

Furthermore, athletes need to know what the performance protocol will be-how the competition will be conducted. This knowledge helps them to mentally prepare for the
performance process they will experience before, during, and
after the competition (i.e., team introductions, the order of
competition or when they will compete as individuals, playing rotation, how to report or check in for the competition,
how the competition will be officiated). All this pre-
performance planning helps athletes gain and maintain
their focus as well as their mental and physical energy. Simple things, such as trying to find the locker room or trainers,
take a conscious effort that can distract athletes and waste
their mental and physical energy.

2. *Attuning to One's Body, Thoughts, and Feelings.* This step in the
    attuning process is essentially carried out during the warm-
    up stage of the competition. During the warm-up athletes
    can begin to listen to their body as they move from making
    simple movements (stretching exercises) to rehearsing more
    complex performance movements and skills that will be
    used in the actual competition. This essential part of the
    attuning process allows athletes to physically activate them-
    selves while becoming more and more mentally passive.

    Prior to competing athletes also need to be aware of or in
    tune to how they are thinking and feeling. The ability to
    think "good" thoughts about an upcoming performance cre-
    ates the positive feelings that will, at least, give an athlete a
    chance to succeed in competition. If an athlete is engaged in
    negative or counterproductive thinking, he or she can use
    thought stoppage and replacement strategies (discussed in
    Chapter 10) to focus or refocus on what they would like to
    have happen during competition (concentration goals and
    cues).

3. *Attuning to Coaches and Teammates.* Athletes can rely on their
    coach to help them stay on task and focused throughout the
    competition. Attuning to the coach helps the athlete to stay
    focused on the team's mission and goals, as well as provides
    the feedback and instruction necessary to achieve an effec-

tive performance. The coach is the athlete's lifeline in the midst of a dynamic performance environment.

Teammates can obviously be an excellent support system for athletes as they approach an upcoming performance. In team sports especially, athletes must attune to their teammates since their overall performance will be influenced by the quality of team interaction. Being aware of each team member's social, emotional, and performance needs, roles, and abilities can only serve to secure effective performances, particularly in highly interactive sports. Each team member needs to ask, "What can I do before, during, and after the competition to help my teammate(s) succeed?" Cooperation is the essence of effective competitive performances.

4. *Attuning to One's Performance Plan.* Lastly, athletes must attune to their personal performance plan. This action plan is essentially the ways and means for achieving effective athletic performance. It is an integration of the various individual performance behaviors that will, when executed with a great attitude and concentrated effort, result in a synergistic or flow performance. While athletes must have a flexible performance plan (developed in the mental preparation stage), it is imperative that they adhere to the plan during competition-the performance plan, comprising of concentration goals and cues, will keep them focused when they are in the middle of demanding and dynamic competitive situations.

Stage 2: The Performance Stage of Concentration

While the first stage of concentration requires that athletes remain mentally active and physically passive as they formulate decisions about their upcoming performance, the second stage of concentration requires them to perform while physically active and mentally passive. The first stage of concentration utilizes decision-making abilities and mental preparation strategies to set an athlete up for success in performance settings by creating an

Stage	Characteristics	Concentration Abilities/ Skills Required
2. Performance Stage	Automatic action	Alertness and trust Mental/physical routines
(Performance)	Body awareness	Attend to performance goals and cues
	Emotional control Internal/external cue recognition	
	Use of feedback (FB)	Selecting the appropriate modes of FB
	Refocusing	Distraction control

atmosphere for effective decision making in high-performance sport settings. The second stage of concentration (see Table 9.1 on page 146) is essentially concerned with the process of applying mentally and physically prepared responses that will help athletes realize their action potential through effective performance.

Stage 2 Concentration Skills

Stage 2 concentration abilities and skills include:
- generating and maintaining an internal focus on body awareness or the physical "feel" of performance;
- generating and maintaining an internal focus on the emotional "feel" of performance;
- the ability to act and react with confidence and trust previous and future decisions regarding performance plans and actions;
- the ability to recognize and react automatically to performance cues that trigger automated movement behaviors and motor programs; and
- the adaptability to perform effectively without being overly concerned about being perfect.

Body and Emotional Awareness

Body and emotional awareness are two critical elements in the performance of automated sport skills. When asked to describe an outstanding performance, athletes often state that it "felt" great. In the middle of a great performance, athlete's often state that they are "feeling" it. In this state the athlete is physically and emotionally aware of his or her every movement. This total awareness or absorption often results in an empowering sense of confidence during performances, in part due to physical and emotional control experienced by the athlete in the midst of performance.

Trusting Performance Plans and Actions

An athlete's ability to trust previously practiced and learned performance skills and abilities and to act and react without second-guessing his or her athletic instincts is at the heart of confident athletic performance (Moore & Stevenson, 1994). Successful and effective athletic performances result from a compilation and combination of automatic responses to performance demands that occur throughout an athletic contest.

Adaptability

The ability to adapt and be flexible throughout athletic performances is the final step in Stage 2 concentration since it reflects the athlete's use of feedback to enhance performance. The athlete must develop his or her sensitivity to both internal (body and emotional awareness) and external feedback (coaches' instructions, visual information from videotapes) to refine and adjust abilities and skills to meet the demands of a dynamic performance environment.

Mastering Stage 2 Concentration Skills

Creating Body Awareness

Body awareness can be initially developed through a variety of practice experiences that emphasize the "feel" of a movement or movement pattern. Many of these drills are aimed at eliminating or restricting the athlete's visual field so he or she is forced to use internal feedback such as body awareness to execute skills and movement patterns. Here are some drills that can be used to create and develop body awareness:

1. *Stork Stand.* Have the athlete stand on one foot, place his or her hands on hips, and place the free foot on the inside of the thigh of the support leg. Have the athlete hold that position for a count of ten. Now ask the athlete to close his or her eyes and hold the stork position for ten seconds. This will be quite challenging once the athlete's visual field is removed since he or she must concentrate on the "feel" of the activity to maintain balance.

2. *Blindfold Drills.* Have athletes perform skills blindfolded. For example, have basketball players shoot foul shots blindfolded or with their eyes closed once they site their target (the basket). This will encourage them to rely on the feel of their shot. This is why basketball players sometimes go through the motions of shooting a foul shot just prior to actually taking their shot.

3. *Visual Restriction Devices.* Basketball point guards, for instance, can practice dribbling the ball while at the same time preparing to pass to a teammate by wearing a device that fits below the nose and prevents them from watching the ball as they dribble. By restricting the player's downward vision, he or she must dribble by "feel." This is a good drill to help athletes master the demands of divided attention.

4. *Weighted Implements.* Have the athlete increase the weight of a performance implement to increase the "feel" of particular movements. A golfer can take practice swings while holding two clubs instead of one. Weighted baseball bats serve the same purpose, that is, to feel the muscle movement required to execute a specific skill or movement pattern.

5. *Slow Motion Movements.* Performing the desired movement patterns and sport skills in slow motion enable the athlete to gain a better "feel" for his or her motor movements.

6. *Removing Outcomes.* Have golfers, for example, remove the outcome of their shots by requiring them to hit into a net. Instead

of being outcome, target, or distance oriented, they will focus on the correct "feel" of their swing (i.e., rhythm, tempo, ball strike, follow-through). Basketball players can shoot against a wall and focus on their release, body alignment, follow-through. Discus throwers can gain a better "feel" for their very complex movements by throwing into a net from both a standing throw and with the spin that is required of a full throw.

7. *Weightless Movements.* Have athletes perform their skills in a weightless environment such as a swimming pool. Sport skills can be performed underwater on the pool bottom. Since the water also provides a gentle resistance to body movements, it also serves to develop an athlete's feel for certain movement patterns.

8. *Flexibility Exercises.* Incorporate body awareness into warm up routines by having the athlete focus on the movements of his or her body as flexibility or stretching exercises are conducted. Encourage athletes to actually feel the muscles in their bodies stretch as they perform various flexibility exercises.

Emotional Control

One of the most overlooked aspects of concentration is that of emotional readiness or intensity. Athletes who are overemotional about their performances have a tendency to overconcentrate or overfocus and perform poorly because they are uptight rather than loose and relaxed. Emotionally uptight and overfocused athletes miss performance cues and perform mechanically or out of sync—they essentially overplay at their sport.

To play as effectively as possible, athletes need to be aware of their level of excitability. Identifying and controlling the level of excitability is essential in creating the appropriate arousal level for each athlete's performance. The composure skill of arousal control is covered in depth in Chapter 11, but one of the best ways to help athletes recognize appropriate emotional levels for performance is to have them reflect on their best performances ever. Have them describe their emotional states and feeling before and during the competition. Ask them to associate a number with those particular feelings, 1 being low emotional intensity and 10 being the highest level. Athletes can then relate their most effective emotional preparation and performance experiences to the current performance situation. They can control their emotional intensity or excitement levels by recalling and matching past emotional levels with their current levels.

Automatic Responses and the Development of Trust

Ultimately effective athletes perform at their best when they stop trying to make things happen and merely let themselves automatically perform the physical skills they have practiced for so long. Trust is the key that unlocks an athlete's ability to "try less" on those important days. Releasing conscious control of the motor programs and movement patterns that will realize performance goals can only occur when an athlete frees him or herself from the fear of making mistakes (Moore & Stevenson, 1991). Trust in one's training, preparation, and talent are essential prerequisites for achieving effective athletic performances.

"Trust as a mental performance skill involves freeing oneself of expectations, fears, or other conscious activity and maintaining a clear and present focus necessary to attend to higher aspects of sports competition, such as cue utilization and strategy" (Moore & Stevenson, 1994, p. 3).

 Mental Key to Success

Trust is the letting go of conscious control, free of expectations, thinking, and fear.

Automatic athletic performances signify that an athlete is in a state of trust when performing, that is, he or she is free from the overthinking and overtrying that so often undermine effective execution. Athletes are not trusting their training, preparation, and talent when they commit one or more of the following errors-jamming, aiming, pressing, and/or controlling (Moore & Stevenson, 1994). These concentration errors are usually present when the athlete is mechanical rather than flowing when performing.

Jamming results from overthinking, which in turn creates a cognitive overload or paralysis by analysis. *Aiming* results from excessive concern for the target or outcome of one's performance. *Pressing* results from excessive tension created by an athlete trying to generate unnecessary force when performing. In essence, they are forcing it, or trying too hard as a result of perceived performance pressures. If we write out the word *pressure* and eliminate the last three letters of the word (pressure), we are pressing. Finally, *controlling* results when athletes exert excessive control over the sequence of their performance skills and movements, once again, trying to be too precise or exacting, only to find themselves frustrated and performing in a mechanical and ineffective way (Moore & Stevenson, 1994).

Moore and Stevenson (1994) recommend three concentration drills to help athletes prevent breakdowns in trust. Two of these drills, "feel" and "connect" drills, are aimed at heightening body awareness or helping athletes perform their skills without conscious thought. Specific "feel" drills were presented in a previous section, addressing the creation and development of body awareness.

The other type of drills, "quiet" drills, are used to eliminate judgmental and distracting thoughts that can interfere with fluid performances (Moore & Stevenson, 1994). These distraction-control drills enable the athlete to refocus on performance goals and cues as well as the "feel" of the desired performance. Thought stoppage and replacement skills, which will be described in Chapter 10, are a must for eliminating the distracting effects on negative self-talk. Concentration drills presented earlier in this chapter that teach an athlete to clear his or her mind when it becomes cluttered and overworked are essential. Mental toughness training, also described earlier, can create the mental calmness, serenity, and security that result from anticipation and preparation strategies that address the "what ifs" that often accompany precompetitive thoughts.

Creating Automatic Responses Using Mental/Physical Routines

The ability to perform with a clear and present focus that will result in automatic and effective athletic performances is achieved by combining mental and physical concentration routines. Cook's model of concentration, as described earlier in this chapter, provides the mental framework that compliments and supports the physical setup an athlete uses just prior to performing a skill. For example, a baseball player has an at-bat routine. He or she does the same thing each and every time before and between each pitch. This physical routine helps to relax the athlete and helps him or her to concentrate without being distracted. Figure 9.2 is an example of a baseball player's combined mental and physical routine.

In a similar way a golfer would use a mental/physical routine to strike a shot with a clear, quiet, confident, and focused mind (Figure 9.3).

OBSERVE
(in dugout and on deck)
Absorb the surroundings
Baserunners, signals, count, inning, defense, score

STRATEGY
(on deck)
What do I have to do to make it happen ?
Your pitch, place in the strike zone, target some in the field, tracking the pitch

---

ALL DECISIONS BUT ONE
HAVE BEEN MADE AT THIS POINT

SEE IT
Visualize putting the fat part of the bat on the ball
and hitting to a certain part of the field

FEEL IT
Feel the swing needed to produce
the visualized hit

SETUP AND TRUST IT
Take a breath, smooth the dirt, step into box, focus on the
pitcher, look at your focal point, swing at your pitch

Figure 9.2   Mental/Physical Routine for Hitting

OBSERVE

Absorb the surroundings

layout, trouble, wind, grass, break

STRATEGY

What do I have to do to make it happen ?

Choose the target, type of shot, the club

ALL DECISIONS HAVE BEEN MADE AT THIS POINT

SEE IT

Visualize the shot

FEEL IT

Feel the swing needed to produce
the visualized shot

SETUP AND TRUST IT

Use the cue word *Trust* to trigger the shot
Choose to *trust* your shot

Figure 9.3   Mental/Physical Routine for Golf

In both of these examples the athletes set themselves up for success by controlling how they shift their focus (taking in all information necessary to be effective and narrowing it down to one focus or trigger cue) and what specifically they will focus on (task relevant cues and information). Concentration creates control in performance settings and the feeling of being in control creates confidence. Distractions are eliminated and replaced by a mental and physical structure that, if adhered to, gives the athlete the best chance to achieve effective athletic performances.

Refocusing and Staying Alert

The most important mental Stage 2 concentration skill is the ability to refocus. The ability to focus counts in sport, but the ability to refocus counts most. Focusing and refocusing go hand in hand—athletes can't perform effectively in sport without acquiring and mastering both of these skills.

Many factors can break an athlete's concentration. Athletic competition has numerous potential distractions, unexpected happenings, and circumstances that require even the most experienced athlete to regroup and refocus to get his or her game plan back on track. Certainly mental toughness training can help athletes prepare for the physical, environmental, and emotional obstacles that can distract them before and during a performance. Besides mental toughness training, other refocusing strategies include the skill of *anchoring* and the ability to maintain alertness.

Anchoring requires that athletes select an object on themselves, a piece of equipment, or an object on the playing field or court that they can look at when they feel distracted or lose concentration. A baseball player can focus on the label on the glove when playing the field or on the label of the bat when hitting, others use a wristband as an anchor or look at a point behind home plate as an anchor. Focusing on an anchor in the midst of confusing or distracting circumstances can remind an athlete of his or her performance goals and cues, and performance plan. Anchors serve as triggers to help athletes focus once again on what they would like to do (skills) and how they "would like to make it happen" (strategy) in certain situations. They can control these aspects of their performance (skills and strategy) when they lack focus and are feeling out of control.

Maintaining alertness or "mental readiness" so that an athlete can both recognize and react to performance cues is another key mental skill. Complete concentration or total concentration involve three steps: (1) knowing what to do in performance settings (performance behaviors, goals, and cues); (2) recognizing the cues that will trigger the appropriate skills and movements (cue recognition); and (3) knowing when to employ skills and movements (cue utilization). This process takes a tremendous amount of mental discipline to master because athletic contests include a great deal of monotony (repetition) and inactivity (time between plays, halftime) that dull the ability to sustain concentration. Many players can get caught "napping" or "sleeping" because they weren't paying attention, and so we often hear coaches give the "heads up" call in crucial game situations—they want to make sure their players are paying attention and are mentally and physically ready.

Athletes can maintain their alertness by keeping their minds active during the course of the athletic contest. Mentally interacting with the flow and plays of a game can enhance performance effectiveness. For example, between plays an outfielder in baseball can review the tendencies of the batter in an effort to anticipate where a ball may be hit or can review cutoff plays if a ball is hit in the gap or over his or her head. In basketball, players who are not in the game can watch opposing players and prepare defensive and offensive strategies that they will use once they are substituted into the game (many players enter the game physically and are still on the bench mentally). In track, distance runners must be aware of opponent strategies, so they won't be caught off guard by a sudden surge by an opponent and lose ground in the critical part of a race.

Although there may not be a lot of time between plays in a game, there is always the opportunity to relax. Trying to concentrate every second of the game, contest, or event can only lead to overconcentrating, which is characterized by increased muscle tension and both mental and physical fatigue. A deep breath or two can serve to physically and mentally help an athlete to relax before refocusing on the task at hand.

Similarly, sometimes an athlete should divert his or her attention in order to relax. Letting one's mind wander in a *purposeful* way can provide a needed break from the repetition and ritual of athletic contests. Repetition and ritual can lead to boredom, and boredom is a distraction that can lead to concentration-related performance errors. If an athlete employs "mind wandering" as a relaxation strategy it is important that he or she use it in a structured way and with a purpose. Between plays an athlete may allow his or her mind to wander to a specific place or thought that is unrelated to the game (e.g., a billboard, trees beyond the outfield fence, a building, the flag, positive and refreshing mental images or thoughts) for a brief time and then return his or her focus once again to the task at hand.

One of the best ways to maintain an athlete's alertness during training and performances is to provide him or her with feedback and results after repetitive trials. Coaches can give information feedback that will be helpful for the next play or help the athlete keep focused on important cues. This encourages the athlete to keep mentally active as he or she awaits feedback from the coach or teammates. Athletes can refine and adjust their performances throughout the course of an athletic contest by learning to use self-generated feedback as they analyze the outcomes and results of their performances from play to play.

Using Feedback to Enhance Concentration

Stage 1 concentration skills require the use of feedforward, such as mental rehearsal, mental routines, and mental toughness training, to set an athlete up for success. Stage 2 concentration skills require the athlete to use feedback in a timely manner to maintain and sharpen their performance focus.

Chapter 7 presented the concepts and applications of both feedforward and feedback as learning and performance techniques that can enhance the learning and performance of motor skills. Figure 9.4 takes the concept of feedback a step further by outlining the relationship between concentration and the various types, modes, and timing of feedback components that are available to coaches and athletes during competition.

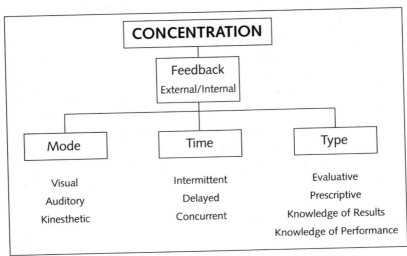

Figure 9.4   Concentration and Feedback

Effective concentration strategies are enhanced by the athlete's ability to recognize and utilize feedback. Feedback (FB) or information about one's performance can come from coaches or teammates, videotaped performances, (external FB) or self-analysis by the athlete (internal FB). Furthermore, athletes and coaches need to be aware of how they can best receive FB (mode). Visual learners prefer to be shown what they did and what they need to do to improve or fix their performance—by viewing demonstrations of the sport skill or technique performed correctly or by using visualization techniques to understand or image how they would like to perform. Other athletes are auditory learners and like to have skills verbally explained to them—they are from the "listen, learn, and perform" school of sport skill acquisition. Still others prefer to use kinesthetic FB to "get the feel" of how the sport skill is to be performed. Most athletes can learn in all three modes but have one primary mode that helps them concentrate best.

Athletes also need to be aware of the best time for them to receive FB. For example, a baseball player may want feedback after an entire at bat (delayed FB), after every pitch (intermittent FB), or while they are batting—FB in the form of cue words yelled by a coach (concurrent FB). One or all of these FB delivery methods can provide timely information to an athlete and help him or her to gain a sharper focus or more effective level of concentration.

Finally coaches and athletes need to be aware of the type of FB that works best for them. Knowing how effective one has been in performance (evaluative FB) helps an athlete to either establish an improvement baseline or simply tells him or her how effective a particular performance has been. Athletes can self-evaluate their performance and then seek out the coach's evaluation to attain more realistic and objective FB. Some athletes like to use feedforward information (performance goals and cues) to gain direction or give themselves something to focus on before a game or immediately prior to a play (prescriptive FB).

The two types of FB that are most valuable to an athlete are knowledge of results and knowledge of performance. These types of FB enable athletes to analyze the outcomes of their performances, detect errors in their performance techniques and strategies, and make corrections. The ability to detect and correct errors is a learned attribute of the best athletic performers. Using FB to adjust, adapt, and change patterns that are not working in performance settings requires a great deal of athletic intelligence and concentration.

Stage 3: The Evaluation Stage

Stages	Characteristics	Concentration Abilities/ Skills Required
3. Evaluation Stage	Constructive evaluation	Improvement strategies based on performance
(Post-performance)		Feedback

After performing, athletes can improve their performance effectiveness by seeking constructive evaluation (Orlick, 1996). Post-competitive evaluations provide the feedback necessary to help athletes to improve their performance effectiveness, especially regarding their ability to focus before and during competition (Stages 1 and 2 of the concentration model).

Orlick (2000) has developed a Focus Control Rating Scale (see pages 180–181) that can be helpful in assessing an athlete's ability to manage and control his or her emotions, confidence, ability to refocus or maintain focus, and ability to focus in the present. The focus control rating scale can be an integral part of an athlete's post-competitive routine and can provide athletes and coaches with important self-evaluative feedback regarding the implementation of concentration skills during competition.

Athletes who excel rate themselves higher on the focus control scale than less accomplished athletes. They tend to have total scores of 80 or above on the focus control scale or average scores of 4 for individual items (Orlick, 2000).

Item 1 helps the athlete evaluate his or her ability to totally focus. Items 2–4 help the performer evaluate his or her ability to refocus both in practice and during competition. Refocusing skills and strategies have been described earlier in this chapter.

Item 5 evaluates the athlete's confidence level, and confidence-building strategies are presented in the next chapter. Item 6 addresses the athlete's ability to take feedback in a constructive way. Athletes with low self-confidence may tend to take criticism personally and may not be able to process performance improvement information. Items 7 and 8 give the athlete a read on how he or she responds to distractions in the performance setting. Response to distractions, unexpected happenings, and adversity is directly related to motivation levels.

Items 9 and 10 evaluate the athlete's ability to remain focused in the present and regain a present focus when distracted by errors. Once again the ability to refocus by viewing mistakes as feedback that is needed to be more effective and to improve performance is a learned characteristic of effective athletic performers.

Peak Performance Exercise 9.1

Focus Control Rating Scale
(adapted from Orlick, 2000, pp. 81–82)

Instructions: The following self-assessment scale is based on qualities that leading coaches and athletes around the world use to describe the kind of self-control that separates the good player from the great player. A rating of 10 means that the statement is completely true, and a rating of 1 means that it is completely false, and rating of 5 means that it is sometimes true and sometimes false.

Rate yourself on each item. Then go back and look at your strengths as well as the areas in which you need to improve.

1. I get so absorbed in my performance (or experiences) that everything else disappears.

    1　　2　　3　　4　　5　　6　　7　　8　　9　　10
    never　　　　　　　　　　　　　　　　　　　always

2. I can direct or redirect my focus so that it does me the greatest
    good, even if I become nervous or uptight in performance situa-
    tions.

    1   2   3   4   5   6   7   8   9   10
    never   always

3. I maintain or quickly regain a high-quality focus in practice or
    preparation sessions.

    1   2   3   4   5   6   7   8   9   10
    never   always

4. I maintain or quickly regain a high-quality focus control in per-
    formances or competitions.

    1   2   3   4   5   6   7   8   9   10
    never   always

5. I have a strong inner confidence or inner strength, a feeling that I
    can do anything I put my mind to.

    1   2   3   4   5   6   7   8   9   10
    never   always

6. I learn from criticism and take it as an opportunity to improve.

    1   2   3   4   5   6   7   8   9   10
    never   always

7. I handle bad calls or situations that go against me by getting right
    back on a positive path.

    1   2   3   4   5   6   7   8   9   10
    never   always

8. I can stay motivated when behind or down in points.

    1   2   3   4   5   6   7   8   9   10
    never   always

9. I maintain my performance focus totally in the present, living in the here and now (for example, one shot, one step, one moment at a time).

    1   2   3   4   5   6   7   8   9   10
    never   always

10. I can quickly regain my best-performance focus even after an error or setback.

    1   2   3   4   5   6   7   8   9   10
    never   always

Total Focus Control Score_____

10

Confidence
The Ultimate Attitude in Sport

Although the concept or phenomenon of confidence is described in a variety of ways, it is perhaps most often explained as an individual's feeling that he or she can successfully accomplish a particular task. An "I can" attitude is an essential mental attribute for an athlete. Confidence must be integrated into an athlete's performance if successful competitive efforts are to be realized.

The following quote by professional boxer Mike Tyson, after he lost his first match, provides a poignant, realistic, and revealing definition of confidence:

> I never lost my confidence, even after Tokyo. . . . A lot of people would love to see that happen—to see this cocky, arrogant, successful black kid who's always talking about how he can kill anybody, beat anybody, all of a sudden say, yeah, well I lost to a better man. Bull! I'm the best. . . . (Putnam, 1990, p. 37)

To be a confident athlete can carry with it many negative labels that result from the social misperception of what being confident actually means. Therefore a confident athlete may be negatively labeled as cocky and arrogant or as someone who feels he or she is more important than other people, particularly opponents. The fact of the matter is that to succeed in sport it is essential that you think and feel you are better at your sport than your opponent. But feeling that you are *better* at your sport than your opponent does not mean that you are more important than your opponents or anyone else, or bigger than what sport is about (Rotella, 1990c). Unfortunately many athletes, as in the case of Mike Tyson, never learn this distinction; they play hard but do not play fair, or they live hard but do not live within society's laws.

In essence it is socially desirable but not socially acceptable to be confident in our society, which is why the athlete who understands confidence soon learns "to be outstanding but not to stand out." For this reason most enduring confident athletes learn to adopt an attitude of quiet confidence as they competently and consistently meet challenges in the athletic arena. These athletes prefer to speak through their actions and deeds because their words are often misunderstood, mostly by persons who are themselves lacking in confidence.

Controlling Confidence vs. Building Confidence

If we are to understand the concept of confidence, we must understand the relationship of self-esteem to self-confidence. Self-esteem or self-worth is at the core of self-confidence. An athlete's feelings of self-worth regarding his or her abilities have a significant influence on the consistent demonstration of confidence and subsequently on performance.

We need to recognize the difference between controlling the confidence levels of athletes and building the confidence level of athletes. Controlling confidence or an "outside-in" orientation to confidence is achieved through the perpetuation of low self-

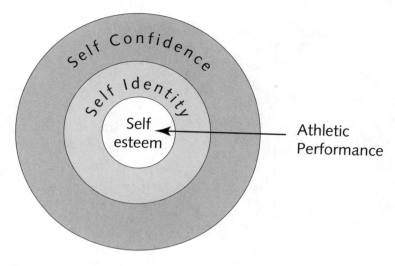

Figure 10.1   An :Outside-In" Approach to Confidence

esteem and comparative self-worth as well as through such motivational techniques as fear and guilt (Figure 10.1). Although a very effective and commonly used technique in athletics, it is not recommended because it serves only to perpetuate low self-esteem among athletes. This technique is effective because it makes athletes feel that no matter how well they perform they are not quite good enough and are only as good as their last or next performance. If they perform poorly, they can't wait to redeem themselves, and if they perform well, they are relieved but apprehensive about future performances. Their feelings of self-worth depend upon their performance effectiveness and the evaluations of others—their friends, their teammates, their parents, and most importantly, their coach.

Building confidence involves cultivating an "inside-out" performance approach, which begins with feeling good about one's self and ends with feeling good about one's self irrespective of outcomes (Figure 10.2). This is not to say that the athlete isn't disappointed with an unsuccessful or ineffective performance. In the inside-out approach the athlete retains his or her feelings of competence and looks forward to performing again, since future performances are viewed as self-enhancing rather than self-

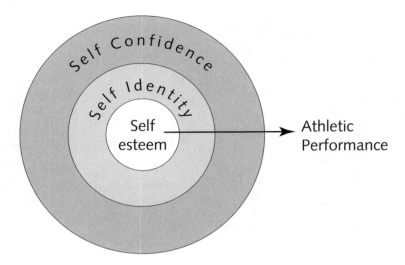

Figure 10.2 An "Inside-Out" Approach to Confidence Building

threatening. Inside-out oriented athletes learn to accept responsibility for their performances, play to their strengths, and view their weaknesses as challenges while making no excuses for their mistakes or poor performances.

Being Human in Sport

Inside-out oriented athletes view their mistakes as feedback, which they can utilize to improve themselves and their abilities as an athlete. In contrast, outside-in oriented athletes take their mistakes and failures personally, thus feeling worthless about themselves because they fail to realize that sport involves games of mistakes. The critical realization for athletes is that their ultimate ability to perform effectively in sport is not determined by their mistakes but how they perform after making a mistake.

Athletes with low self-confidence dwell on their mistakes and carry their negative emotional impact with them to their next performance effort. On the other hand, self-confident athletes realize that they are human, anticipate making a minimum of mistakes, vow not to repeat their mistakes, and move on emotionally to the next challenge.

Comparing Ourselves to Others

Athletes can perpetuate low self-esteem and guilt by constantly comparing themselves to other athletes and teams. This is only natural since sport has a built in comparison mechanism that is magnified by the media and fans. Athletes can be easily misled to focus on a "would have, should have, could have, didn't" mentality—a focus that can lead only to frustration and feelings of incompetence and worthlessness.

Yes, athletes do compete against one another, and the athlete who is the best on that particular day usually wins the competition, but it is wrong to accept the idea that the "best *person* won" (McGuire, 1998). We are all at our best when we are giving our best, and even though one person wins over another, everyone is to be equally valued and respected for their performance efforts as well as their willingness to "put it all on the line" (McGuire, 1996 a, b). Most important in this process is self-respect for one's efforts and preparation since this is the first step to developing self-confidence.

A former Olympic track and field athlete gave this response when asked what advice he would have for young athletes who aspire to be Olympians:

I would say don't compare yourself to anyone else. Compare yourself to yourself. Look deep within yourself and always know that every time you go out on the track, if you run to the best of your ability, look in the mirror after you get through running and say, "I ran the best that I can run." Be happy and satisfied with that and go on about your business, because I think a lot of times we put pressure on ourselves that we shouldn't put on ourselves. Don't put pressure on yourself that you wouldn't want someone else to put on you. . . . Compare yourself to yourself. Do the best that you can do. . . . when you go to the meets, if you do what it took to get you to the meet, you'll do fine. (Vernacchia, McGuire, Reardon & Templin, 2000, p. 19)

Being Normal vs. Being Extraordinary

The view of an athlete's performance depends on the viewer. An athlete's performance may be viewed as exceptional or extraordinary by others (i.e., fans, parents, coaches, teammates, media), but the athlete usually views the same performance as being normal. The performance merely reflects what the athlete normally can do as a result of his or her training and experience.

The point here is that people who are average or below average athletically can't understand or really relate to excellent athletic performances, and so they are soon in awe of anyone who can perform at a very high level. These people tend to make a successful athlete feel self-conscious with his or her normal but very effective athletic skills and prowess. Attention, and in some cases, adulation, tends to set the successful athlete apart from peers and can foster the misperception on the part of the athlete that his or her past performances were extraordinary. It is normal for great athletes who are ordinary to do extraordinary things.

The danger is that exceptional athletes may relinquish their confidence because they feel uncomfortable with the attention they receive because of their athletic prowess. They would rather be average because being their normal selves athletically draws too much attention and adulation and creates on the part of the athlete with low self-esteem a fear of success or a reluctance to perform effectively in order to avoid the limelight that accompanies successful athletic performances.

The coach and sport psychology consultant can influence the emerging exceptional athlete to understand this component of confidence, so that the athlete doesn't unknowingly sabotage his or her performances because of feeling uncomfortable with success.

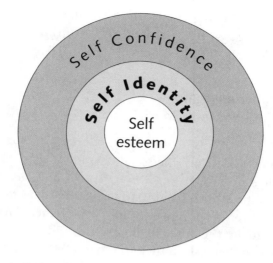

Figure 10.3   Self-Identity

Acting Confident vs. Being Confident

Self-identity resides halfway between self-esteem and self-confidence—see Figure 10.3. Athletes who choose the outside-in approach to performance and confidence are acutely aware of the mannerisms of a confident individual and subsequently feel that if they can act confident then they will be confident. This phenomenon is best demonstrated in the verbal behaviors of the many professional boxers who chose to imitate the legendary Muhammad Ali by adopting his pet phrase, "I am the greatest." This sounds good, but as many boxers who were searching for confidence by employing this phrase found out, it doesn't or didn't work in the ring.

Recall again the statement by Mike Tyson earlier in this chapter. The last few words, "I'm the best," reflect an athlete who truly believes in his abilities and talent.

Athletes who lack confidence identify with someone else's accomplishments and abilities rather than taking pride in their own past accomplishments and present abilities. They believe they can become ready by acting confident, and down deep they really aren't confident. These athletes believe in everyone else's abilities but their own. They tend to become coach dependent because self-motivation is impossible.

Tough-mindedness and Tender-mindedness in Sport

Early studies of successful athletes by sport psychologists showed that the most discerning personality trait of these athletes was tough-mindedness (Ogilvie, 1968). Tough-mindedness can be described as the athlete's ability to take criticism as feedback that can be employed to improve future performances. Tough-mindedness is actually the outer shell of self-confidence (Figure 10.4).

Tender-mindedness on the other hand refers to a tendency to take criticism personally, in the sense that the athlete resists processing performance feedback that would enable him or her to improve. The tender-minded athlete is often labeled a quitter since the inability to accept criticism or feedback constructively results in alienation toward coaches and continued ineffective performances. Tender-minded athletes are reluctant to make changes or corrections in their training or performance behaviors because they feel that the feedback is about them as well as about their skills and strategies. Tender-minded athletes react to their mistakes with self-doubt and worry, mistrust their previously formulated performance strategies and physical skills, and feel helpless or out of control in performance situations.

Eventually tender-minded athletes or "thin-skinned" athletes are eliminated or rendered ineffective in the athletic world, whereas "thick-skinned" or tough-minded athletes continue to flourish with the help of performance feedback from coaches. Essentially this issue is about being coachable as much as it is about coaching.

As stated before, self-confident athletes realize that they are human and will make mistakes in performance settings. They realize that sports are games of mistakes. Coaches can cultivate this attitude and mind-set by making athletes aware that being perfect in sport is an unrealistic expectation. In most cases you have to "win ugly" to be successful in sport.

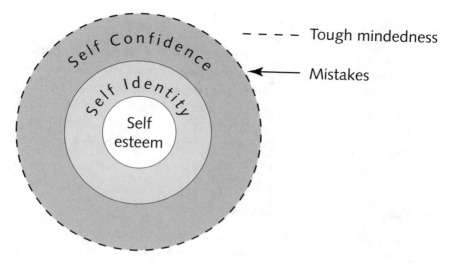

Figure 10.4   Tough-mindedness

If mistakes are made, focus on error correction rather than dwelling on past failures. Athletes must learn from mistakes, make changes, adapt, and focus on present performance behaviors or strategies that will increase the probability of future success in sport.

Self-Conscious vs. Unconscious in Sport

To perform well, athletes must learn to release themselves from the self-criticism they use daily in practice situations. We are very judgmental and critical of ourselves in practice, which is great for practice because self-evaluation and analysis lead to improvement. The problem is that too many athletes carry their practice mind-set into the game. They are very self-conscious of their every move and action, and they fail because they continue to practice when they are in the game.

A good example of this phenomenon is reflected in the following quote by professional golfer Andrew McGee after shooting a course record 28 on the front nine and a 38 on the back nine during the first round of the 1991 Los Angeles Open: "You are not thinking when you shoot 28, but when you shoot 38 . . . My goal was to be unconscious" (Quote, 1991).

Being unconscious while performing is the most important mental concept coaches can cultivate in their athletes. The athlete must learn to trust his or her preparation, skills, and feelings. Sport psychologists refer to this aspect of athletic performance as "winning the battle within," that is, the battle between thinking and feeling—after a successful performance an athlete will say "It felt great" not "It thought great."

Protecting the Athlete's Self-Esteem

Most athletes, particularly the young and developing athlete, may not have the experience and maturity necessary to completely understand many of the confidence-related concepts discussed in this chapter. For this reason the coach's role is to protect the athlete's self-esteem as he or she develops a mind-set for confidence as a result of the successes and failures of athletic competition.

Coaches can take the pressure off their athletes by accepting the responsibility for poor performances, especially when mistakes or failures occur in crucial situations. A simple, "that's OK, it was my fault" attitude on the coach's part will ease the traumatic emotional burden of a disappointing or poor performance. The key is to help the athlete learn from mistakes, rather than dwell on them and take them personally.

The coach can help the athlete focus on the trust they both have in the athlete's skills, abilities, and talents. When self-esteem and self-confidence are low, and an athlete is in a slump, it is often because talent is present but trust is lacking (Rotella, 1990d).

Allowing Athletes to Become Self-Confident

Coaches who truly understand confidence-building understand what is meant by the saying, "A watched pot never boils" as it pertains to sport. In the final analysis the coach must allow their athletes to develop, become, and emerge as self-confident individuals.

To illustrate this point let's review a coach's and athlete's reaction during a confidence-related situation, which this writer actually witnessed. Several years ago, our university basketball team was playing its chief rival in a very close and thrilling game. Our team was down one point in the final minute of the game, and the opposing team had the ball with only 54 seconds left in the game. What strategy would you employ if you were the opposing coach? Would you slow down and control play, run down the clock and wait for a good shot with approximately 10 seconds left in the game? Or would you allow the team to play according to what they felt was the best play to make?

Here's the newspaper account of what actually happened:

> From deep along the left baseline—a spot from which he had drilled two shots—the senior let fly with a 3-point bomb even though 26 seconds remained on the shot clock. . . . That mattered little when the ball swished through the net. . . . "I was hot and it's my favorite place to shoot. . . . I really didn't even think about it. If I'd thought about it, I probably wouldn't have shot. (Lee, 1991, p. D1)

When asked about the athlete's decision, his coach had a quick response: "No comment," he said, offering an ever-so-sly grin. "I admire his confidence if not his intelligence. He's the player of the game in my book" (Lee, 1991, p. D1).

This scenario is played out many times on many basketball courts each year, but in this case the player had a truly confident response because he was in an unconscious frame of mind in which he trusted his talents. The player felt in control of the situation and sure of himself while at the same time not being intimidated by the possible negative consequences of his actions.

Even more interesting is the fact that the same player had missed all nine of his shots in a losing team effort during the last game he had played. Fortunately his coach trusted him enough to allow him to trust in himself.

Peak Performance Exercise 10.1

Assessing Your Confidence

On a scale of 1(low)-10(high), rate your confidence level first in sport, and second, in everyday life. List , explain, and justify all the reasons you have to believe in and trust yourself. Think back to your greatest moments in sport and describe how you were thinking and feeling on days prior to competition. Think of your everyday life activities, are you just as confident in yourself as a person as you are in yourself as an athlete? Why? Why not? Compare and contrast those thoughts and feelings to your worst days in competition or in life. List the most confidence-enhancing statements that have been made to you by those around you-coaches, friends, teammates, teachers, and family. List the most confidence-enhancing statements you recall making to yourself. How do you handle destructive statements by others and yourself regarding your confidence and ability to achieve your goals both in sport and life? Are your sport confidence and life confidence one and the same or do your scores differ? Does your confidence as a person affect your athletic performance and vice versa? (Adapted from Rotella, 1990a).

The best coaches understand this aspect of confidence-building—they let their athletes play their game. Al Hairston, a very successful basketball coach at Garfield High School in Seattle, Washington (267–61), made the following statement when asked about the success of one his teams: "I just stayed out of the way and let them go undefeated" (Kugiya, 1991, p. C11).

Increasing Self-Confidence

After assessing their confidence levels, athletes should spend some time determining whether they need to become more confident by imaging and describing the most confident person they know. They should be imaging and describing themselves. If not, they may need some active confidence-increasing measures.

In addition to understanding confidence as both a social and athletic attribute that will enhance athletic performance, aspiring effective performers must understand and implement the following principles to increase self-confidence:

1. Confidence = Control × Competence × Consistency

2. Confidence requires support

3. Confidence is a learned attribute

4. Confident athletes focus on success

5. Confident athletes have a plan of action

Confidence = Control × Competence × Consistency

Confident athletes soon learn that a lot of things will happen to them and around them that they can't control, but they can control how they respond to what happens to them and around them. For this reason confident athletes learn to focus on what they can control in each and every performance setting and situation. This ability or *response-ability* results from a conscious choice, known as willpower, that an athlete makes to stay within his or her circle of control (Figure 10.5).

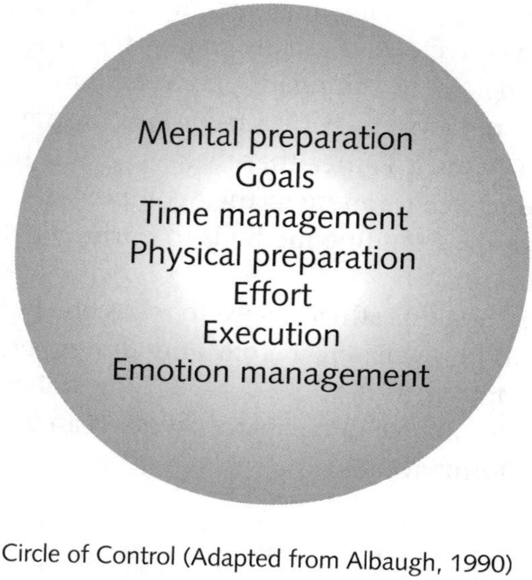

Mental preparation
Goals
Time management
Physical preparation
Effort
Execution
Emotion management

Figure 10.5   Circle of Control (Adapted from Albaugh, 1990)

While athletes can't control the things that are outside their circle of control such as the weather, quality of facilities and equipment, officiating, and crowds, they can choose to maximize the control they can exert by focusing on their physical, mental, and emotional attributes and skills. We will revisit this issue in the following chapter on composure.

Mastery of physical and mental skills through quality training and practice is the first step to increase an athlete's feelings of competency. Mastery of skills as a result of conscientious preparation provides reassurance for any athlete who is about to test his or her skills in athletic competition. Preparation and self-improvement go hand in hand and by focusing on the progress he or she has made from day to day, week to week, month to month, and year to year, an athlete can create a feeling not only of competence but of consistency. Consistency under the pressure of performance situations is the mark of a confident, competent, and well-trained athletic performer. At the heart of establishing competence and consistency is the commitment that an athlete makes to believing in his or her preparation. There are no right or wrong preparation methods (training techniques, drills, conditioning practices, etc.); there are only different methods, and athletes must choose to believe in *their* method of preparation or training (Cook, 1996b).

Athletes who are lacking in confidence are not quite sure they have prepared correctly and usually change their methods of performing just before or during the competition. They tend to always be searching for the perfect technique or strategy that will make them a winner. Rather than believing and trusting their preparation they believe more in their competitor's method and readily change their training methods to mirror what their competitors are doing.

In the final analysis athletes need to focus on effort and trusting their skills immediately before and during performances. Doubt and worry created by second-guessing training methods and performance preparation can only weaken an athlete's confidence and performance resolve.

Confidence Requires Support

Confident athletes need social support to maintain their confidence. Being confident in a vacuum does little to enhance athletic performance. The support of teammates, coaches, and administrators is an extremely important and often overlooked advocacy for an athlete. External support such as social support and resource support are instrumental in helping an athlete reach his or her goals and athletic dream, and this is especially true in team sports.

Athletes whose individual performances are singled out by the media and fans often overlook and take for granted the people in the background who have contributed to their moment in the spotlight. Confident athletes believe in sharing the spotlight with all those who have made their success possible. Sharing the glory and spotlight of successful performances will ensure continued support from their family, coaches, teachers, teammates, and athletic administrators.

Confident athletes are also very good at recruiting internal support for their training and performance efforts. Self-support composed of positive self-talk and affirmations (Cook, 1996b) is a necessary element of confidence building because "what you say to yourself is what you get."

Confidence building or increasing one's feeling of competency, control, and consistency can be enhanced by using positive self-talk and restraining from engaging in negative self-talk. Self-talk is statements we make to ourselves about ourselves in the privacy of our own minds. Self-talk can be used to enhance performance by helping athletes: to focus in the present; to avoid dwelling on mistakes and failures; to raise self-esteem; to improve motor skill acquisition; to change bad habits; to maintain concentration; to create or change an athlete's mood (Zinsser, Bunker, & Williams, 2001).

Affirmations and positive self-talk can help athletes focus on their strengths rather than their weaknesses as they approach competitive challenges. Focusing on weaknesses just prior to performing can only create doubt, fear, and worry in an athlete's mind. For this reason self-supportive statements such as "I'm a great defender" or "I am relaxed and confident" or "I feel strong, powerful, and in control" are a large part of a confident athlete's inner vocabulary.

Negative thoughts can soon escalate into attitudes that predispose an athlete to failure. Common negative self-talk such as "I hope I do well" leads to doubt and worry. Likewise, negative self-talk such as "I have to do well" can lead to stress and anxiety. Positive self-talk, such as "I'm looking forward to doing well" or "I can do well" reflect and reaffirm an athlete's confidence in his or her skills (Vernacchia, 1996b).

This does not mean that an athlete will not experience negative thoughts or engage in negative thinking in the weeks, days, hours, minutes, and moments prior to performing. The mental trick here is not to entertain these negative thoughts by dwelling on them, but instead to make the choice to interrupt and replace negative thoughts with positive thoughts and affirmations. Practice and master the following thought stoppage and replacement techniques (Vernacchia, 1996b):

1. *Recognize negative thinking and decide to think positive.* Athletes need to be aware that they are thinking negatively and that they can choose not to think this way. Negative thoughts are a natural part of athletic performance, but the athlete can dispel such thoughts and refocus his or her thoughts on a successful performance.

2. *Physically and/or visually and/or verbally interrupt negative thoughts.* Athletes can interrupt and stop negative thoughts by clapping their hands sharply, snapping their fingers, or firmly squeezing the forefinger and thumb together. Some athletes wear a rubber band on their wrist and snap it against their wrist once a negative thought enters their mind. Visually oriented athletes can picture a "STOP" sign or perhaps just the word "STOP" in their mind's eye. Auditory oriented athletes can just say the word "STOP" out loud in a low voice that only they can hear. These and other

physical, visual, and verbal thought stoppers should be used as soon as an athlete becomes aware of counterproductive thinking.

3. *Replace negative thoughts with positive thoughts.* The final step of this process requires the athlete to positively focus his or her thoughts on the task at hand. "I am relaxed, energized, and ready to perform effectively today" is a positive replacement for thoughts of worry, doubt, and anxiety.

Confidence is a Learned Attribute

Successful athletes look forward to displaying their talents in competitive settings but that wasn't always so. When children first begin in sport, they know little about it except that they love to play and that it is fun to be with their friends. Once they enter the world of organized sport and more demands are placed on them, they begin to experience feelings of doubt, fear, and worry as they wonder if they will make the team, get to play, not strike out, please their parents and coaches, make a mistake, or look stupid in front of their friends.

Feelings generated by doubt, fear, and worry are natural when a child begins in sport but soon dissipate as they learn more about their sport, become more skillful, and gain more competitive experience. They become more confident, less self-conscious, and more effective as a result of good coaching and good thinking.

While this type of coaching and mentoring for developing athletes is desirable it isn't always the case. Athletes can learn to fear sport and the outcome of their performances because they are taught and reminded to focus on what can go wrong rather than what can go right. They become afraid to fail or afraid to become successful and tend to avoid rather embrace the sport experience. Young athletes can soon learn to second-guess their decisions and instincts regarding how they play their sport. This hesitation to trust their preparation and talent undermines their confidence.

Mental Key to Success

Confidence is a learned attribute of effective athletes.

Confidence is learned from coaches, family, and teammates, all of whom strive to teach developing athletes to be human, practice hard, play fair, learn from their mistakes, always give their best effort, and to ultimately feel good about their performance and themselves regardless of whether they won or lost.

Confident Athletes Focus on Success

As stated in Chapter 5: Visualization—"Successful athletes see what they would like to have happen, and unsuccessful athletes see what they don't want to have happen." Athletes can picture themselves at any point on the confidence continuum:

Less Confident   Confident

◄───►

Fear, Doubt, Worry   Trust

Athletes can choose to be confident by flooding their minds with thoughts and images of what can go right with their performances, by trusting their talent and training, and by recognizing that they are as prepared for the challenges of competition as is humanly possible. The power of visualization to enhance athletic performance (see Chapter 5) is one of the most effective confidence-building techniques available to athletes who desire to increase their levels of confidence. Athletes can dwell on what they would like to do by combining sound physical preparation with positive self-talk and visualization, which will put them well on the way to becoming confident performers.

Take, for example, the case of Mike Powell, the track and field athlete who broke the 23-year-old long jump world record by jumping 29'4½" at the 1991 World Track and Field Championships. Powell had been pursuing this record throughout his career and talked about how he walked through his images of success in his own home :

> . . . By the time I got to the dining room I would jump, and I would visualize myself breaking the world record. . . . I could actually feel it, feel the rush in my head. I've imagined that moment in my living room a hundred times. (Newman, 1991, pp. 36–37)

Once he actually broke the record, he reflected on the need for persistent positive visualization:

> I've been dreaming about this for two years, and when I'd tell people they would laugh in my face. . . . Nobody gave me credit. So not to say "in your face". . . . but in your face. (Newman, 1991, p. 37)

Even more revealing about Powell's confident attitude was the way he signed pre-meet autographs with the figure "8.95 meters," which translates to 29'4½", the exact distance he jumped (Moore, 1991). Who knows, perhaps he limited himself and it would have been more appropriate to sign "8.95 meters or better."

Confident Athletes Have a Plan of Action

Confident athletes have an achievement plan for attaining success—they achieve success by design and not by chance. An action plan for success is a blueprint of the steps, ways, and means for attaining performance goals and realizing athletic dreams (Cook, 1996b).

Goal attainment strategies and techniques have been covered in depth in a Chapter 6. It is worth mentioning again that goal attainment plans are only as effective as the willingness of the athlete to act or "get busy" making the plan a reality. Once an athlete realizes that he or she has the aptitude and passion to pursue and achieve athletic excellence, he or she must *plan* to reach this goal. In effect the athlete must find a coach, practice, perform, evaluate performances, and commit to improving, maintaining, and refining his or her performance effectiveness.

An action plan for athletic success involves the following phases:

Learn ⟶ Expect ⟶ Practice ⟶ Perform ⟶ Evaluate

Athletes should strive to be "students" of their sport by placing themselves under the guidance of a qualified and competent coach and by learning as much about their sport that they possibly can. Coaches are the teachers of sport, and the athlete meets sport at the coach (McGuire, 1996a,b). The coach possesses the knowledge of sport that the aspiring athlete needs to improve his or her athletic ability. The coach becomes the athlete's mentor, the one who monitors and regulates the athlete's development as he or she experiences the journey of achieving athletic excellence. The coach can help formulate and ultimately make or break the athlete's action plan for achieving athletic excellence.

While athletes engage in demanding practice sessions to learn and master athletic skills and performance strategies, they must realize that learning is an invisible process that is confined to the practice environment. To see what one has learned, athletes need to display their skills in performance settings. Athletes and coaches have certain reasonable expectations regarding how they will perform skills. These expectations depend on the athletes' skill level and experience and are the reason why coaches place athletes in certain situations and assign them certain tasks or roles. Once the athletes have performed, the effectiveness of their skills is evaluated, so that they can be improved, refined, or maintained as a result of further practice and competitive experience.

11

Composure
Creating and Accessing the Emotional Energy for Success

In practice many athletes are calm, focused, and relaxed, but in the performance setting they find themselves uncertain, distracted, and tense. The reason for this type of ineffective performance response is that athletic performances occur in an emotional climate that reflects the drama of sport. Outcomes are uncertain in an emotionally distracting environment of media attention, rivalries, and intense competition. Highly effective athletic performers learn to keep their composure, that is, to manage their emotional responses; when it is time to deliver their best performance—they seem to flourish rather than perish in the performance setting.

Part of the emotional response during performance lies in the way we are socialized, that is, what we are taught as we grow up. Emotionality differs by culture—some children are raised to express themselves with emotion while others learn to hide their emotions because expressing them is viewed as a sign of weakness and lack of self-control. Depending on how an athlete is raised, emotion can energize or diffuse performance.

Sport emotion is a derivative of passion—the deep-seated love of sport. Performing with passion is a key element in producing peak performances—the balance between emotion and passion produces the energy to perform at one's highest level, free from doubt, fear, and worry. Peak performers are relaxed, confident, and energized—excited about upcoming performances. Contrary to popular belief, peak performers do not need to be "psyched up" to perform at their best, they need to be "psyched down," in effect, to maintain their composure and emotional energy.

 Mental Key to Success

"A lot of things are going to happen to you and around you that you can't control, but you can control your response to what happens to you"

Peak performers also recognize the importance of creating the proper emotional climate for themselves before, during, and after competitive efforts. They recognize that each athlete has an emotional style that works best for him or her—this style is unique to the individual's life and athletic experiences. Highly effective performers strive to create and replicate a physical, mental, and emotional climate that gives them the best chance to succeed in various performance settings. Some athletes, for example, rely on music during their warm-up to generate a comfortable emotional and rhythmic climate for high-performance sport. These athletes couple this climate with their physical and mental warm-up routines to create a state of balance performance readiness—a state of total physical, mental, and emotional focus. *Most importantly, peak performers make a conscious effort to choose positive emotion before, during, and after competitive efforts.*

Composure and Peak Performance

The diagram on the next page outlines the key mental and physical factors that, if mastered through mental skills training, can lead to composed, energized, and effective performances. Many of these skills have been addressed in previous chapters, and some will be addressed in this chapter. Athletes must keep in mind that attaining and maintaining composure is a three-step process that involves first, making a concentrated effort to perform well; second, adopting a confident and "in control" attitude; and third, keeping emotional poise in performance situations.

Pre-performance Concerns

Prior to performing, athletes deal with a variety of factors and issues that can spill over into their performances resulting in poor or ineffective competitive efforts. Facing the unknown of performance conditions, situations, and outcomes can make athletes anxious, apprehensive, tense, and worried—certainly not a mindset and physical state that lead to optimal performances. Athletes can learn that it is OK to have butterflies as long as they fly in formation. Nervousness is a natural part of athletic performance and competition; it tells the performer that he or she is ready to perform and actually enhances performance because the athlete is in a state of physiological and psychological readiness. A low level of pre-performance tension enhances performance similar to a properly strung bow—puts it on line to strike the intended target.

On the other hand, being overready and keyed up can inhibit the natural performance flow of an athlete. In psychological terms this is known as the "fight or flight" syndrome.

 Mental Key to Success

It's OK to be nervous but don't lose your nerve.

Specific strategies and techniques to control and manage anxiety and stress will be presented in an upcoming section of this chapter.

Composure and Peak Performance

Pre-performance composure skills	Performance composure skills	Post-performance emotions
Anxiety and stress management	Maintain positive self-talk	Euphoria
Arousal control	Thought stoppage and replacement	Ambivalence
Relaxation training		Disappointment
Simulation training	Arousal control	Apathy
Physical skill rehearsal	Focus on perform-ance cues	Depression
Rest	Concentration (focusing and re-focusing)	Frustration and anger
Attitudes		Self-fulfillment and happiness
Confidence	Mental/physical routines	
Positive self talk	Process orientation	
Thought stoppage and replacement	Enjoyment and fun based on mastery	
Review of performance goals/cues and plans	Relaxation strategies and techniques	

Quality training can relax an athlete and set him or her up for success through conscientious practice composed of simulation training, physical skill rehearsal, and, of course, quality rest between training sessions and prior to competitive efforts. In similar fashion, a great attitude toward upcoming performance that focuses on giving one's best can be supported by positive self-talk and thought stoppage and replacement techniques.

Finally, as the athlete moves from doubt, stress, worry, anxiety, and hesitation to an excited and confident approach to an upcoming performance, control of his or her emotional energy becomes imperative. Energy conservation and distribution become key factors during the actual performance. Dissipating physical and emotional energy prior to performing or in the early stage(s) of a performance can leave an athlete "flat" during the critical zone(s) of a potential peak performance. Emotional energy management or arousal control training will be covered in greater depth in a following section.

Performance Concerns

In the middle of a performance, an athlete must have the presence of mind to apply the mental and physical skills they had activated prior to performing. This is the athlete's greatest challenge—applying his or her mental and physical skills in the middle of an emotionally charged performance. Keeping one's composure during a competitive performance allows an athlete to think clearly and make effective decisions "in the heat of the battle."

During a performance an athlete can keep his or her composure by maintaining positive self-talk and thought stoppage and replacement techniques. Staying positive through self-talk techniques, including positive affirmations, will help an athlete maintain confidence by focusing on his or her abilities and strengths.

Focusing on performance goals rather than outcome goals during a performance is another way athletes can remain in control of their physical skills. Furthermore, reviewing performance cues will help athletes stay on task or even to refocus in the face of distractions and unexpected happenings. In addition emotional energy can be retained by athletes through the use of physical and mental routines.

Athletes can also stay relaxed during competitive performances by listening to their bodies, recognizing counterproductive physical and mental tension that may be building, and utilizing deep breathing techniques to "stay loose" and maintain the flow of their performance. Sensitivity to one's excitability level during competition is an essential aspect of maintaining composure and will be covered in depth later in this chapter.

Finally, to maintain composure an athlete can focus on the mastery of his or her skills, that is, the exhilaration and joy of being effective in competitive performance settings. Focusing on the "process" of performance—being in the spotlight of the competitive arena and recognizing the performance setting as an opportunity: to be with teammates; to work toward team and personal goals; to travel; and to experience the support of fans, family, and coaches. These are all "process" factors to focus on during performance if an athlete is to remain emotionally energized.

Post-performance Concerns

One of the most overlooked aspects of composure is how emotions are addressed once an athletic competition is completed. We spend a great deal of time preparing for performance and designing strategies to use during competition but very little time, if any, addressing post-competitivecompetitive stress.

Prior to competition we would like an athlete to be on an even keel emotionally so that he or she can compete with a calm, quiet, and confident mind and controlled physical readiness. Once the competition has been completed, it is important that an athlete returns to his or her emotional baseline, similar to the one prior to competition—calm, quiet, confident, and physically relaxed, free from feelings that can lead to increased physical and emotional tension and personal disharmony.

Coaches and parents can play an integral role in helping athletes, especially young athletes, place their performance in perspective. Athlete centered coaches spend time with their athletes immediately after a contest or individual performance to make sure that emotions are dealt with in a healthy way. The highs and lows of athletic competition can sometimes put athletes on an emotional roller coaster.

Following a game, an athlete needs time to either come down from a great and exhilarating performance or come back up from a disappointing performance. In either case, win or lose, most athletes experience a post-competitivecompetitive let down. They must allow themselves to recover emotionally as well as physically before they can adequately resume the mental and physical preparation for the next athletic contest. Failure to recognize the need to emotionally recover following intensive competitive efforts can lead to emotional overload and overtraining (Vernacchia, 1997).

Identifying Sources of Stress

Since athletes are challenge and mastery oriented, they often place themselves in stressful situations, in fact, they can be considered "stress seekers." Recognizing the sources of personal stress for each athlete is an important first step to developing strategies to respond to stress in a healthy and empowering way. The exercise "Sources of Stress" below can help athletes identify the sources of stress that may be adversely effecting or enhancing their performance.

Peak Performance Exercise 11.1

Sources of Stress

What are some of the sources of stress (persons, situations, demands, fears, etc.) that cause you to feel uptight, anxious, and nervous prior to a competition? Do these situations enhance or detract from your performance? Are there stresses in your life or lifestyle that seem to spill over into your performance? Does this "spillover" enhance or detract from your performance? Are you able to gain control over these stresses, by learning to react to them in a way that will enhance your performance? Do you view these stressors as challenges rather than fears? (Adapted from Rotella, 1990a).

10 Ways to Master Pre-performance Stress

Athletes are often overwhelmed by feelings of uncertainty prior to competition; in some cases, they become so nervous, tense, and worried their ability to perform effectively is compromised. Facing the unknown of competition outcomes can create certain fears, perceived or real, that interfere with the fluid and confident execution of sport skills and performance strategies.

Pre-performance stress is a natural occurrence for all athletes—the trick is to be able to manage this stress so that it *enhances* athletic performance. Stress and tension can activate an athlete to perform at optimal physical and mental levels—but controlling the stress response is essential. Here are several techniques to exert personal control in stressful athletic performance situations (Vernacchia, 1996b):

1. *Revisit your philosophy of performance and athletic participation.* Reviewing their mission statement and foundational beliefs will help athletes put their performance in perspective and give a deeper meaning to their reasons for pursuing athletic excellence.

2. *Master relaxation training.* Athletes should listen to their body and know when their thoughts and feelings are creating unwanted physical tension. They should use progressive relaxation and deep breathing exercises to reduce the physical and mental tension associated with competitive athletic performances.

3. *Use simulation training in practice sessions.* Athletes can replicate and incorporate in practice, the exact conditions they will face in competition. This will help them adapt to similar conditions on game day.

4. *Avoid overemotionalizing about the upcoming performance.* Making the competition bigger than it really is by focusing on winning can only set an athlete up for failure and increase stress. Athletes can take a more composed approach to their upcoming performance by focusing on things they can control—proper execution of the performance goals, cues, and plans that will lead to successful outcomes. A good thought

for athletes to refocus upon once they become seemingly overwhelmed by an upcoming competition is, "Whatever you did to get to this level worked, do the same thing that got you to this level, it'll work again."

5. *Use mental and physical routines to relax.* Routines set an athlete up for success because they do not have to give conscious thought to their performance. They merely trigger their performance by doing the same thing over and over in the form of a routine; in this the execution of athletic skills become "natural," automatic, and instinctive.

6. *Use visualization or mental rehearsal to anticipate and prepare for competition.* Rather than worrying about what will happen once the game begins, athletes can picture themselves in various performance situations and mentally rehearse an effective response to the "what ifs" of athletic performance. Formal mental visualization techniques (discussed in depth in Chapter 5) that can help athletes mentally prepare for competition include imitation, highlight music videotapes, repetitious visualization, and creative concentration audiotapes and CD's.

7. *Overlearn physical skills through prolonged drill.* Overlearning performance skills can set an athlete up for success because it builds confidence through skill mastery. Automatic responses resulting from prolonged practice remove the hesitation an athlete may have as he or she moves from thinking about performing skills to acting on instinct and cues that trigger effective motor patterns.

8. *Create diversions if stress is too great.* Provide diversions such as listening to music, casual conversation, and humor to help athletes relieve the stress they are experiencing.

9. *Use mild exercise to relax and reduce stress.* Going for a walk or participating in a light practice helps relieve stress and "shake out" mentally and physically prior to a performance.

10. *Surround yourself with a support group that is in control, calm, and confident.* Most importantly, being around supportive

people will provide emotional support as the competition draws closer. Coaches, family, and friends can provide emotional security, encouragement, reassurance for athletes.

Creating the Emotional Climate for Athletic Excellence

As stated above, it is important for aspiring athletes to surround themselves with individuals who can provide support for their athletic pursuits. For this reason, successful athletes do all that is possible to create a support group or athletic advocacy for themselves. This group (coaches, teammates, family, friends, community members, administrators, etc.) can provide an athlete with emotional security, empathy (understanding what an athlete is feeling and experiencing), and encouragement in stressful situations.

Most importantly, an athlete's support team can set the stage for generating the proper emotional climate necessary to succeed in demanding training and performance settings. Practicing in isolation, training in various climatic conditions, injuries, poor performances or performance slumps, balancing life and academic demands are but a few of the occurrences that can influence and interfere with the attainment of personal performance goals. Social support can facilitate athletic performance by providing athletes with opportunities for social and emotional growth within the demanding context of the athletic arena (Rosenfeld & Richman, 1997).

Social support can provide the encouragement and resources necessary to reduce stress, combat overtraining and burnout, increase feelings of well-being, and overcome feelings of isolation associated with training (Rosenfeld & Richman, 1997). Support, encouragement, care, and concern provided by the athlete's support team are essential in providing the motivational fuel and emotional energy necessary to overcome adversity and to provide meaning for an athlete's quest for performance excellence.

Here are some ways friends, coaches, and family can provide appropriate social support for aspiring athletes (Rosenfeld & Richman, 1997):

- **Listening Support** (*athletes feel someone can listen to their concerns and problems without giving advice and being judgmental*): give nonjudgmental advice regarding the stress of training and performance demands; provide group social events for coaches, staff, and athletes so they can "step out of sport" and their roles within the team and relate to each other on a more personal level; promote informal contacts between team members, the coaching staff, and other support personnel; structure the practice environment to convey warmth, friendliness, and acceptance.

- **Emotional Support** (*provides athletes with a feeling of care and concern, that someone is on their side*): stress the importance of emotional support to team leaders so they can provide and model such support for team members; encourage emotional support for injured athletes; encourage the support staff to be available to team members away from practice; make the services of a sport psychologist available to the team and staff.

- **Emotional Challenge Support** (*athletes feel that others challenge them to evaluate their attitudes, values, and feelings*): this type of support is provided by friends, parents, and coaches, not teammates; use of team meetings, team talks, and team themes, etc. to help team members focus, or in some cases, refocus their emotional energy on their performance.

- **Task Appreciation Support** (*acknowledes the efforts of athletes and displays an appreciation for their work ethic*): team members and coaches reinforce and affirm the training effort of teammates who are striving to master their sport skills through conscientious and dedicated practice; provide awards ceremonies—reward improvement, as well as outstanding performances; use the media to convey the value and significance of performance accomplishments.

- **Task Challenge Support** (*athletes are made to feel that coaches and teammates will challenge them to challenge themselves in* *terms of improving their ability and performance effectiveness*): coaches and teammates can provide positive reinforcement and information/corrective feedback to challenge athletes to enhance training and performance efforts; use of technology (e.g., videotaping) to provide feedback and enhance performance; encourage athletes to accept task challenge as a team responsibility and norm.

- **Tangible Assistance Support** (*provision of support resources*): training equipment and facilities, economic support when appropriate (scholarships); support for travel to competitions.

- **Personal Assistance Support** (*assistance with lifestyle needs unrelated to sport*): athletes and support team members help with academic interests (peer advising), transportation to social events, errands, personal needs during injury rehabilitation.

Creating and Maintaining the Excite-Ability for Athletic Excellence

In the days and hours preceding an athletic performance it is crucial that an athlete creates an emotional climate that will provide support for upcoming performance. This is a climate of looking forward with excitement to the challenges of athletic competition. Excite-ability refers to an athlete's ability to create and maintain emotional energy for effective competitive efforts— excite-ability is often referred to as an athlete's arousal or level of activation.

In general, the successful athlete is self-confident, relaxed, and only *moderately* aroused. On a scale of 1–10, most athletes maintain an arousal level between 5–7 when performing in competitive situations. Two other factors athletes must take into consideration when determining their levels of performance excitement or activation are: (1) the type of sport skill that is to be performed (simple or complex); and (2) the audience effect.

low level	**Excite-Ability Levels**	high level

1 ← _____ → 10

complex sport skills   simple sport skills

Depending on the sport or motor skill complexity, an athlete should be aroused to a level above his or her normal resting level, but not to the level of overarousal. Athletes who are apathetic or underaroused may need to increase their arousal level (psyching up), while athletes whose arousal levels are already high prior to competition may benefit from reducing their arousal level (psyching down).

For example, a football quarterback executing a pass play (a sport skills composed of a series of movements) would require an arousal level of 3-4. The quarterback would have to approach the line after calling the pass play, access the defense, make adjustments by calling an audible if necessary, take the snap from center, fake a handoff while dropping back in the pocket, look at primary and secondary receivers, deciding to whom and whether or not to throw the pass, and throw the pass to a moving target.

On the other hand a basketball player playing the post position may need to be aroused at a very high level (10) as she goes for a rebound. As the player comes down with the rebound she may decide to go right back up with it to score a basket. To do this effectively the player must launch herself with a high level of arousal (10) and actually reduce her level of arousal to about 3 when she shoots the ball. It is not uncommon to see a rebounder go up for a close range shot and miss the basket completely by shooting "over it" because she has not adjusted her arousal level during a series of sport skills such as offensive rebounding and shooting.

In addition, performing in front of an audience may over-arouse an athlete and require that he or she "calm down" or reduce his or her level of excite-ability.

Arousal control training can be taken a step further by creating an emotion management program for athletes based on the athlete's past, present, and future performances (Vernacchia,

Austin, VandenHazel & Roe, 1992). Athletes can recall and visualize a previous peak performance and associate this feeling with a number from 1 to 10 that approximates their arousal or exciteability level at the time of the performance. The idea is that athletes who are readying for competition can replicate the physical and emotional arousal state achieved in a prior personal best performance. Using a number to represent this arousal level helps the athlete to remember an ideal arousal state (Vernacchia, 1996b).

Mastering the 4R's of Emotion Management

Developing a postplay emotional routine is extremely helpful in maintaining an athlete's composure throughout the course of a competitive performance. Some athletes perform poorly once they make a mistake or are unsuccessful in a particular performance attempt—they lose their composure and dwell on the ineffective performance rather than "playing on." A basketball player can make a poor play on offense (have a pass intercepted or miss an "easy" shot) and have the negative feelings associated with the previous play carry over to the next defensive play. Physically the player may transition to defense but makes another mistake or poor play on defense because he or she is dwelling emotionally on the poor outcome of the previous offensive play.

Performing in any competitive athletic event is a process of making one play at a time with an emotionally focused mind. Just as a mental routine can aid an athlete in making a concentrated effort to perform effectively (see Chapter 9), so too can a postplay emotional routine help an athlete to perform effectively play by play throughout an athletic competition. Figure 11.1 illustrates the four phases to a postplay performance routine (Ravizza & Hanson, 1995; Ravizza & Osborne, 1991).

The first phase (*Respond*) requires athletes to perform their skills with a quiet, clear, and confident mind. The second phase (*Release*) requires athletes to "let go" or "get over" the emotions that come with an effective or ineffective performance. Of the

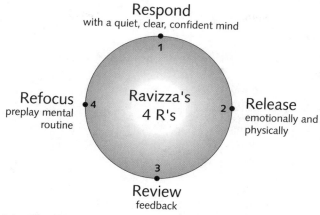

Figure 11.1   The 4R's of Emotion Management
(Adapted from Ravizza & Hanson, 1995; Ravizza & Osborne, 1991)

4R's *Release* is the most crucial since many athletes get emotionally hung up in this phase and never "play on." Two choices are made in the release phase: (1) If a good or effective play is made, the player must "lock it in" physically so that the play is reinforced, recognized, and rewarded. Many players pump their fist in recognition or celebration of a great play, others such as golfers, lock in a great shot by "posing" after the shot. In essence these athletes are having a "love affair" with their most effective plays and use this feeling to increase their emotional energy. (2) If a poor or ineffective play is made, the player must release him or herself from the negative feelings and play on. A conscious effort must be made to dump the negative emotions that can be associated with a failed or ineffective performance.

The third phase (*Review*) requires the athlete to get feedback regarding each play immediately after the play is made and prior to making the next play. This is very difficult, if not impossible to do if the player fails to release him or herself from the previous play because he or she cannot effectively evaluate what went right (what worked) or what went wrong (what didn't work). Getting the appropriate feedback after each play can help the athlete detect and correct errors, or to maintain effective performance behaviors. The final phase (*Refocus*) allows the athlete to "reset"

Figure 11.2   Postshot Routine: GOLF

for the next play by adhering to and initiating the preplay mental/physical routines.

A postshot routine for a golfer is shown in Figure 11.2.

Prominent Emotional Distractors

Many distractors can break an athlete's emotional focus and shatter the calm and composed climate he or she has created. Maintaining an effective emotional and mental focus, that is, thinking and feeling what can go right vs. what can go wrong, is essential for effective athletic performances. Unfortunately this is not as easy as it sounds because many potential emotional distractors that can ultimately sabotage composure surround athletes. Some of these prominent distractors include: (1) feelings of fear, doubt, worry, and hesitation; (2) the emotional reminiscence effect; (3) winning and losing; (4) emotional conflict; (5) emotional response to injury; (6) media; and (7) family and friends.

Fear, Doubt, Worry, and Hesitation

The most common emotional distractors or feelings experienced by athletes are fear, doubt, and worry about the outcome of upcoming performances. These feelings create a climate of uncertainty in an athlete's mind that leads to ineffective decision-making, hesitation, and second-guessing before, during, and after performance. As the adage goes, "Indecision is the sign of a fearful mind."

Focusing on what can be controlled in the performance setting can conquer fear. Confidence based on mental and physical preparation (reviewing one's circle of control) can go a long way in helping athletes refocus their emotional responses in stressful situations. Rather than worrying about what happened in the past or what might happen in the future, the athlete needs to focus in the moment and on the task at hand. Reviewing performance goals, cues and strategies will help an athlete who is experiencing pre-performance stress.

Rather than have their imagination run away with them, athletes can determine what is real and what is imagined about the outcomes of upcoming performances. Fear is often generated by personal perceptions about upcoming events that are sometimes threatening, hence the acronym for fear:

Mental Key to Success

False **E**vidence **A**ppearing **R**eal

Using mental rehearsal strategies that will help them anticipate and prepare, that is, develop various contingency plans and performance strategies for possible or unexpected competitive happenings, can dispel fear and apprehension. Improved concentration will lead to a better sense of control in performance settings—mastering the various mental skills related to concentration is a prime prerequisite to establishing both athletic confidence and a resilient sense of athletic composure.

Fear is a common distractor of athletes who lack competitive experience, especially young athletes. Experience conquers fear, but experience alone is not enough. Experience coupled with the patience to use performance feedback to improve and develop more effective performance responses are the keys to overcoming fear, doubt, worry, and hesitation.

Emotional Reminiscence

One of the best strategies to dispel anxiety and apprehension regarding an upcoming performance is to have an athlete recall his or her best performance ever. The athlete can mentally recall and describe every specific aspect of the performance. He or she may have been "in the zone" and feeling invincible. Reminiscing about past successes calls up feelings of control and competence for athletes and gives them a confident and more positive and emotional focus on an upcoming performance.

Intense athletic performances have an intense effect on an athlete's emotional memory. In some cases, negative feelings associated with failed or ineffective performances can create an emotional block in future performance situations that are similar to the original situation. For example, if a basketball player misses a free throw at the end of the game that would give his or her team a victory in the season-ending championship game, he or she may be reminded of his or her miss once again in the following year's championship game. The athlete may play less assertively on offense or defense in order not to be placed in the same situation again. Similarly, a rehabilitated athlete who had received a career-threatening injury may avoid or not perform intensely enough to be effective in future situations that remind him or her of the past injury.

The tendency to avoid potential emotionally intense performance situations can be overcome by the athlete mentally and emotionally rehearsing in advance how he or she would handle himself or herself if the situation should occur again. It is only human not to want to think about unpleasant past outcomes, but not doing it ahead of time means that unpleasant thoughts and feelings may resurface in similar or the exact same situations during an actual future competition. This type of emotional interference can adversely affect an athlete's performance.

To avoid the negative effects of emotional reminiscence, effective players learn to "let go" of ineffective or poor performances. They flush the memory of ineffective or poor performance from their mind and memories and take from such performances the feedback that will help them adjust and adapt their performance so they are more effective in the future. In essence, "Keep the best, and flush the rest."

Emotional reminiscence can help strengthen an athlete's belief and trust in his or her talents, skills, and performance effectiveness. Athletes at all levels, particularly elite athletes, have a love affair with their best performances or certain aspects of a performance. For example, a golfer will pose after a great shot, holding his or her finish while savoring the excitement and feel of a great shot (postshot routine). All this helps the athlete to replicate a similar shot in a different situation. Some players emotionally "lock in" the feeling of a great performance by pumping a fist or engaging in a similar minicelebration.

Winning and Losing

In some cases, winning or delivering a successful athletic performance can catch an athlete by surprise. The athlete either can be unwilling to accept the fact that he or she deserved to win or simply "can't believe" he or she was successful. A response to an athlete who refers to a successful performance by saying, "I can't believe it, I won!" should be, "That was the idea, wasn't it ?"

Winning and success can be uncomfortable for those athletes who have not really planned to be successful. These are the athletes who are in love with the ritual and routine of sport rather than attaining their best performance. They seem to undermine their best performances or achieve excellence sporadically and then return to the world of average performances—they are unable to maintain ongoing excellence. They are the overmotivated underachievers who work hard and train to train rather than training to perform.

Learning to acknowledge successful performances and accept the responsibility and adulation that accompany such performances is a first step to feeling comfortable with success. Accepting the congratulations of others rather than replying, "Thanks, but I should have. . ." or "I could have. . ." or "Yeah, that was OK but I didn't do this or that (insert a negative or ineffective aspect of the overall performance)." Remember the goal in performance settings is to be effective and not perfect.

Athletes who are emotionally uncomfortable with success can learn to focus on continuing to improve on their personal best rather than to compare their performance to their competitors. "Improving on your best" is a performance theme that helps athletes focus on self-improvement rather than on comparative self-worth. Comparative self-worth (always comparing one's self to others rather than to one's own best self or best performance) can lead to lowered self-confidence and feelings of performance inadequacy. In most cases, there will always be someone in the athletic world who will perform better on any given day—athletes cannot control this, but they can control how they perform.

Losing, on the other hand, can be devastating for those athletes who judge themselves by how they perform. All committed athletes are disappointed after a losing or poor performance, but they are not devastated. Once the feelings of disappointment have receded, success-oriented athletes begin to tap into the performance resolve that has made them so successful in the past—they refocus on self-improvement and how they can be more effective in future competitive situations.

Understanding the emotional impact of losing can go a long way in helping athletes rebound from unsuccessful or ineffective performances. Losing a game, losing a place in the starting lineup, losing one's physical abilities due to injury, or ending an athletic career can bring on a series of unpleasant and confusing feelings and thoughts. The natural feelings of disappointment, depression, frustration, or sometimes anger following a loss can be mastered through the support, understanding, and encouragement of coaches, family teammates, and friends, as well as good sportspersonship and a performance resolve to learn from mistakes and focus on self-improvement.

Emotional Conflict

Staying on an even keel emotionally prior to performance is an attribute of effective athletic performances. Creating an emotional climate of calmness and balance can often be thwarted by interpersonal conflicts with coaches, teammates, family, friends, fans, or the media. Conflict and disagreement are natural happenings in sport because emotions run high in high-performance settings—athletes and coaches tend to be emotionally keyed up in an effort to access their physical and mental abilities, especially as they move closer to game or performance time.

Athletes can diffuse potential conflict situations by avoiding them or by not adding fuel to the fire of conflict by remaining calm when faced with confronting information or individuals. Having a clear mind and being able to step back emotionally in the face of conflict and confrontation are important attributes because miscommunication and misinterpretation usually cause them. Clarifying the reasons for interpersonal or intrateam conflict can be accomplished by implementing the following conflict resolution strategies (Vernacchia, 1996c):

1. Understand that conflict is healthy when dealt with in a mature, respectful, and open manner and that it can actually enhance understanding among individuals and teams.

2. Speak to each other in a neutral setting away from the playing field, locker room, or coach's office. Go for a walk, have lunch together, etc.

3. Address the conflict directly, calmly, honestly, and as soon as possible after it occurs but once emotions have settled.

4. Listen to the other person, listen to all sides of the person's complaint(s) without interrupting and then present your concerns and perspectives.

5. Repeat the issues and continue to address the problem until the emotional component of the conflict is diffused.

6. Review how your behaviors are affecting not only each other but teammates and others around you. Most importantly, address how conflict is affecting your performance.

7. Work out a solution to the conflict/problem that is acceptable to everyone involved. Create a win-win situation for everyone.

8. If necessary have an objective person (e.g., athletic director, sport psychology consultant) facilitate conflict resolution. A

good method is to have the objective person create a 5 on 5 situation. Allow one person to explain his or her complaints for 5 minutes without being interrupted. Then the other person has 5 minutes to voice his or her complaints, once again without being interrupted. The objective person can summarize the points of conflict and serve as an emotional buffer to help all involved reach resolution.

9. Use informal (conversation) or formal (meetings) follow-up sessions to evaluate the effectiveness of previously agreed upon solution(s) to particular conflicts. Continue to meet if necessary.

Emotional Response to Injury

One of the most common emotional distractors reported by athletes is coping with injury (Vernacchia, McGuire, Reardon & Templin, 2000). Just as intense, or perhaps more intense, than losing an athletic contest are the emotional feelings associated with injuries and the loss of physical abilities or prowess. Athletes must learn how to respond in a healthy way to injury since at one time or another all athletes experience an athletic injury (Brewer, 2001; Heil, 1993).

An athlete will experience or progress through several emotional stages after being injured (Kübler-Ross, 1969; Williams, Rotella & Scherzer, 2001). As a general rule, these stages are experienced sequentially or sometimes in random order and include the following feelings:

1. *Denial, disbelief, and isolation.* An athlete's first response to injury is often, "I can't believe I got injured," or "Why does this always have to happen to me?" An athlete often feels that he or she is no longer a member of the team because he or she can no longer contribute to team goals and performance outcomes. Athletes are often lost and feel alone following an injury because there is nowhere for them to seemingly go—they can't practice and play so what's the sense of going to practice.

2. *Frustration and anger.* Obviously an athlete will experience frustration and oftentimes become angry as a result of being injured. Anger, especially anger that is turned inward, can do little to help an athlete in the healing process. Some athletes may even strike out verbally toward athletic trainers, physicians, and loved ones as a result of the frustration and anger they are experiencing—they simply will not accept the fact that they were injured.

3. *Bargaining.* Some athletes realize they are injured but still feel they can play. They may compensate to accommodate an injury and in doing so set themselves up for new injuries or possibly reinjury. Still in denial in this stage, athletes may experience further frustration when their adjustment to injury renders them ineffective in performance settings even though they are able to play.

4. *Depression.* Once the athlete faces the fact that he or she is "really" injured, reality sets in and soon he or she feels as though there is no hope for recovery, at least, in the way of returning to play. As a result of this realization an athlete can feel even more alone and emotionally "down" about his or her future as both an athlete and a person.

5. *Resignation.* Finally, the athlete will resign himself or herself to the fact that he or she is injured. At this point the athlete will engage in both the physical and psychological rehabilitation that will help him or her heal and eventually, if possible, return to practice and play.

Additional theories are related to the emotional impact of athletic injury, but the stage model presented here serves well to help athletes understand the emotions they may experience if injured. Specific strategies for psychoemotional rehabilitation from athletic injury are addressed in Chapter 8.

Media

Many athletes and coaches have a love-hate relationship with the media. The media can be a powerful and influential advocate or adversary—the choice is up to you. Here are some basic guidelines to follow when interacting with the media (U.S. Olympic Committee, 1999):

Television. Television is looking for answers in the 10-20 second range. Be presentable, make eye contact (remove sunglasses for example), and have a friendly smile. Speak clearly and distinctly when on camera, be direct, and use slight pauses to reinforce important statements. Maintain eye contact with the interviewer, sit up straight, and look attentive and eager to talk. Body language is important—*how* you say what you say is as important as what you say. Arrive early for your interview so you can become familiar with the interview format and technology that will be used. Dress appropriately. The image you present will remain on film for your lifetime, to be seen again and again.

Radio. An radio interview is very informal and is more like a conversation; answers can range from 30-second sound bites to hours of on-air dialogue. Give good solid answers but don't ramble. Determine in advance whether an interview is live, taped, or edited. If it's to be taped or edited, keep your answers within 10-20 seconds. Beware of long audible pauses—"uhs" that creep into speech—because they are accentuated on radio.

Print. With the immediacy of television and radio, newspapers must dig deeper to keep their readers interested. Be prepared to spend more time on your answers. Try to give the print media the most in-depth personal view of the competition—a more detailed version of what happened in the competition. Every athlete has a fascinating story outside the competition arena—refer to your hobbies and personal interests and activities. The print interview presents the greatest challenge because your spoken word is translated. Finish up a print interview with, "Are there any questions I can clear up?" It's a good way to finish on the right note and clear up any misunderstandings.

Press Conference. A press conference is used at major sporting events. You will be at a podium with a microphone, and questions will come from the audience. Compose yourself—you may be coming off a disappointing or poor performance and will be asked to face the press shortly thereafter. Dress appropriately, you are creating an image. Speak into the microphone and speak up. If it's a big room, it can be helpful to everyone to repeat a question so that the entire audience understands your answer. Accept follow-up interviews after the formal press conference. Many of the best questions will come in this setting.

The Press Box

Interview Do's and Don'ts (U.S. Olympic Committee, 1999)

DO'S
- Relax. It's not brain surgery.
- Keep your cool. You are in charge of the interview.
- Educate reporters about your sport but don't lecture them.
- Praise your teammates, credit your coaches, and thank your sponsors, if appropriate.
- Keep appointments and return phone calls. If you can't keep an appointment, don't schedule it.
- Recognize the fact that reporters are under deadline pressure and have a job to do.
- Think before you speak. Silence can be your friend.
- Feel free to say, "I'd rather not go into that," or "I don't feel comfortable talking about that." Sometimes a "no comment" sends up a red flag. There are better ways to say that you don't want to talk about a subject.
- Make yourself presentable. Your appearance counts.
- Anticipate questions you may be asked and plan your responses.
- Project authority. You're the expert. Use eye contact.
- If a question doesn't make sense, come up with an answer that makes sense. Save everyone the embarrassment of a bad question and give a good answer.
- Volunteer background information that the interviewer doesn't know, if appropriate.
- Develop a game plan prior to the interview. Identify the two or three essential points that you want to get across. Stay with those points.

- How you behave when you lose may be more important than your actions when you win. Remember to step back and get your mind ready before an interview.
- Ask a reporter his or her name or where he or she is from. Next time say "hi." You don't have to be best friends, but recognition is a courtesy.

DON'TS

- Don't think of the media as adversaries.
- Don't talk too fast.
- Don't be worried about the pauses between questions. People are writing or recording. Be patient.
- If you don't know the answer to a question, say "I don't know." Don't ramble on about it. Offer to find out the answer and move on.
- Don't use technical language or sports jargon that the reporter and the general public doesn't understand. If necessary, give a full explanation.
- Don't ever presume to know what someone else thinks. Speak only for yourself.
- Don't look at your feet. (They'll be there when the interview is over.)
- Don't swear.
- Don't play favorites among the media when granting interviews.
- Don't play referee and blame judges or officials.
- Don't go down a road you don't want to travel. Redirect the tone of the interview.
- Don't start every answer with, "Well. . . " Don't use "uhh. . . " or "you know. . . " Just answer the question.
- Don't treat the media like your best friend, telling all your deep dark secrets. Keep a friendly and professional distance.
- Don't go "off the record." If you don't want to see it in the morning newspaper, don't say it. Start with the fact that if you say it, expect to see it somewhere, somehow, someway, sometime.

- Don't forget you're always on. Microphones are extremely sensitive and cameras have zoom lenses.
- Don't let your guard down for an informal moment.
- Don't try to make serious points through humor. It can often be misinterpreted or translate very badly in print.
- Don't say things that could come back to haunt you. Never say never.

Family and Friends

Another prominent distractor is frequently an athlete's family. Family members do not mean to be a distractor, it just happens. An athlete's family will also benefit from his or her accomplishments. Families may unwittingly ask for special favors that impact an athlete (speaking, appearances, social functions, getting tickets for games or events, or other "special favors"). An athlete needs to be respectful of his or her family but must also make it perfectly clear that he or she is dedicated to performance goals. An athlete needs to be the master of his or her own time and not be committed to various social functions with his or her family. Athletes can do what they feel is appropriate, but the minute they feel pressured by family social commitments, they need to cut back on attending them. Social commitments can become superficial and detrimental to what an athlete is attempting to accomplish.

Friends can also be a distractor as an athlete's competition draws closer. Again, friends mean well but can exert unwanted pressures. Many friends will call or contact an athlete to offer sincere congratulations on his or her success, but then ask for some of the athlete's time (lunch, coffee, etc.). As critical performance situations approach, it is not the time to become a socialite. The athlete must be pleasant in these situations, and he or she can ask friends to call again after the competition, when he or she has more time to be a regular person.

Athletes may also hear from people they have not talked to or seen for quite a while. These may be friends whom an athlete really would like to spend some time with, but again, it is important for the athlete to be conservative and try to put them off until after the competition. True friends will enjoy an athlete's successes and also understand his or her dedication to excellence.

12

Commitment
Putting It All Together

Commitment, in any endeavor, is all about follow-through and pride. Commitment is a pledge, a vow, a promise, or a declared intention that one strives to fulfill or complete (Bennett & Pravitz, 1987). Merely completing a task is not enough, the quality of the completed effort and task also reflects the level of commitment—the time, energy, talent, and emotion that separates a committed effort from merely "getting the job done." The committed performer is a craftsperson, one who takes pride in his or her work and efforts and one who is dedicated not only to quality performance but also to building and maintaining his or her reputation for excellence.

Committed athletes generate and deliver signature performances on a consistent basis—in the sport world this is known as pride. Commitment and pride are inseparable links in the chain of performance excellence.

"Commitment is the condition you enter immediately after jumping from a diving board."—James Bennett

Many athletes are involved in the processes of sport that stimulate self-improvement, but only a few are committed to these same processes of achieving performance excellence. Commitment, it has been said, is likened to a bacon and eggs breakfast— the hen is involved, the pig is committed. As Orlick (1996, p. 5) states:

> Excellence requires an incredible commitment to persist through the ups and downs associated with becoming your best and maintaining your best performance. You must ignite something within that drives you to excel. You must not only commit yourself to the goal of excelling, but you must also commit yourself to act on a daily basis in ways that lead you to excel.

Commitment is not a "light switch" concept—you just don't turn it on one day and then everything is fine from that day on. Commitment is an educational process of awareness, and awareness is the first step to changing from one's current personal investment in his or her sport to the thought of being the very best at the sport that he or she can be. This process of self-improvement has been addressed in earlier chapters and is characteristic of high achievers in sport who dedicate themselves daily to being just a little better than they were the previous day.

Sport performance researchers have found that sport commitment was highest in athletes who enjoyed their sport (fun) and who made personal investments in their sport (sacrifice). Furthermore, the enjoyment of sport rose when body awareness occurred, thereby resulting in moments of enriched personal meaning or moments of total immersion in sport that provided a sense of self-fulfillment (Scanlan, Carpenter, Schmidt, Simons & Keeler (1993).

A Formula for Instilling Commitment

Commitment = Challenge × Pride × Sacrifice × Fortitude

Committed individuals enjoy mastering the challenge of their undertakings. Sport or any other endeavor becomes fun when our skills and abilities successfully meet the challenge(s) that face us. This is real "fun" in sport. Commitment is also situationally specific, and certain situations awaken commitment in us—committed athletes display this emergent quality in adverse or seemingly impossible situations.

We really don't know how committed an individual is until he or she is placed in a challenging situation. In the final analysis, committed athletes thrive on challenge, especially when people tell them a certain performance task "can't be done" or has "never been done before." In many cases the accomplishments of great athletes are defined by overcoming the naysayers and "boobirds" of the sporting world.

Feelings of mastery that an individual develops as challenging tasks are accomplished results in a deep sense of pride. This sense of pride embraces the artistic side of athletic performance—an athlete views him or herself as an artist, whose performances stem from self-expression and lead to self-fulfillment. Proud and committed athletes autograph their performances with excellence.

Commitment requires sacrifice to maintain a tenacious mental grip on performance goals, no matter how long it takes to accomplish them, especially in light of the personal setbacks that are experienced or the personal comforts that are given up in the quest for personal and athletic excellence. The disappointment of failing in sport cannot be eased by such statements as "it was a good learning experience." This statement may be true for the person observing the athlete's performance, but for the committed athlete to fail is to experience a "learning ordeal." Poor or failed performances are taken to heart by committed athletes as a result of their tremendous sense of pride and personal investment in achieving performance excellence.

Most good athletic performers have a sound work ethic but truly great athletic performers also possess and demonstrate the mental, physical, and emotional fortitude necessary to become high achievers in sport. This fortitude is reflected in their desire to overcome personal and performance challenges with an attitude that reflects a great sense of pride, determination, and dedication. High achievers in sport make a committed or extra effort toward achieving their goals.

For the committed athlete, it is not enough to get the "idea" of what is needed to perform effectively in competitive situations, he or she will stay after formal practice to master a challenging skill, or take the initiative to seek out a coach or performance consultant that can help them master a challenging skill. Committed athletes endure and embrace the inconvenience of inadequate facilities, limited budgets, poor equipment, etc. to make the "extra effort" to attain their athletic dreams and goals.

Finally, the ability to endure adversity, that is, to continue to actively pursue their dreams in light of hardship and setbacks is characteristic of high achievers in a variety of endeavors. One such high achiever was Ernest Shackleton, the legendary Antarctic explorer who, in the face of overwhelming odds, led his crew to safety after being shipwrecked by an ice floe (Lansing, 1959). Shackleton's incredible journey and tale of superhuman survival was inspired by his family motto (Lansing, 1959, p. 14):

Fortitudine Vincimus—"By endurance we conquer."

The exercise on the facing page evaluates an athlete's personal commitment to excellence.

Peak Performance Exercise 12.1

Rating Your Personal Commitment
(Adapted from Orlick, 2000, p. 42)

How important is it for you to excel in your sport
(or other chosen pursuit)?

←——————————————————————————————————————→

No commitment	Involved but not committed	Commitment

1	2	3	4	5	6	7	8	9	10

Not very important   The most important
                                      thing in my life

While reading this chapter, keep in mind that:

- *Education enables commitment.* A peak performer needs to learn and practice the ways and means of success before he or she can commit to performing them on a daily and ongoing basis. This learning includes many of the mental training techniques introduced in previous chapters: positive imagery, positive self-talk, emotion and time management, goal attainment strategies, learned effective behavior, and a great attitude.

- *Effort enhances commitment.* Making a consistent, concentrated, and quality effort to practice, master, and perform the physical and mental skills of highly effective athletic performers is characteristic of an athlete's inner drive to excel at his or her sport. Commitment requires the traditional achievement attributes of dedication, hard work, deferred gratification, and a continual striving to improve one's performance effectiveness. There are no short cuts to success.

- *Will power ensures commitment.* The willingness of an athlete to make the extra effort necessary to succeed in his or her sport, or at least, give him or herself a chance to succeed is also characteristic of an athlete's inner drive to excel at his or her sport.

Athletes can use the following exercise to further explore their commitment to their sport or other endeavor(s) they are pursuing.

Peak Performance Exercise 12.2

Commitment

Think about someone or some endeavor that you are passionate about. Are you committed to this person or activity? If so, what are some of the dimensions of your commitment—what things do you do on a consistent basis to honor your commitment to this person or endeavor? If you are not committed, how is your lack of total commitment displayed?

What attributes or actions tend to help you maintain your commitment? What factors and actions tend to diminish your personal commitment to be the best you can be at what you do?

Are there times when you need to reexamine and recommit to your goals and plans for success? What changes can you make in your attitude and lifestyle that will enhance your ability to become committed to your goals and vision of personal and/or athletic excellence?

Visit Pockets of Commitment to Experience True Greatness

In addition to the commitment exercises above, athletes can spend some time reflecting on various commitment examples that demonstrated total commitment to an individual's beliefs. Such a total commitment to one's beliefs is often characterized by tremendous investments of dedication and personal sacrifice. Athletes can gain an even deeper understanding of the personal commitment needed to achieve true greatness by visiting the actual places in the United States of America where examples of committed excellence are on display. These sites can serve as true inspiration for personal commitment.

One such pocket of commitment can be found in Atlanta, Georgia, at the Martin Luther King Jr. Center for Nonviolent Social Change. Visitors can see the tomb, church, neighborhood, and childhood home of a man who gave his life for his dedication to the promotion of civil rights for all peoples. Dr. King's dream was altruistic and idealistic: "I have a dream that my four little children will one day live in a nation where they will not be judged by the color of their skin, but by the content of their character." His commitment to his dream and his beliefs reflect one of his most famous statements: "A man who won't die for something is not fit to live." He, in fact, did give his life for his dream and beliefs.

At the Franklin Roosevelt Memorial in Washington, DC, visitors can review the accomplishments and words of a great statesman and political leader. Roosevelt moved a nation from despair to hope and out of the Great Depression with his famous saying, "We have nothing to fear but fear itself."

In Washington, DC, various war memorials honor those men and women who made the ultimate sacrifice of their lives to defend our country and all that it stands for. A similar visit to Gettysburg, Pennsylvania, serves as a sobering and somber reminder of the power of commitment. On the battlefield of Gettysburg more American men died than in the Vietnam war.

Another inspirational pocket of commitment can be experienced at Ellis Island, New York. Here immigrants from foreign countries arrived in great numbers during the early part of the twentieth century with dreams of a better life for their immediate families and future generations. This dream was realized through the hard work and the personal sacrifice that was required to overcome the adversity, and sometimes discrimination, that they faced in pursuit of their dream. These immigrants committed themselves to the mission of living and giving their todays for other people's tomorrows.

Commitment Is a Lifestyle Choice

Commitment involves a constant focus on excellence in a particular area for extended periods of time (Orlick, 1996). Deciding to commit one's self to his or her sport or any other chosen endeavor requires that certain adjustments in lifestyle be made to accommodate a genuine committed effort toward self-improvement and effective performance outcomes. Here is a five-step process that will facilitate commitment:

1. *Look before you leap into the waters of commitment.* If commitment is the state that you find yourself in once you leave the diving board, then it is wise to "look before you leap." Know what efforts are required while you are in the air and what awaits you once you enter the water. It is often helpful to know what lies beneath the water's surface. Athletes should enter the waters of commitment with their eyes open to the realities of the challenges they are about to undertake in the quest for self-improvement and performance excellence.

   Committed athletes anticipate and prepare for the challenges, rewards, and personal setbacks that often accompany a prolonged effort toward a particular goal. Adhering to the principles of goal attainment that are described in Chapter 6 can help athletes establish a realistic perspective toward the challenges they will face on the road to athletic and personal excellence.

2. *Simplify your lifestyle to create an atmosphere for commitment.* Athletic excellence, as with any other worthwhile endeavor, requires an athlete to lead a less complex lifestyle in order to pursue his or her dream(s) in a very nondistractible way. The pursuit of athletic excellence requires an athlete to lead a rather Spartan lifestyle that focuses primarily on working, training, performing, and resting.

   To achieve athletic excellence, athletes seek the comfort of their passion as they commit themselves to dedicated efforts on a consistent basis. In some cases, such as with professional athletics, an athlete is able to make a living while "playing" his or her sport. Simplicity of lifestyle and sacrifice go hand in hand with striving for performance excellence— you really can't have one without the other. Sacrifice, an uncomfortable concomitant requirement of success, is best described by the saying, "everyone wants to go to heaven, but no one wants to die."

3. *Develop a network for success.* High achievers in sport soon learn to build an advocacy or support system to help them reach their goals and dreams. This success network is composed of: *social support* (family and friends); *financial support*

to live, train, and perform (attained from sport and nonsport employment or sources); *medical support* (physicians, athletic trainers, etc.); *training support* (coaching, facilities, and equipment); and *spiritual support* (the maintenance of faith and hope, especially in the face of adversity). Of all these support systems, the coach is the most essential element in the athlete's success. The coach is instrumental in generating and recruiting the support and resources for an athlete—the coach is the conductor of the support symphony.

4. *Rest for success.* Most athletes can focus on training hard and even engage in quality training, but the key to ongoing success is committing to time periods for rest, recovery, and regeneration. Rest is best for remaining healthy in the face of intense training and competitive efforts. As simple as it sounds, it is very hard to stay healthy, that is, injury- and illness–free in the demanding world of competitive athletics. Sometimes the best athlete doesn't win, the healthiest does. All things being equal, however, the rested, recovered, and regenerated athlete has the best chance to win.

5. *Develop interests and pursuits outside of sport.* The ability to step out of sport once interruptions such as injury, illness, disappointing performances occur can go a long way to protect and preserve an athlete's willingness to continue to follow dreams of athletic success. Professional career interests unrelated to sport, as well as hobbies, community service, and education can provide a healthy distraction and sanctuary from the oftentimes single-minded pursuit of excellence. Overcommitment does little to achieve excellence.

Commitment Is an Easy—Hard Process

Just the thought of committing to a certain endeavor can deter people from pursuing excellence. In many cases, commitment is viewed as a demanding "all or none" concept. In reality there are degrees of commitment that lie on a continuum from easy to hard. This idea is somewhat different from more traditional approaches to understanding commitment, which describe levels of deepening commitment.

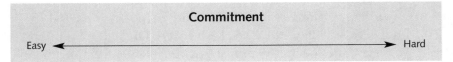

Commitment

Easy ◄————————————————————————————► Hard

Think of things or endeavors that are easy to commit to, such as taking a day off from work, spending time with friends at an enjoyable social activity, watching your favorite TV show, or perhaps taking a vacation, or watching a sunset at the seashore. These types of committed endeavors may be more attractive to us because they require less training, effort, or work to participate in them—they are easy to commit to—"no sweat."

On the other hand, many endeavors are very hard to commit to because they require extensive energy and effort over a prolonged period of time. Mastery is actually commitment made visible—it is the point at which one's skill and ability are equal to the challenge of a particular activity. For athletes, the ability to perform effectively and efficiently in challenging competitive situations requires great investments of time, energy, and emotion. The processes of sport that are predicated on trial and error learning and the refinement of physical and mental skills temper effective and efficient athletic performances. Making a committed effort to perform effectively in challenging competitive situations is hard—if it were easy everyone would be able to do it.

The point here is that everyone is committed to doing certain things, a certain way, at certain times, but only a few are committed to do a challenging thing well on a consistent basis. It takes time to develop the willingness of an athlete to engage in hard commitment endeavors. Major leaguers took their first commitment steps in the little leagues of their sport. At each progressive level of play—high school, college, semi-professional, minor leagues—their commitment to the process of mastering their sport became more challenging and demanding. At each level of play the athlete must make more and more sacrifices and devote more time and energy to his or her sport. Experience and commitment go hand in hand in tempering athletic talent.

The Confidence, Belief, and Commitment Relationship

An athlete's best chance to attain performance excellence occurs when commitment and belief intersect (Orlick, 1996). This intersection point is referred to as confidence. At this point an athlete truly trusts him or herself and surrenders all doubt, fear, worry, anxiety, or hesitation regarding the process and outcome of performance. Committed athletes trust and believe:

- In themselves
- In their methods (how they train and develop their skills and abilities)
- In their talent and abilities
- In their plan for success
- In their ability to deliver the best performance that they are capable of at that moment
- In their ability to deliver a consistent and concentrated effort
- In the thought that everything will turn out for the better when you give your best.

The following quote by Duncan Goodhew, an Olympic gold medal swimmer, best illustrates the importance of believing in one's self:

> The difference between winning and losing was simply belief. You have to be able to get up on the block and say to yourself, "I am the best in the world!" You have to believe it one hundred percent. To break a world record, you have to say, "Not only am I the best in the world, but I may be the very best that has ever been! In fact, I may be the best that will ever live!" Now to get your teeth onto that kind of thinking is very difficult to do. In fact, it is near impossible. Very few people can do it. (*The Little Book of Olympic Inspiration*, 1996, p. 82)

In his quest for excellence, Duncan Goodhew overcame a great deal of adversity to achieve his athletic goals and dreams

(Hemery, 1986). As a young boy he became an introvert and was made to feel self-conscious and even inferior as a result of being diagnosed with severe dyslexia. In addition, at the age of 8 he fell out of a tree and suffered nerve damage that resulted in the loss of all of his hair. Fortunately he found his sanctuary in sport and at the age of 14 stepped out of the pool one day and exclaimed to his classmates that one day he was going to the Olympics (Hemery, 1986).

Mastering the "Intangibles" of Commitment

Certain "make or break" attributes are characteristic of peak performers and separate them from the rest of the pack. Five of these attributes are reflected in an athlete's attitude and character and are essential to master if peak and effective performances are to be achieved on a consistent basis. The attributes or "intangibles" that characterize the most effective and consistent performers in sport are patience, courage, persistence, perseverance, and spirituality.

Patience

Many athletes get close to what they want to achieve in sport on sheer will power. This *active* will power has been instrumental in bringing about successful outcomes for many athletes who rise through the ranks of their sports to achieve athletic excellence at very high levels. A few high achievers in sport reach the very highest levels of their sport by exercising *passive* will power or patience in high-performance settings.

Patience allows athletes to "play their game" with confidence—patient athletes allow themselves to let their performance flow rather than trying to make their performance happen. Patient athletes allow the game to come to them—they try *less* at what they are attempting to accomplish. They know that trying harder, rather than waiting patiently for their opportunity, only leads to forced performances that result in frustration and botched opportunities. As Rotella (1990c) states, "you've got to try less on the most important day of your life."

Patience helps to unify and integrate the four main mental attributes of peak performers that are described throughout this book—concentration, confidence, composure, and commitment. Without patience the techniques used to learn, master, and apply each of these mental attributes are rendered useless and ineffective. It takes time to become a focused, confident, composed, and committed athletic performer. Bennett and Pravitz (1987, p. 255) state, "To be patient is to be able to wait calmly for something you desire while at the same time actively working with all the creative steps of your plan to achieve desired goals." As the saying goes, "You've got to take a rowboat before you get to the yacht."

Patient athletic performers remain calm, believing, and focused in a sport world that is very impatient and driven by a constant sense of urgency. Impatient athletic performers, on the other hand, are restless and have a "wait" problem. They can't wait to perform or to show their "stuff." Impatient athletic performers often rush their performance and become ineffective—their timing is off, and in the world of high-performance sport, timing is everything.

Impatient athletes who rush their performances feel that they don't have enough time to perform their skills effectively in intense competitive situations and settings. They press in pressure situations and do, in fact, become ineffective. Impatient athletes need to remember that while they don't have a lot of time, they have more time than they think. Patience produces a performance rhythm that is appropriate for the timely execution of athletic skills, especially in intense competitive settings. This performance principle is reflected in the saying, "You can't rush the great ones."

Impatient performers often become irritable when scheduled performances are delayed, or they can display signs of perfectionism, especially when performance protocols aren't just right prior and during competition (Nideffer, 1992). Often, impatience surfaces as a key or important performance approaches because it may be the moment in an athlete's career that he or she has been longing for. The athlete is eager to perform—too eager—and this overexcitement dissipates the emotional energy that fuels performance effectiveness. The impatient athlete will sometimes comment that he or she "just wants to get it over with."

Courage

A great deal, if not the majority of athletes, are concerned about the fear factor in sport. They do all they can to manage it and steer clear of it, but the fact of the matter is that to experience courage you must first experience fear (Gordin, 2000).

Courage in sport can be defined as the ability of an athlete to conquer fear. This does not mean the best athletes are fearless, but that they are confident and in control of those performance factors (physical, mental, and emotional) they can directly influence. They also anticipate and prepare for their responses to the performance factors (officiating, weather, gamesmanship) that may be out of their control in competitive situations.

In regards to courage, Dr. Martin Luther King Jr. stated:

> Courage faces fear and thereby masters it. Courageous men never lose the zest for living even though their life situation is zestless; cowardly men, overwhelmed by the uncertainties of life, lose the will to live. We must constantly build dykes of courage to hold back the flood of fear. (King, 1987, p. 24)

Courageous athletes are *encouraged* as they view the possible outcomes of their performance efforts, because they are mentally and physically prepared to meet competitive challenges. Unprepared athletes are *discouraged*, worried, doubtful, and fearful in the face of upcoming competitive challenges. Some athletes who are mentally and physically prepared still remain fearful in the face of upcoming performances. These athletes are making a conscious choice to select fear over courage. Courage involves the conscious choice or the will power to select confidence over fear.

It is also important to understand the relationship between confidence and courage. Courage serves to guard against overconfidence—a tinge of fear in every athlete prior to performing helps him or her pay attention or refocus, if necessary, on performance plan details.

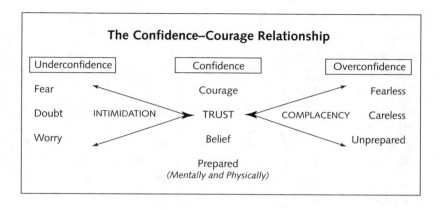

The overconfident athlete can easily become complacent and lose a healthy respect for his or her opponents or the necessity of sound mental, physical, and emotional preparation. This type of mental laziness is often the cause of subpar performances in sport and occurs when athletes are performing effectively or on a winning streak. To preserve and protect their confidence athletes need to be constantly vigilant about the details of their performance and respectful of the competitive challenges they are about to undertake. Most importantly, confident athletes are respectful of their opponent's abilities and capabilities and realize that victory is earned as a result of conscientious mental and physical preparation.

Persistence and Perseverance

An athlete's inner drive to succeed at sport is characterized by two key performance traits—persistence and perseverance.

Persistence or continual striving in the face of adversity and the setbacks that accompany the process of achieving worthwhile performance goals in sport is another characteristic of effective athletic performers. Persistent athletes have a stubborn streak in them that is a by-product of their belief in themselves and in their ability to achieve goals.

Sometimes athletes can be stubborn to a fault; they become close-minded in pursuit of their goals. The overly stubborn athlete continues to do the same thing and expects to achieve a different result. The "don't confuse me with the facts" principle comes to mind here as the athlete ignores feedback from others and from his or her performance outcomes. A different approach to training or a new performance strategy may need to be integrated into the athlete's preparation and game plan in order to be more effective.

Perseverance is the athlete's ability to overcome adversity, that is, to persist in spite of or in the face of difficulties. Disappointment and setbacks are the speed bumps every athlete experiences on his or her journey to achieving athletic excellence. Perseverance requires the athlete to have a great attitude and a sound character in order to endure the trials and tribulations of athletic training and performance.

Persistence and perseverance are often found in the company of sacrifice. Sacrifice enables an athlete to return to the basics when confronted by a challenging event or circumstance. This is why athletes are encouraged to simplify their lifestyles—it helps to eliminate distractions and to focus on the bare essentials of training and performance to be mastered, or in some cases, relearned, if an athlete can progress to higher performance levels.

While persistence, perseverance, and sacrifice are measures of an athlete's inner drive, they are not self-sustaining. These commitment attributes require support systems to remain operable. The demands of athletic training and competition intensify as an athlete's effectiveness and competency increase. Quality training and quality rest alone cannot sustain athletes who live at the highest levels of their sport; they must have quality support networks if they are to remain healthy and energized. The five-step process to facilitate commitment identified earlier in this chapter can help athletes preserve perseverance and persist at persistence.

Spirituality

Mind–body–spirit unity in sport has its roots in ancient Greek philosophies of athletic performance. Today, the spiritual side of sport is becoming a more identified and recognizable determinant of peak performance (Balague, 1999; Cooper, 1998; Jackson & Delehanty, 1995; Murphy & White, 1995; Vernacchia, McGuire, Reardon, & Templin, 2000).

Herb Elliot, an Olympic gold medalist in track and field, reflected on the role that spirituality played in his performances:

> It (competition/racing) appealed to the basic, animal part of me, the part that wanted to grind people to dust. . . . That's what I ran for at first. But then I realized the battle wasn't against others. It was against myself. It was in defeating my own weakness, in demonstrating that my spirit could master my body. . . . I came to realize that spirit, as much as or more than physical conditioning, had to be stored up before a race. I would avoid running on tracks because tracks were spiritually depleting. I never studied my opponents—they were an irrelevancy to me. Poetry, music, forest, ocean, solitude—they were what developed enormous physical strength. How do modern professional runners today find that, when most everything they do would seem to deplete that simplicity, that spirituality? (Smith, 1994, p. 80)

This quote reflects a sense of inner focus that an athlete can attain through athletic participation and performance. It is sometimes referred to as a mental state of harmony or oneness that occurs when an athlete is in the moment or in the present, focused and centered on the performance task at hand, and feeling at the height of athletic prowess and powers (Ravizza, 1984).

For some athletes, spirituality is an integral and integrated component of the sport experience. This experience produces a sense of unity of self with the environment as well as a loss of time and space or an absence of mind and effort that can produce "flow" or peak experience and performance in sport (Privette & Bundrick, 1991; Scanlan et al., 1993).

Contemporary sport slogans such as "be the best you can be" illustrate the use of sport participation as vehicle for self-actualization and self-fulfillment. The prominent psychologist Abraham Maslow (1968, 1969, 1971) believed that for a person to become all that he or she is capable of becoming, the person needs to be consciously aware of the "intrinsic values" of truth, goodness, beauty, excellence, dignity, and commitment.

In some cases, commitment can only be achieved when an athlete experiences spiritual transcendence beyond the actual sport performance as a result of physical commitment, sacrifice, forces of nature, passion as well as the ecstasy and beauty that can accompany athletic performance (Slusher, 1966).

Spirituality, whether accessed by nature, music, solitude, religion, or physical movement, can play a prominent role in an athlete's life and performance (Balague, 1999). Spirituality can help an athlete access his or her true inner strength and provide meaning, value, comfort, and purpose to the rigors of an athletic lifestyle that includes conscientious training, prolonged periods of practice, success and failure, demanding performances, and an ongoing commitment to excellence.

Accessing one's inner strength requires an athletic performer to go back to the basics. Revisiting one's foundational beliefs, values, goals, and mission can help an athlete not only focus more clearly on an upcoming performance but provide the inspiration necessary to fuel the most effective performance (Orlick, 1998).

Physically revisiting places and people who have been a part of past successful performances, especially past personal best performances is also helpful. Reliving the thoughts, images, and feelings that are generated by former coaches, teammates, stadiums, and past highlight performances can serve as an inspirational reminder to athletes that they do have what it takes to give their best effort and be successful.

Recalling and reliving past successful performances can also help generate the mental, emotional, and spiritual energy and performance focus that will be necessary to master the challenges of an upcoming athletic competition. In some cases, just visiting family members, places where one grew up, or former friends may awaken the positive thoughts, images, and feelings of happy and fulfilling past experiences in life as well as in sport. We tend to perform better when we are happy, optimistic, and full of hope about our future endeavors.

Mastering Commitment Through Personal and Performance Evaluation

Developing inner strength through commitment is a measurable process. Commitment requires a total approach to sport or athletic performance that begins with the intent to perform effectively in any given situation and ends with an appraisal or evaluation of the actual effectiveness of that performance. The goal of the committed peak performer is to match desired performance intentions with the actual performance outcome.

Since commitment is all about follow-through and effectiveness, peak performers need feedback not only about the outcomes of their performance but also about the process that they used to achieve their performances. Performance evaluation provides the accountability factor necessary to define, shape, and duplicate effective committed performance efforts and outcomes.

Athletes are encouraged to engage in a competitive evaluation process each time they perform (Orlick, 1986). Such an evaluation is actually considered to be a part of the performance —unevaluated performances are incomplete. Performance evaluations are used by athletes to identify their weaknesses and strengths. Coaches often provide external evaluations of an athlete's performance by reviewing game videotapes to improve an athlete's physical skills in competitive settings and situations. Athletes should also engage in an internal evaluation process that accesses their mental preparation as well as the effectiveness of the application of particular mental skills during an athletic performance.

On pages 250–254 is an example of a competitive evaluation form that would be helpful for an athlete to complete after each competitive performance:

Exercise

Competition Evaluation
(adapted from Orlick, 1986)

Name: _____

Event: _____

Date: _____

Results: _____

Site: _____

Complete this form as soon as possible or feasible after the completion of each event.

1. How did you feel about your performance in this event?

2. Did you have a performance outcome goal (or result goal) for this event? If so, what was it?

To what extent did you achieve this outcome goal?

0	1	2	3	4	5	6	7	8	9	10

Did not achieve
goal at all

Achieved goal
completely

3. What was your attitude going into this competition?

To what degree did you maintain this attitude during the competition?

0	1	2	3	4	5	6	7	8	9	10

Did not maintain

Maintained

4. Circle your feelings going into this event.

Goal Determination

0	1	2	3	4	5	6	7	8	9	10

No determination

Completely determined
to achieve goal

Activation

0	1	2	3	4	5	6	7	8	9	10

No physical
activation (flat)

Highly physically activated
(charged)

Worry

0	1	2	3	4	5	6	7	8	9	10

Extremely worried,
scared, or afraid

No worries
or fears

Control

0	1	2	3	4	5	6	7	8	9	10

Completely out
of control

In complete control

Uptight

0	1	2	3	4	5	6	7	8	9	10

Mentally uptight

Mentally calm

Focused on Task

0	1	2	3	4	5	6	7	8	9	10

No task focus

Complete task focus

Commitment to Push (Limit)

0	1	2	3	4	5	6	7	8	9	10

No commitment
to fully extend
myself

Complete commitment
to fully extend
myself

Confidence in Physical Preparation

0	1	2	3	4	5	6	7	8	9	10

No confidence
in my physical
preparation (doubts)

Complete confidence
in my physical
preparation

Confidence in Psych Preparation

0	1	2	3	4	5	6	7	8	9	10

No confidence
in my mental
preparation

Complete confidence
in my mental
preparation

Confidence in Abilities

0	1	2	3	4	5	6	7	8	9	10

No confidence
in my abilities
(to achieve goal)

Complete confidence
in my abilities
(to achieve goal)

Risk Taking

0	1	2	3	4	5	6	7	8	9	10

Not willing to
take necessary risks

Willing to take
necessary risks

5. Did you follow a previously practiced *pre-competition plan* (e.g., specific pre-event warm-up, positive self-talk)?

_____Yes   _____No, not at all   _____Partly

If partly, which parts were followed and which not followed?

6. What were you saying to yourself (or thinking) *immediately* before the start of the event?

7. Were you able to follow your preplanned *competition focus plan*?

_____Yes   _____No, not at all   _____Partly

If partly, which parts were followed and which not followed?

8.   Rate your overall feeling of effectiveness at the competition site and during the different segments of your pre-event preparation and performance. Use a scale from 0 to 10 where 10 is "going great" (right on target), and 0 is the "absolute pits" (right off target) and 5 is somewhere in between.

30–60 min. before event
(general warm-up)

Warm-up before
start

Moments before
you start

Rating _____

Rating _____

Rating _____

Start Rating _____

Event Rating _____

Finish Rating _____

9.   Were you able to fully extend yourself to the limit during the event?

Extend limits

0	1	2	3	4	5	6	7	8	9	10

Did not extend
myself at all

Completely extended
myself (to the limit)

10.   What were you saying to yourself or focused on to extend to the limits? (or to try to extend limits?)

11.   During the event did your focus of attention stay on your performance (following event focus plan) or drift to other things?

Event focus

0	1	2	3	4	5	6	7	8	9	10

Drifting most
of the time

Completely focused,
absorbed in performance
(following event plan)

12. When you were going best, where was your focus?

13. If you were going less well in parts, where was your focus?

14. Did you have to make a recovery to get back on track during the event? (or before the competition?) If so, were you able to recover and focus again quickly? If you used a "cue word" to refocus, did it work?

15. Did *anything* unforeseen or unexpected happen (or anyone say anything to you) either before or during the event that may have had an impact on your performance (for better or for worse)?

16. Should anything be changed or adapted for the next competition?

17. Other performance observations and comments

Commitment and evaluation are inseparable partners in the quest for performance excellence in sport. Peak performers must always retain the courage to review and evaluate the effectiveness of their performances. Evaluation is, in fact, the final phase of the dream cycle that can lead to the attainment and achievement of athletic excellence.

Dream Cycle and Athletic Excellence

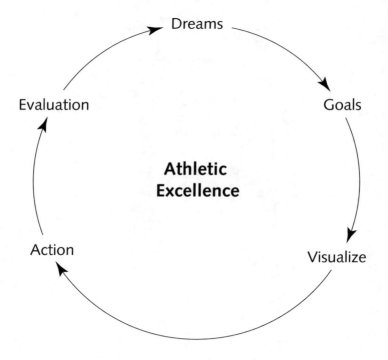

Commitment is the keystone mental skill that athletes must practice consistently to make their athletic dreams a reality. Commitment requires that an athlete live his or her dream on a daily basis. In the final analysis, commitment enables an athlete to focus and refocus on the process of success (goals, visualization, action, evaluation) and releases the inner strength necessary to attain peak performances consistently.

PEAK PERFORMANCE

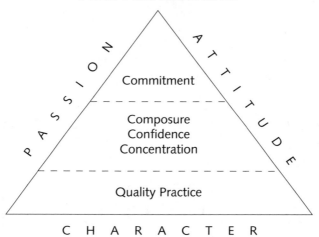

Creative Concentration Script

Basketball

We are four games away from accomplishing our season goal—to play all days in the state tournament. We have already accomplished many other goals we set earlier in the season and I have personally met the challenges of my own goals. We are now heading off to our final destination, the place where dreams are realized.

I put on my headphones and run through our game plan. I focus on defense first, I can picture the other team's plays and I go through each man on the scouting report, noting their strengths and weaknesses. I picture myself performing each duty of a point guard: setting up the play, passing, dribbling, shooting, rebounding.

I feel excitement surge through my body as the arena comes

into view. As we file out of the vans, confidence leads us in. Anticipation lingers in the locker room as we gear up for the game.

During warm-ups my shots fall straight through the hoop. I find my rhythm. I dribble around and get used to the feel of the court. I feel loose and ready. My body is tuned and my mind is prepared. The atmosphere is electric. I hear the band playing and the sounds of the game on the opposite court.

We quickly file into the locker room for a last minute game plan run-over.

Sitting on the bench waiting for the starting line-ups, I relax my mind—I trust my training and can't wait for the game to begin.

After we score off tip-off I get in position in the zone. I trap in the corner and force a turnover. We are playing a good team—it is a quick game. I bring the ball up the floor—I meet my defender and drive past him. I dish the ball to our center who puts in the lay-in. I feel energized on defense, yet in control. I anticipate a pass and steal the ball for a fast break. I am heavily guarded but I convert. The game goes back and forth. I am working hard but my body is feeling good.

At half we are up by six. My muscles are loose and although I've played all half, I am fresh and strong.

I come back out and find my touch. I hit a three from the corner. Bringing the ball up the court, I fake to the left and go around my defender to the right and pull up to cash a jumper. My body tries to call out signs of fatigue, but I refuse to give in. I push on and run harder, hustle more on each play.

We have a comfortable lead with the clock winding down. I keep my focus. I know the floor; I know the position of everyone on it. Even in fast action transition I can feel the court as if watching from the stands.

The buzzer sounds. My jersey is soaked—my body exhilarated. We have won. I have given it my all—I left everything on the court. I can hear the crowd cheer. My teammates and I congratulate each other. I am confident, I am ready for the next challenge—the next game.

References

Albaugh, G. (1990, June 29). *Perspectives on sport psychology*. Presentation given at the University of Virginia Sport Psychology Conference, Charlottesville, VA.

Andronicos, M. (1979). The role of athletics in the education of the young. In N. Yalouris (Ed.), *The eternal Olympics: The art and history of sport* (pp. 41–65). New Rochelle, NY: Caratzas Brothers, Publishers.

Anshel, M. (1990). An information processing approach to teaching motor skills. *The Journal of Physical Education, Recreation and Dance, 61*, 70–75.

Austin, D. (1981). The teacher burnout issue. *Journal of Physical Education, Recreation and Dance, 52*, 35–36

Baker, W. J. (1986). *Jesse Owens: An American life*. New York: The Free Press.

Balague, G. (1999). Understanding identity, value, and meaning when working with elite athletes. *The Sport Psychologist, 13*, 89–98.

Bannister, R. (1955). *The four minute mile*. New York: Dodd, Mead.

Bennett, J. G., & Pravitz, J. E. (1987). *Profile of a winner: Advanced mental training for athletes*. Ithaca, NY: Sport Science International and Bets Ltd.

257

Brawley, L. B., & Roberts, G. (1984). Attributions in sport: Research foundations, characteristics, and limitations. In J. M. Silva & R. S. Weinberg (Eds.), *Psychological foundations in sport* (pp. 197–213). Champaign, IL: Human Kinetics.

Brewer, B. W. (2001). Psychology of sport injury rehabilitation. In R. N. `Singer, H. A. Hausenblas, & C. M. Janelle, *Handbook of sport psychology* (2nd ed., pp. 766–786). New York: John Wiley & Sons.

Burns, D. D. (1980, November). The perfectionist's script for self-defeat. *Psychology Today*, pp. 34–52.

Christina, R. W., & Corcos, D. M. (1988). *Coaches guide to teaching sport skills*. Champaign, IL: Human Kinetics.

Chighisola, D. A. (1989). Coaching with video tape. *Scholastic Coach, 58* (8), 76–77, 110.

Connelly, D. (1992). Understanding/coaching athletes hooked on perfection. *Track and Field Quarterly Review, 92 (1)*, 37–39.

Cook, D. L. (1989, September). *Current strategies for the prediction and implementation of individualized audio rehearsal tapes*. Paper presented at the annual conference of the Association for the Advancement of Applied Sport Psychology, Seattle, WA.

Cook, D. L. (1996a). Effective motivation. In R. A. Vernacchia, R. T. McGuire, & D. L. Cook, *Coaching mental excellence: It does matter whether you win or lose*, (pp. 61–71). Portola Valley, CA: Warde Publishers.

Cook, D. L. (1996b). The composition of confidence. In R. A. Vernacchia, R. T. McGuire, & D. L. Cook, *Coaching mental excellence: "It does matter whether you win or lose . . ."*, (pp. 81–89). Portola Valley, CA: Warde Publishers.

Cook, D. L. (1996c). Creative concentration. In R. A. Vernacchia, R. T. McGuire, & D. L. Cook, *Coaching mental excellence: "It does matter whether you win or lose . . ."*, (pp. 72–80). Portola Valley, CA: Warde Publishers.

Cratty, B. J. (1989). *Psychology in contemporary sport* (3rd ed.). Englewood Cliffs, NJ: Prentice Hall.

Cooper, A. (1998). *Playing in the zone: Exploring the spiritual dimensions of the zone*. Boston: Shambhala Publications.

Csikszentmihalyi, M. (1990). *Flow: The psychology of optimal experience*. New York: Harper & Row, Publishers, Inc.

Dale, J. & Weinberg, R. (1990). Burnout in sport: A review and critique. *Journal of Applied Sport Psychology, 1*, 67–83.

Dweck, C. S. (1975). The role and expectations and attributions in the alleviation of helpessness. *The Journal of Personality and Social Psychology, 31*, 674–685.

Dweck, C. S. (1978). Achievement. In M. E. Lamb (Ed.), *Social and personality development*, (pp. 114–130). New York: Holt, Rinehart and Winston.

Dweck, C. S. (1980). Learned helplessness in sport. In C. M. Hadeau, W. R. Halliwell, K. M. Newell, & G. C. Roberts (Eds.), *Psychology of motor behavior and sport-1979*, (pp. 1–11). Champaign, IL: Human Kinetics.

Earley, P. (1988). *Attributional retraining and the performance of intercollegiate football players*. Unpublished master's thesis, Western Washington University, Bellingham, WA.

Eitzen, S. & Sage, G. (1993). *The sociology of north American sport* (5th ed.). Dubuque, IA: Brown & Benchmark.

Feltz, D. L., & Landers, D. M. (1983). The effects of mental practice on motor skill learning and performance: A meta-analysis. *Journal of Sport Psychology, 5*, 25–57.

Franks, I. M., & Maile, L. J. (1991). The use of video in sport skill acquisition. In P. W. Dowrick (Ed.), *Practical guide to using video in the behavioral sciences* (pp. 231–243). New York: Wiley.

Gill, D. (1980). Success-failure attributions in competitive groups: An exception to egocentrism. *Journal of Sport Psychology, 2*, 106–114.

Gill, D. (1986). *Psychological dynamics of sport*. Champaign, IL: Human Kinetics.

Girdano, D., Everly, G., & Dusek, D. (1990*). Controlling stress and tension: A holistic approach* (3rd ed.). Englewood Cliffs, NJ: Prentice Hall.

Gordin, R. (2000, December). *Sport psychology seminar presentation*. USATF National Convention, Albuquerque, NM.

Gordin, R., & Reardon, J. (1995). Achieving the zone: The study of flow in sport. In K. P. Henschen & W. F. Straub (Eds.), *Sport psychology: An analysis of athlete behavior* (3rd ed., pp.223–230). Longmeadow, MA: Mouvement Publications.

Gould, D. (2001). Goal setting for peak performance. In J. M. Williams (Ed.), *Applied sport psychology: Personal growth to peak performance*, (4th ed., pp.190–205). Mountain View, CA: Mayfield Publishing Co.

Grove, J., & Pargman, D. (1986). Attributions and performance during competition. *Journal of Sport Psychology, 8*, 129–134.

Halliwell, W. (1990). Providing sport psychology consulting services in professional hockey. *The Sport Psychologist, 4*, 369–377.

Heil, J. (1993). *Psychology of sport injury*. Champaign, IL: Human Kinetics.

Hemery, D. (1986). *The pursuit of sporting excellence: A study of sport's highest achievers*. Champaign, IL: Human Kinetics.

Henschen, K. P. (1995). Attention and concentration skills for performance. In K. P. Henschen & W. F. Straub (Eds.), Sport psychology: An analysis of athlete behavior (3rd ed., pp. 177–182). Longmeadow, MA: Mouvement Publications.

Henschen, K. (2001). Athletic staleness and burnout: Diagnosis, Prevention, and Treatment. In J. Williams (Ed.), *Applied sport psychology: Personal growth to peak performance* (4th ed., pp. 445–455), Mountain View, CA: Mayfield Publishing Co.

Jackson, P., & Delehanty, H. (1995). *Sacred hoops: Spiritual lessons of a hardwood warrior.* New York: Hyperion.

Jackson, S. A. (1992). Athletes in flow: A qualitative investigation of flow states in elite athletes. *Journal of Applied Sport Psychology, 4,* 161–180.

Jackson, S. A. (1995). Factors influencing the occurance of flow state in elite athletes. *Journal of Applied Sport Psychology, 2,* 138–166.

Jackson, S. A. (1996). Toward a conceptual understanding of the flow experience in elite athletes. *Research Quarterly for Exercise and Sport, 67,* 76–90.

Jackson, S. A., & Csikszentmihalyi, M. (1999). *Flow in sport.* Champaign, IL: Human Kinetics.

King, C. S. (1987). *The words of Martin Luther King, Jr.* New York: Newmarket Press.

Kubler-Ross, E. (1969). *On death and dying.* New York: Macmillan.

Kugiya, H. (1991, March 3). Purple reign. The Seattle Times/Seattle Post-Intelligencer, pp. C1, C11.

Lansing, A. (1959). *Endurance: Shackleton's incredible voyage.* New York: Carroll & Graf Publishers.

Leavitt, J., Young, J., & Connelly, D. (1989). The effects of videotape highlights on state self-confidence. *Journal of Applied Research in Coaching and Athletics, 4,* 225–232.

Lee, A. (1991, January 20). CWU holds off Viks comeback. Bellingham Herald, D1.

Magill, R. A. (1989). *Motor learning: Concepts and applications* (3rd ed.). Dubuque, IA: Wm. C. Brown Publishers.

Mahoney, M. J., Gabriel, T. J., & Perkins, T. S. (1987). Psychological skills and exceptional athletic performance. *The Sport Psycholologist, 1,* 181–199.

Malone, C., & Rotella, R. (1981). Preventing coaching burnout. *Journal of Physical Education, Recreation and Dance, 52,* 22.

Malroy, T. (2000). *The effect of mental skills training on performance of a basketball skill.* Unpublished master's thesis, Western Washington University, Bellingham, WA.

Mark, J., Mutrie, N., Brooks, D., & Harris, D. (1984). Causal attributions of winners and losers in individual competitive sports: Towards a reformulation of te self-serving bias in sport. *Journal of Sport Psychology, 6,* 184–196.

Maslow, A. H. (1968). *Toward psychology of being.* Princeton, NJ: Van Nostrand.

Maslow, A. H. (1969). Various meanings of transcendence. *Journal of Transpersonal Psychology, 1,* 56–66.

Maslow, A. H. (1971). *The farther reaches of human nature.* New York: The Viking Press.

McCauley, E., & Gross, J.(1983). Perceptions of causality in sport: An application of the causal dimension scale. *Journal of Sport Psychology, 5*, 72–76.

McGuire, R. (1992). Concentration for the field event athlete: An application of Cook's model of concentration. *Track and Field Quarterly Review, 92*(1), 49–51.

McGuire, R. (1996a). The coach, someone special. In R. Vernacchia, R. McGuire, & D. Cook, *Coaching mental excellence: "It does matter whether you win or lose . . ."* (pp. 3–14). Portola Valley, CA: Warde Publishers.

McGuire, R. (1996b). The coach's philosophy: Establishing foundational beliefs. In R. Vernacchia, R. McGuire, & D. Cook, *Coaching mental excellence: "It does matter whether you win or lose . . ."* (pp. 15–31). Portola Valley, CA: Warde Publishers.

McGuire, R. (1996c). The coach and family: The stress of success. In R. Vernacchia, R. McGuire, & D. Cook, *Coaching mental excellence: "It does matter whether you win or lose . . ."* (pp. 154–179). Portola Valley, CA: Warde Publishers.

McGuire, R. (1997, December 4). Motivating the track and field athlete. Presentation at the *United States Track and Field (USATF) National Convention*, San Francisco, CA.

McGuire, R. (1998, April 6). A "construction" model for positive coaching. Keynote presentation given at the *American Alliance for Health, Physical Education, Recreation and Dance (AAHPERD) National Convention*, Reno, NV.

Moore, K. (1991, September 9). Great leap forward. *Sports Illustrated, 75*, pp. 14–19.

Moore, W. E., & Stevenson, J. R. (1991). Understanding trust in the performance of complex automatic sport skills. *The Sport Psychologist, 5*, 281–289.

Moore, W. E., & Stevenson, J. R. (1994). Training for trust in sport skills. *The Sport Psychologist, 8*, 1–12.

Moran, A. P. (1996). *The psychology of concentration in sport performers: A cognitive analysis*. East Sussex, United Kingdom: Psychology Press.

Morgan, W. (1992). Monitoring and prevention of staleness. *Track and Field Quarterly Review, 92*(1), 47–48.

Murphy, S. M., & Jowdy, D. P. (1992). Imagery and mental practice. In T. S. Horn (Ed.), *Advances in sport psychology* (pp. 221–245). Champaign, IL: Human Kinetics.

Murphy, M., & White, R. A. (1995). *In the zone: Transcendent experience in sports*. New York: Penguin Books.

Neubauer, J. P., Miller, L., & Vernacchia, R. A. (1994). A prospective view on mental practice research: The logic and use of the cognitive rehearsal technique of creative concentration. *Applied Research in Coaching and Athletics Annual*, 119–141.

Newman, B., (1991, September 16). At long last. *Sports Illustrated, 75,* pp. 36–39.

Nideffer, R. M. (1976). *The inner athlete: Mind plus muscle for winning.* New York: Thomas Y. Crowell, Publishers.

Nideffer, R. (1985). *Athletes' guide to mental training.* Champaign, IL: Human Kinetics.

Nideffer, R. M. (1992). *Psyched to win: How to master mental skills to improve your physical performance.* Champaign, IL: Leisure Press.

Nideffer, R. M., & Sagal, M. S. (2001). Concentration and attention control training. In J. M. Williams (Ed.), *Applied sport psychology: Personal growth to peak performance* (4th ed., pp. 312–332). Mountain View, CA: Mayfield Publishing Company.

Nougier, V., Stein, J. F., & Bonnel, A. M. (1991). Information processing in sport and "orienting of attention". *International Journal of Sport Psychology, 22,* 307–327.

Odom, S., & Perrin, T. (1985). Coach and athlete burnout. In L. Bunker, R. Rottela, & A. Reilly, *Sport psychology: Psychological considerations on maximizing sport performance.* Longmeadow, MA: Mouvement Publications.

Ogilvie, B. (1968). Psychological consistencies within the personality of high-level competitors. *Journal of the American Medical Association, 205,* 156–162.

Orlick, T. (1986). *Psyching for sport: Mental training for athletes.* Champaign, IL: Leisure Press.

Orlick, T. (1992). The psychology of personal excellence. *Contemporary Thought on Performance Enhancement, 1,* 109–122.

Orlick, T. (1996). The wheel of excellence. *Journal of Performance Education, 1,* 3–18.

Orlick, T. (1998). *Embracing your potential.* Champaign, IL: Human Kinetics.

Orlick, T. (2000). *In pursuit of excellence: How to win in sport and life through mental training* (3rd ed.). Champaign, IL: Human Kinetics.

Orlick, T., & Partington, J. (1988). Mental links to excellence. *The Sport Psychologist, 2,* 105–130.

Oxendine, J. B. (1986). Motor skill learning for effective sport performance. In J. M. Williams (Ed.), *Applied sport psychology: Personal growth to peak performance* (pp. 17–33). Mountain View, CA: Mayfield Publishing Co.

Perry, D. (2001). *The effect of a mental training program on the performance of offensive soccer skills.* Unpublished master's thesis, Western Washington University, Bellingham, WA.

Prapavessis, H., & Carron, A. (1988). Learned helplessness in sport. *The Sport Psychologist, 2,* 189–201.

Privette, G., & Bundrick, C. M. (1991). Peak experience, peak performance, and flow: Correspondence of personal descriptions and theoretical constructs. *Journal of Social Behavior and Personality, 6,* 169–188.

Putnam, P. (1990, December 17). Fire and fury. *Sports Illustrated,*pp. 32–37.

Quote. (1991, February 23). Seattle Post-Intelligencer, p. D1.

Ravizza, K. (1984). Qualities of the peak experience in sport. In J. M. Silva III & R. S. Weinberg (Eds.), *Psychological foundations of sport* (pp. 452–461). Champaign, IL: Human Kinetics.

Ravizza, K., & Hanson, T. (1995). *Heads-up baseball: Playing the game one pitch at a time.* Indianapolis, IN: Masters Press.

Ravizza, K., & Osborne, T. (1991). Nebraska's 3R's: One play-at-a-time preperformance routine for college football. *The Sport Psychologist, 5,* 256–265.

Reardon, J., & Gordin, R. (1992). Psychological skill development leading to a peak performance "flow state". *Track and Field Quarterly Review, 92,* 22–25.

Roberts, G. (1982). Achievement motivation in sport. *Exercise Science and Sport Reviews, 10,* 236–269.

Roberts, G., & Pascuzzi, D. (1979). Causal attributions in sport: Some theoretical implications. *Journal of Sport Psychology, 1,* 203–211.

Rosenfeld, L. B., & Richman, J. M. (1997). Developing effective social support: Team building and the social support process. *Journal of Applied Sport Psychology, 9,* 133–153.

Rotella, R. (1981). Learned helplessness: A model for maximizing potential. In L. Bunker & R. Rotella (Eds.), *Sport psychology: Psychological considerations in maximizing sport performance.* Charlottesville, VA: University of Virginia.

Rotella, R. (1990a). *Self-improvement program.* Unpublished manuscript. University of Virginia, Charlottesville, VA.

Rotella, R. (1990b). Providing psychology consulting services to professional athletes. *The Sport Psychologist, 4,* 409–417

Rotella, R. (1990c). *Class notes: Case studies in sport psychology.* University of Virginia, Charlottesville, VA.

Rotella, R. (1990d). *Class notes: Introduction to sport psychology.* University of Virginia, Charlottesville, VA.

Samuelson, J., & Averbuch, G. (1995). *Joan Samuelson's running for women.* Emmaus, PA: Rodale Press.

Savis, J. C. (1994). Sleep and athletic performance: Overview and implications for sport psychology. *The Sport Psychologist, 8,* 111–125.

Scanlan, T. K., Carpenter, P. J., Schmidt, G. W., Simons, J. P., & Keeler, B. (1993). An introduction to the sport commitment model. *Journal of Sport and Exercise Psychology, 15,* 1–15.

Schmidt, R. A. (1991). *Motor learning and performance.* Champaign, IL: Human Kinetics Publishers.

Silva, J. (1990). An analysis of the training stress syndrome in competitive athletics. *Journal of Applied Sport Psychology, 2*, 5–20.

Singer, R. (1980). *Motor learning and human performance: An application to motor skills and movement behaviors*. New York: MacMillan Publishing Co.

Simons, J. (1998). Concentration. In M. A. Thompson, R. A. Vernacchia, & W. E. Moore (Eds.), *Case studies in applied sport psychology: An educational approach*. Dubuque, IA: Kendall/Hunt Publishers.

Singer, R. N., Cauraugh, J. H., Murphey, M., Chen, D., & Lidor, R. (1991). Attentional control, distractors, and motor performance. *Human Performance, 4*, 55–69.

Slusher, H. S. (1966, March). *Sport and existence: An analysis of being*. Paper presented at the meeting of the American Association for Health, Physical Education and Recreation National Convention, Chicago, IL.

Smith, G. (1994, June 27). An exclusive club. *Sports Illustrated, 80*, 70–82.

Spink, K., & Roberts, G. (1980). Ambiguity of outcome and causal attributions. *Journal of Sport Psychology, 2*, 237–244.

Suinn, R. M. (1976). Body thinking: Psychology for Olympic champs. In R. M. Suinn (Ed.), *Psychology in sports: Methods and applications* (pp. 306–315). Minneapolis, MN: Burgess.

Stallings, L. M. (1982). *Motor learning: From theory to practice*. St. Louis: The C. V. Mosby Co.

Syre, J., & Connolly, C. (1987). *Sporting body, sporting mind: An athlete's guide to mental training*. Englewood Cliffs, NJ: Prentice Hall.

The little book of Olympic inspriration (1996). Tulsa, OK: Trade Life.

Templin, D. P., & Vernacchia, R. A. (1995). The effect of highlight music videotapes upon the game performance of intercollegiate basketball players. *The Sport Psychologist, 9*, 41–50.

Unestahl, L. E. (1986). Self hypnosis. In J. M. Williams (Ed.), *Applied sport psychology: Personal growth to peak performance* (pp. 285–300). Mountain View, CA: Mayfield Publishing Company.

U. S. Olympic Committee (1999). *Media interview guidelines*. Colorado Springs, CO: U. S. Olympic Committee.

Vanek, M., & Cratty, B. J. (1970). *The psychology of the superior athlete*. New York: MacMillan.

Vealey, R. S., & Greenleaf, C. A. (2001). Seeing is believing: Understanding and using imagery. In J. M. Williams (Ed.), *Applied sport psychology: Personal growth to peak performance* (4th ed., pp. 247–283). Mountain View, CA: Mayfield Publishing Co.

Vernacchia, R. A. (1992). Overcoming overcoaching: The key to beating burnout. *Track and Field Quarterly Review, 92*(1), 44–46.

Vernacchia, R. A. (1995). "They used to call me coach": Burnout and the career termination of coaches. In K. P. Henschen & W. F. Straub, *Sport psychology: An analysis of athlete behavior* (3rd ed., pp. 361–370). Long-meadow, MA: Mouvement Publications.

Vernacchia, R. A. (1996a). Conducting effective practices. In R. A. Vernacchia, R. T. McGuire, D. L. Cook, *Coaching mental excellence: "It does matter whether you win or lose . . ."* (pp.113–135). Portola Valley, CA: Warde Publishers.

Vernacchia, R. A. (1996b). Composure. In R. A. Vernacchia, R. T. McGuire, D. L. Cook, *Coaching mental excellence: "It does matter whether you win or lose . . ."* (pp.93–112). Portola Valley, CA: Warde Publishers.

Vernacchia, R. A. (1996c). Leadership and team building. In R. A. Vernacchia, R. T. McGuire, D. L. Cook, *Coaching mental excellence: "It does matter whether you win or lose . . ."* (pp. 35–58). Portola Valley, CA: Warde Publishers.

Vernacchia, R. A. (1996d). Preventing and reversing coaching burnout. In R. A. Vernacchia, R. T. McGuire, & D. L. Cook, *Coaching mental excellence: "It does matter whether you win or lose . . ."* (pp.139–153). Portolla Valley, CA: Warde Publishers.

Vernacchia, R.A. (1997). Psychological perspectives on overtraining. *Track Coach, 138,* 4393–4399, 4420.

Vernacchia, R. A. (1998). Competitive refocusing and the performance of USA international junior elite track and field athletes. *New Studies in Athletics, 13,* 25–30.

Vernacchia, R. A., Austin, S., VandenHazel, M., & Roe, R. (1992). The influence of self-hypnosis upon the arousal and performance of intercollegiate track and field athletes. *Applied Research in Coaching and Athletics Annual,* 77–91

Vernacchia, R. A., & Cook, D. L. (1993). The influence of a mental training technique upon the performance of selected intercollegiate basketball players. *Applied Research in Coaching and Athletic Annual,* 188–200.

Vernacchia, R. A., & Henschen, K. (2001). *Coping with the reality of athletic injury: Working with track and field athletes at the Olympic games.* Proceedings of the Association for the Advancement of Applied Sport Psychology (AAASP) National Conference, 104.

Vernacchia, R. A., McGuire, R. T., & Cook, D. L. (1996). *Coaching mental excellence: "It does matter whether you win or lose . . ."* Portola Valley, CA: Warde Publishers.

Vernacchia, R. A., McGuire, R. T., Reardon, J. P., & Templin, D. P. (2000). Psychosocial characteristics of Olympic track and field athletes. *The International Journal of Sport Psychology, 31,* 5–23.

Weinberg, R. S., & Gould, D. (1999). *Foundations of sport and exercise psychology* (2nd ed.). Champaign, IL: Human Kinetics.

Weinberg, R. S., & Williams, J. M. (2001). Integrating and implementing a psychological skills training program. In J. M. Williams (Ed.),

Applied sport psychology: Personal growth to peak performance (4th ed., pp. 347–377). Mountain View, CA: Mayfield Publishing Co.

Weiner, B. (1972). *Theories of motivation: From mechanism to cognition.* Chicago: Markham.

Weiner, B. (1974). *Achievement motivation and attribution theory.* Morristown, NJ: General Learning Press.

Weiner, B. (1979). A theory of motivation for some classroom experiences. *Journal of Educational Psychology, 71,* 3–25.

Weiner, B., Hierenberg, R., & Goldstein, M. (1976). Social learning (locus of control) versus attributional (causal stability) interpretations of expectancy success. *Journal of Personality, 44,* 52–68.

Weiner, B., Russell, D., & Lerman, D. (1979). The cognition-emotion process in achievement related contexts. *Journal of Personality and Social Psychology, 37,* 1211–1220.

Williams, J. M., & Krane, V. (2001). Psychological characteristics of peak performance. In J. M. Williams (Ed.), *Applied sport psychology: Personal growth to peak performance* (4th ed., pp. 162–178). Mountain View, CA: Mayfield Publishing Company.

Williams, J. M., Rotella, R. J., & Scherzer, C. B. (2001). Injury risk and rehabilitation: Psychological considerations. In J. M. Williams (Ed.), *Applied sport psychology: Personal growth to peak performance* (4rd ed., pp. 456–479). Mountain View, CA: Mayfield Publishing Company.

Zinsser, N., Bunker, L., & Williams, J. (2001). Cognitive techniques for building confidence and enhancing performance. In J. M. Williams (Ed.), *Applied sport psychology: Personal growth to peak performance* (4th ed., pp.284–311). Mountain View, CA: Mayfield Publishing Co.

Index

About the Author

Ralph A. Vernacchia, Ph.D. directs the undergraduate and graduate programs in sport psychology at Western Washington University, as well as WWU's Center for Performance Excellence. He has presented extensively on a variety of sport psychology topics. His publications include numerous articles and chapters related to performance psychology and he as co-authored/edited two previous textbooks in sport psychology. He is a fellow and certified consultant of the Association for the Advancement of Applied Sport Psychology (AAASP) and a member of the United States Olympic Committee (USOC) Sport Psychology Registry. Dr. Vernacchia serves as a performance consultant to the Western Washington University Athletic Department and is a former Chair of the Sport Psychology Academy of the American Alliance for Health, Physical Education, Recreation and Dance (AAH-PERD). He is also co-chair of the USA Track and Field (USATF) Sport Psychology Sub-Committee and has traveled internationally as a performance consultant with several USA track and field teams, including the 2000 USA Olympic Track and Field Teams that competed in Sydney, Australia. He has been inducted into the Western Washington University Athletic Hall of Fame, in honor of his accomplishments as Western's cross country and track and field coach from 1973 to 1987. He has also been selected as a 2003-2004 Distinguished Visiting Professor in Physical Education at the United States Military Academy, West Point, New York.